# THE BEST TEST PREPARATION FOR THE

# GRE

GRADUATE

RECORD

EXAMINATION

# COMPUTER SCIENCE

**Ruknet Cezzar, Ph.D.**
Visiting Professor of Computer Science
Hampton University, Hampton, Virginia

**Li-hsiang Aria Cheo, Ph.D.**
Chairperson, Computer Science and Quantitative Analysis Department
William Paterson College of New Jersey, Wayne, New Jersey

**John Najarian, Ph.D.**
Associate Professor of Computer Science
William Paterson College of New Jersey, Wayne, New Jersey

**Gary Wester, Ph.D.**
Computer Science Consultant
Normal, Illinois

Research and Education Association
61 Ethel Road West
Piscataway, New Jersey 08854

The Best Test Preparation for the
GRADUATE RECORD EXAMINATION (GRE)
in COMPUTER SCIENCE

1998 PRINTING

Printed in the United States of America

Library of Congress Catalog Card Number 96-69296

International Standard Book Number 0-87891-847-7

Research & Education Association
61 Ethel Road West
Piscataway, New Jersey 08854

REA supports the effort to conserve and
protect environmental resources by
printing on recycled papers.

# CONTENTS

**PREFACE**  v

**ABOUT THE TEST**  v

**SCORING THE TEST**  vi

**NOTATIONS AND CONVENTIONS**  vii

**GRE Computer Science Test 1**  1
Answer Sheet Form 1    2
Test 1    3
Answer Key    36
Detailed Explanations of Answers    37

**GRE Computer Science Test 2**  71
Answer Sheet Form 2    72
Test 2    73
Answer Key    104
Detailed Explanations of Answers    105

## GRE Computer Science Test 3  127

    Answer Sheet Form 3  128
    Test 3  129
    Answer Key  156
    Detailed Explanations of Answers  157

## GRE Computer Science Test 4  187

    Answer Sheet Form 4  188
    Test 4  189
    Answer Key  217
    Detailed Explanations of Answers  218

## Glossary of Terms  238

# ABOUT RESEARCH & EDUCATION ASSOCIATION

Research and Education Association (REA) is an organization of educators, scientists, and engineers specializing in various academic fields. Founded in 1959 with the purpose of disseminating the most recently developed scientific information to groups in industry, government, high schools, and universities, REA has since become a successful and highly respected publisher of study aids, test preps, handbooks, and reference works.

REA's Test Preparation series includes study guides for all academic levels in almost all disciplines. Research and Education Association publishes test preps for students who have not yet completed high school, as well as high school students preparing to enter college. Students from countries around the world seeking to attend college in the United States will find the assistance they need in REA's publications. For college students seeking advanced degrees, REA publishes test preps for many major graduate school admission examinations in a wide variety of disciplines, including engineering, law, and medicine. Students at every level, in every field, with every ambition can find what they are looking for among REA's publications.

Unlike most Test Preparation books that present only a few practice tests which bear little resemblance to the actual exams, REA's series presents tests which accurately depict the official exams in both degree of difficulty and types of questions. REA's practice tests are always based upon the most recently administered exams, and include every type of question that can be expected on the actual exams.

REA's publications and educational materials are highly regarded and continually receive an unprecedented amount of praise from professionals, instructors, librarians, parents, and students. Our authors are as diverse as the subjects and fields represented in the books we publish. They are well-known in their respective fields and serve on the faculties of prestigious universities throughout the United States.

# ACKNOWLEDGMENTS

In addition to our authors, we would like to thank Dr. Max Fogiel, President, for his overall guidance which has brought this publication to its completion; John Paul Cording, Project Modernization Manager, and Larry B. Kling, Revisions Editor, for their editorial review; and Randall Raus for his editorial contributions.

# PREFACE

This book provides an accurate and complete representation of the Graduate Record Examination in Computer Science. The four practice exams provided are based on the format of the most recently administered Graduate Record Examinations in Computer Science. Each test is two hours and fifty minutes in length and includes every type of question that can be expected in the actual exam. Following each exam is an answer key, complete with detailed explanations designed to clarify the material to the student. By completing all four exams and studying the explanations that follow them, students can discover their strengths and weaknesses and thereby become well prepared for the actual exam. As an additional study aid, we have provided a helpful glossary of computer science terms at the end of this book.

# ABOUT THE TEST

The Graduate Record Examination in Computer Science is offered four times a year by the Educational Testing Service, under the direction of the Graduate Record Examinations Board. Applicants for graduate school submit GRE test results together with other undergraduate records as part of the highly competitive admission process to graduate school. The GRE tests are intended to provide the graduate school admissions committee with a means of evaluating students' competence in certain subject areas.

The questions on the test are composed by experts in the field of computer science who teach at various undergraduate and graduate institutions throughout the United States. The questions are designed to determine students' understanding of computer science concepts, as well as their ability to apply these concepts to specific situations.

The test consists of approximately 80 multiple-choice questions. Some questions are grouped together and refer to a particular diagram, graph, or program fragment. Emphasis is placed on the following major areas of computer science. The given percentages are approximate because these proportions may differ from administration to administration.

Software (35%)
— Organization of Data
— Design and Development
— Languages
— Program Control
— Systems

Theory (20%)
— Program Corrections

— Algorithm Analysis
— Language Theory

Computer Organization and Architecture (20%)
— Processors/Control Units
— I/O Devices
— Interconnection
— Logic Design
— Memories

Computational Mathematics (20%)
— Discrete Structures (Abstract and Boolean Algebra, Graph and Set Theory, Discrete Probability)
— Numerical Mathematics

Special Topics (5%)
— Typical topics may include artificial intelligence, graphics, simulation and modeling, and data communication.

## SCORING THE TEST

After taking one of the sample tests, check your answers against the solution key provided at the end of each test. For each correct answer, give yourself one point. For each incorrect answer, subtract one fourth of a point. Unanswered questions do not affect your score. Round the resulting total to the nearest whole number. This number represents your total raw score. Then use the given table to convert your raw score from the practice tests into a total scaled score. This enables you to compare your performance with that of others.

## CONVERSION TABLE

| Raw Score Range | Scaled Score Range |
|:---:|:---:|
| 70–80 | 930–990 |
| 60–69 | 860–920 |
| 50–59 | 790–850 |
| 40–49 | 720–780 |
| 30–39 | 650–720 |
| 20–29 | 590–650 |
| 10–19 | 520–580 |
| 0–9 | 450–510 |

# Notations and Conventions

In this test a reading knowledge of Pascal-like languages is assumed. All programs are written in a Pascal-like language unless otherwise specified. The following notational conventions are used.

1.  All numbers are assumed to be written in decimal notation unless otherwise indicated.

2.  $\lfloor x \rfloor$ denotes the greatest integer that is less than or equal to $x$.

3.  $\lceil x \rceil$ denotes the least integer that is greater than or equal to $x$.

4.  $g(n) = O(f(n))$ denotes "$g(n)$ has order $f(n)$" and, for purposes of this test, may be taken to mean that $\lim\limits_{n \to \infty} \left| \dfrac{g(n)}{f(n)} \right|$ is finite.

5.  $\exists$     denotes "there exists."

    $\forall$     denotes "for all."

    $\Rightarrow$     denotes "implies."

    $\neg$     denotes "not"; "$A$" is also used as meaning "$\neg A$."

    $\vee$     denotes "inclusive or."

    $\oplus$     denotes "exclusive or."

    $\wedge$     denotes "and"; also, juxtaposition of statements denotes "and," e.g., $PQ$ denotes "$P$ and $Q$."

6.  If $A$ and B denote sets, then:

    $A \cup B$ is the set of all elements that are in $A$ or in $B$ or in both;

    $A \cap B$ is the set of all elements that are in both $A$ and $B$; $AB$ also denotes $A \cap B$;

    $\overline{A}$ is the set of all elements not in $A$ that are in some specified universal set.

7.  In a string expression, if $S$ and $T$ denote strings or sets of strings, then:

    An empty string is denoted by $\varepsilon$ or by $\Lambda$;

    $ST$ denotes the concatenation of $S$ and $T$;

    $S + T$ denotes $S \cup T$ or $\{S, T\}$ depending on context;

$S^n$ denotes $\underbrace{S\,S...S}_{n\ \text{factors}}$;

$S*$ denotes $\varepsilon + S + S^2 + S^3 + ...$

8.   In a grammar:

$\alpha \rightarrow \beta$ represents a production in the grammar.

$\alpha \Rightarrow \beta$ means $\beta$ can be derived from $\alpha$ by the application of exactly one production.

$\alpha \overset{*}{\Rightarrow} \beta$ means $\beta$ can be derived from $\alpha$ by the application of zero or more productions.

Unless otherwise specified

(i)    symbols appearing on the left-hand side of productions are nonterminal symbols, the remaining symbols are terminal symbols,

(ii)   the leftmost symbol of the first production is the start symbol,

(iii)  the start symbol is permitted to appear on the right-hand side of productions,

(iv)   for all grammar problems, choose the strictest or best answer. For example, if a language is context-free, choose context-free rather than the broader class of recursively enumerable, and

(v)    the term "empty" refers to the empty string.

9.   In a logic diagram:

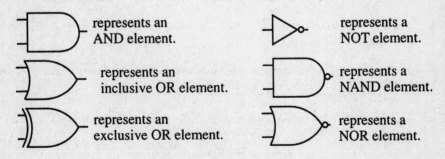

represents an AND element.

represents a NOT element.

represents an inclusive OR element.

represents a NAND element.

represents an exclusive OR element.

represents a NOR element.

10. input 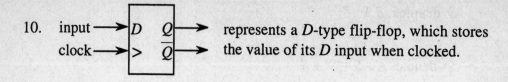 represents a *D*-type flip-flop, which stores the value of its *D* input when clocked.

11. Binary tree traversal is defined recursively as follows:

   preorder — visit the root, traverse the left subtree, traverse the right subtree

   inorder — traverse the left subtree, visit the root, traverse the right subtree

   postorder — traverse the left subtree, traverse the right subtree, visit the root

12. In a finite automation diagram, states are represented by circles, with final (or accepting) states indicated by two concentric circles. The start state is indicated by the word "Start." An arc from state *s* to state *t* labeled *a* indicates a transition from *s* to *t* on input *a*. A label *a / b* indicates that this transition produces an output *b*. A label $a_1, a_2, ..., a_k$ indicates that the transition is made on any of the inputs $a_1, a_2, ..., a_k$.

# The Graduate Record Examination in

# COMPUTER SCIENCE

## Test 1

# THE GRADUATE RECORD EXAMINATION IN
# COMPUTER SCIENCE
# TEST 1
# ANSWER SHEET

1. Ⓐ Ⓑ Ⓒ Ⓓ Ⓔ
2. Ⓐ Ⓑ Ⓒ Ⓓ Ⓔ
3. Ⓐ Ⓑ Ⓒ Ⓓ Ⓔ
4. Ⓐ Ⓑ Ⓒ Ⓓ Ⓔ
5. Ⓐ Ⓑ Ⓒ Ⓓ Ⓔ
6. Ⓐ Ⓑ Ⓒ Ⓓ Ⓔ
7. Ⓐ Ⓑ Ⓒ Ⓓ Ⓔ
8. Ⓐ Ⓑ Ⓒ Ⓓ Ⓔ
9. Ⓐ Ⓑ Ⓒ Ⓓ Ⓔ
10. Ⓐ Ⓑ Ⓒ Ⓓ Ⓔ
11. Ⓐ Ⓑ Ⓒ Ⓓ Ⓔ
12. Ⓐ Ⓑ Ⓒ Ⓓ Ⓔ
13. Ⓐ Ⓑ Ⓒ Ⓓ Ⓔ
14. Ⓐ Ⓑ Ⓒ Ⓓ Ⓔ
15. Ⓐ Ⓑ Ⓒ Ⓓ Ⓔ
16. Ⓐ Ⓑ Ⓒ Ⓓ Ⓔ
17. Ⓐ Ⓑ Ⓒ Ⓓ Ⓔ
18. Ⓐ Ⓑ Ⓒ Ⓓ Ⓔ
19. Ⓐ Ⓑ Ⓒ Ⓓ Ⓔ
20. Ⓐ Ⓑ Ⓒ Ⓓ Ⓔ
21. Ⓐ Ⓑ Ⓒ Ⓓ Ⓔ
22. Ⓐ Ⓑ Ⓒ Ⓓ Ⓔ
23. Ⓐ Ⓑ Ⓒ Ⓓ Ⓔ
24. Ⓐ Ⓑ Ⓒ Ⓓ Ⓔ
25. Ⓐ Ⓑ Ⓒ Ⓓ Ⓔ
26. Ⓐ Ⓑ Ⓒ Ⓓ Ⓔ
27. Ⓐ Ⓑ Ⓒ Ⓓ Ⓔ

28. Ⓐ Ⓑ Ⓒ Ⓓ Ⓔ
29. Ⓐ Ⓑ Ⓒ Ⓓ Ⓔ
30. Ⓐ Ⓑ Ⓒ Ⓓ Ⓔ
31. Ⓐ Ⓑ Ⓒ Ⓓ Ⓔ
32. Ⓐ Ⓑ Ⓒ Ⓓ Ⓔ
33. Ⓐ Ⓑ Ⓒ Ⓓ Ⓔ
34. Ⓐ Ⓑ Ⓒ Ⓓ Ⓔ
35. Ⓐ Ⓑ Ⓒ Ⓓ Ⓔ
36. Ⓐ Ⓑ Ⓒ Ⓓ Ⓔ
37. Ⓐ Ⓑ Ⓒ Ⓓ Ⓔ
38. Ⓐ Ⓑ Ⓒ Ⓓ Ⓔ
39. Ⓐ Ⓑ Ⓒ Ⓓ Ⓔ
40. Ⓐ Ⓑ Ⓒ Ⓓ Ⓔ
41. Ⓐ Ⓑ Ⓒ Ⓓ Ⓔ
42. Ⓐ Ⓑ Ⓒ Ⓓ Ⓔ
43. Ⓐ Ⓑ Ⓒ Ⓓ Ⓔ
44. Ⓐ Ⓑ Ⓒ Ⓓ Ⓔ
45. Ⓐ Ⓑ Ⓒ Ⓓ Ⓔ
46. Ⓐ Ⓑ Ⓒ Ⓓ Ⓔ
47. Ⓐ Ⓑ Ⓒ Ⓓ Ⓔ
48. Ⓐ Ⓑ Ⓒ Ⓓ Ⓔ
49. Ⓐ Ⓑ Ⓒ Ⓓ Ⓔ
50. Ⓐ Ⓑ Ⓒ Ⓓ Ⓔ
51. Ⓐ Ⓑ Ⓒ Ⓓ Ⓔ
52. Ⓐ Ⓑ Ⓒ Ⓓ Ⓔ
53. Ⓐ Ⓑ Ⓒ Ⓓ Ⓔ

54. Ⓐ Ⓑ Ⓒ Ⓓ Ⓔ
55. Ⓐ Ⓑ Ⓒ Ⓓ Ⓔ
56. Ⓐ Ⓑ Ⓒ Ⓓ Ⓔ
57. Ⓐ Ⓑ Ⓒ Ⓓ Ⓔ
58. Ⓐ Ⓑ Ⓒ Ⓓ Ⓔ
59. Ⓐ Ⓑ Ⓒ Ⓓ Ⓔ
60. Ⓐ Ⓑ Ⓒ Ⓓ Ⓔ
61. Ⓐ Ⓑ Ⓒ Ⓓ Ⓔ
62. Ⓐ Ⓑ Ⓒ Ⓓ Ⓔ
63. Ⓐ Ⓑ Ⓒ Ⓓ Ⓔ
64. Ⓐ Ⓑ Ⓒ Ⓓ Ⓔ
65. Ⓐ Ⓑ Ⓒ Ⓓ Ⓔ
66. Ⓐ Ⓑ Ⓒ Ⓓ Ⓔ
67. Ⓐ Ⓑ Ⓒ Ⓓ Ⓔ
68. Ⓐ Ⓑ Ⓒ Ⓓ Ⓔ
69. Ⓐ Ⓑ Ⓒ Ⓓ Ⓔ
70. Ⓐ Ⓑ Ⓒ Ⓓ Ⓔ
71. Ⓐ Ⓑ Ⓒ Ⓓ Ⓔ
72. Ⓐ Ⓑ Ⓒ Ⓓ Ⓔ
73. Ⓐ Ⓑ Ⓒ Ⓓ Ⓔ
74. Ⓐ Ⓑ Ⓒ Ⓓ Ⓔ
75. Ⓐ Ⓑ Ⓒ Ⓓ Ⓔ
76. Ⓐ Ⓑ Ⓒ Ⓓ Ⓔ
77. Ⓐ Ⓑ Ⓒ Ⓓ Ⓔ
78. Ⓐ Ⓑ Ⓒ Ⓓ Ⓔ
79. Ⓐ Ⓑ Ⓒ Ⓓ Ⓔ
80. Ⓐ Ⓑ Ⓒ Ⓓ Ⓔ

# GRE COMPUTER SCIENCE
# TEST 1

**TIME:** 170 Minutes
80 Questions

---

**DIRECTIONS:** Each of the questions or incomplete statements below is followed by five suggested answers or completions. Select the one that is best in each case. Refer to Pages vii – ix for *Notations and Conventions*.

---

1. The binary representation of the hexidecimal number 3B7F is

   (A) 0100 1001 1110 1101     (D) 0110 0011 1011 1100

   (B) 0011 1011 0111 1111     (E) 1101 1100 1011 0101

   (C) 0010 0100 0000 1010

2. Let $A$ be a sorted array of $n=10$ elements. Which of the following denotes the average successful time for finding an arbitrary element $x$ in $A$ using a binary search? Assume that only one comparison is required to determine whether the target is equal to, less than, or greater than $A[i]$.

   (A) 1.6          (D) 5.5

   (B) 2.9          (E) 6.8

   (C) 4.2

3. Consider the following Pascal declarations

   **type**
   
           *byte* = 0..7;
   
           *word* = 0..15;
   
           *num* = *real*;

   **var**
   
           *a*: *byte*;

*b,c: word;*
*d: integer;*
*e: real;*
*f: char;*

Which of the following pairs of variables are compatible but are not identical?

(A)  *a* and *e*　　　　　　　　(D)  *c* and *f*

(B)  *b* and *c*　　　　　　　　(E)  *c* and *d*

(C)  *d* and *e*

4.　Access to moving head disks requires three periods of delay before information is brought into memory. The response that correctly lists the three time delays for the physical access of data in the order of their relative speeds from slowest to fastest is

(A)  latency time, cache overhead time, seek time

(B)  cache overhead time, latency time, seek time

(C)  transmission time, latency time, seek time

(D)  seek time, latency time, transmission time

(E)  queue wait time, cache overhead time, transmission time

5.　Object modules generated by assemblers that contain unresolved external references are resolved for two or more object modules by a/ an

(A)  linker　　　　　　　　(D)  debugger

(B)  loader　　　　　　　　(E)  compiler

(C)  operating system

6.　Consider the following truth table for the Boolean function f:

| a | b | c | d | f |
|---|---|---|---|---|
| 0 | 0 | 0 | 0 | 1 |
| 0 | 0 | 0 | 1 | 0 |
| 0 | 0 | 1 | 0 | 1 |
| 0 | 0 | 1 | 1 | 0 |
| 0 | 1 | 0 | 0 | 0 |

| 0 | 1 | 0 | 1 | 0 |
|---|---|---|---|---|
| 0 | 1 | 1 | 0 | 0 |
| 0 | 1 | 1 | 1 | 1 |
| 1 | 0 | 0 | 0 | 1 |
| 1 | 0 | 0 | 1 | 0 |
| 1 | 0 | 1 | 0 | 1 |
| 1 | 0 | 1 | 1 | 0 |
| 1 | 1 | 0 | 0 | 0 |
| 1 | 1 | 0 | 1 | 0 |
| 1 | 1 | 1 | 0 | 0 |
| 1 | 1 | 1 | 1 | 1 |

Which of the following expressions is the minimal sum of products (SP) representation of the function given in the truth table?

(A)  $abcd$

(B)  $a + a'bcd$

(C)  $b'd' + bcd$

(D)  $a'b'd' + abcd$

(E)  $a'b'c'd' + a'b'cd' + a'bcd + ab'c'd' + ab'cd' + abcd$

**QUESTIONS 7–8** are based on the following Pascal fragment.

```
procedure L1;
        var a,b: integer; {1}
        var c, d: char;

        procedure L2(var e: integer);
                var b,f: real;

        begin
                ___
                ___
        end;

        procedure L3(g:char);
                var b, c: integer;

        begin
                ___
                ___
```

```
        end;
   begin
        ___
        ___
        L2(a);
        L3(c);
        ___
        ___
   end;
```

7. In procedure $L2$ the variable e is best described as a/an

   (A) global variable      (D) variable parameter

   (B) local variable      (E) actual parameter

   (C) recursive variable

8. If the notation $L1$-$L2$ means "the portion of the block $L1$ that is not in block $L2$" and $L1$-$L2$-$L3$ "the portion of the block $L1$ not in blocks $L2$ and $L3$," then the scope of variable b that is declared in the statement numbered {1} is

   (A) $L1$      (D) $L1$-$L2$-$L3$

   (B) $L1$-$L2$      (E) $L2$ and $L3$

   (C) $L1$-$L3$

9. Consider the set {1,2,3} and the binary relation represented by the following digraph. Which of the following properties does the relation represented by this digraph have?

   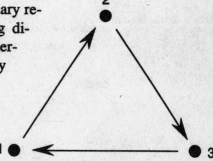

   I. Reflexivity

   II. Symmetry

   III. Transitivity

   (A) I and II only      (D) I, II, and III

   (B) I and III only      (E) None

   (C) II and III only

10. An unpaged or read-ahead cache associates disk domains with the start address of the read and continues for a specific length. The major disadvantage of unpaged cache is that

    (A) it allows cache domains to contain redundant data

    (B) it does not allow writes to be cached

    (C) its access time is greater than that of paged caching

    (D) read-ahead cache domain blocks are necessarily fixed in size

    (E) it may compromise file system consistency if the system crashes

11. A single-user workstation is attached to a local network. The workstation accesses files over the network from a file server. The average access time is 0.09 second per page. A similar stand-alone workstation accesses files from its own local disk with an average access time of 0.03 second per page. A particular program accesses and processes a 300 page file. The time to process the file once the data is in memory is 45 seconds. What is the ratio of the total time to access and process the file for the local network workstation to the total time for the stand-alone workstation?

    (A) 3/1                          (D) 5/2

    (B) 4/3                          (E) 1/1

    (C) 8/5

12. Suppose $\Sigma = \{1\}$ and $\Phi = \Sigma \cup \{a,b\}$. Let $S$ be a system with a single axiom $ab1$ and rules

$$a\boxed{1}b\boxed{2} \longrightarrow a\boxed{2}b\boxed{1}\boxed{2}$$

$$a\boxed{1}b\boxed{2} \longrightarrow \boxed{1}$$

    $L(S)$ is the set of numbers written in base 1. Which of the following sets of numbers correspond to $L(S)$?

    (A) 0, 1, 2, 3, 4, 5, 6, 7, ...        (D) 0, 2, 4, 6, 8, 10, 12, ...

    (B) 0, 1, 4, 9, 16, 25, 36, ...        (E) 0, 3, 5, 7, 9, 11, 13, ...

    (C) 0, 1, 2, 3, 5, 8, 13, ...

13. *Availnode* is a pointer variable that points to the next available node in a singly linked list of available nodes. If p points to a node currently being accessed in a program, then the program fragment

```
if p = nil then
        error
else
        begin
            p^.next:=availnode;
            availnode:=p
        end
```

(A) returns to the Pascal heap the space that is occupied by the node to which *p* is pointing

(B) swaps the nodes to which *p* and *availnode* are pointing

(C) replaces the information stored in the node pointed to by *availnode* with the information stored in the node pointed to by *p*

(D) creates a new node by removing a node from the available node list

(E) disposes of p by inserting it into the front of the available node list

14. Let $\Sigma = \{a,b,c,d,e,f\}$. The number of strings in $\Sigma^*$ of length 4 such that no symbol is used more than once in a string is

(A) 28

(B) 35

(C) 49

(D) 360

(E) 720

15. Consider the following regular expression:

$R = (ab \mid abb)^*bbab$

Which of the following strings is NOT in the set denoted by *R*?

(A) *ababab*

(B) *abbbab*

(C) *abbabbbab*

(D) *ababbabbbab*

(E) *abbabbbabbbab*

16. Consider the following recursive Pascal function where n is a non-negative integer:

```
function calc(n: nonnegint): nonnegint;

begin
        if n = O then
                calc:= O
        else
                calc:= n + calc(n-1)
end;
```

What value will calc return when it is invoked with $n=8$?

(A) 0

(D) 56

(B) 8

(E) 64

(C) 36

17. Derive the function represented by the following circuit:

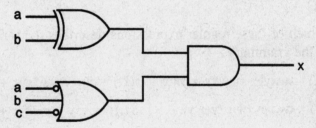

(A) $ab + a'bc'$

(D) $(ab)(a'bc')$

(B) $(a \oplus b)(a' + b + c')$

(E) $bc'$

(C) $ab + a'bc'$

18. In the figure shown, a deterministic finite automaton $M$ has start state $A$ and accepting state $D$. Which of the following regular expressions denotes the set of all words accepted by $M$?

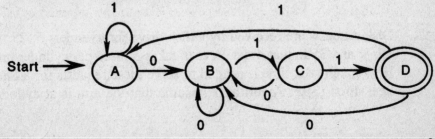

(A) 001            (D) 1\*0\*011

(B) 10\*1\*0         (E) (0|1)\*011

(C) 10\*1\*010

19. A digital search tree is implemented as a tree with n nodes each of which can contain m pointers, corresponding to the m possible symbols in each position of the key. The number of nodes that must be accessed to find a particular key is

(A) $m$           (D) $m^n$

(B) $n$            (E) $\log_m n$

(C) $n^m$

20. Consider the following grammar:

$S \rightarrow Ax \,|\, By$
$A \rightarrow By \,|\, Cw$
$B \rightarrow x \,|\, Bw$
$C \rightarrow y$

Which of these regular expressions describes the same set of strings as the grammar?

(A) $xwxy + xww^*y + ywx$     (D) $xwy + xw^*xyx + ywx$

(B) $xwx + xww^*y + yw$       (E) $xw^*y + xw^*yx + ywx$

(C) $xw^*y + xwxyx + ywx$

21. Two square matrices $A$ and $B$ represent the same linear transformation if and only if there is a matrix $P$ such that

(A) $AP = BP$          (D) $B = P^{-1}AP$

(B) $\det(A) = \det(P^{-1}BP)$     (E) $AP = BP^{-1}$

(C) $B = AP$

22. Disk requests are received by a disk drive for cylinders 5, 25, 18, 3, 39, 8, and 35 in that order. A seek takes 5 msec per cylinder moved. How much seek time is needed to serve these requests for a Shortest Seek First (SSF) Algorithm? Assume that the arm is at cylinder 20

when the last of these requests is made with none of the requests yet served.

(A)  125                    (D)  750

(B)  295                    (E)  935

(C)  575

23.  The clock interrupt handler on the SOS computer requires 2 msec per clock tick. The clock runs at 60 Hz. What percent of the CPU is devoted to the clock?

(A)  1.2                    (D)  18.5

(B)  7.5                    (E)  24

(C)  12

24.  The Squash Computer Model uses the following 32-bit floating-point representation of real numbers:

| S | Mantissa | | Exponent |
|---|----------|---|----------|

31 30                                    7 6              0

In a redesign of the Squash Computer, the Model 200 uses the following floating point representation scheme:

| S | Mantissa | | Exponent |
|---|----------|---|----------|

31 30                                    8 7              0

Which of the following statements is true with regard to the Model 200 method of representing floating-point numbers over the Model 100 method?

(A)  both the range and precision are increased

(B)  the range is increased but the precision is decreased

(C)  the range is decreased but the precision is increased

(D)  both the range and precision are decreased

(E)  both the range and precision remain the same

25.  Consider the following set of micro-operations:

t0:      MAR ← (PC)

t1:     $IR \leftarrow (MDR), PC \leftarrow (PC + 1)$
t2:     $Decoder \leftarrow (IR)$
t3:     $ABUS \leftarrow (R1), BBUS \leftarrow (R2)$
t4:     $ALU \leftarrow (R1 + R2)$
t5:     $CBUS \leftarrow (ALU)$
t6:     $R1 \leftarrow CBUS$

The operation(s) that make up the entire fetch phase of the instruction cycle include

(A) $t3$

(B) $t4$

(C) $t5, t6$

(D) $t0, t1$

(E) $t0, t1, t2$

26. Four $256 \times 8$ PROM chips are used to produce a total capacity of $1024 \times 8$. How many address bus lines are required?

(A) 4

(B) 8

(C) 10

(D) 16

(E) 32

27. Every computer can represent a limited number of real numbers exactly in any floating-point representation. The Tomato Computer represents floating-point numbers in normalized, base 2 format shown below:

| S | Mantissa | Exponent |
|---|----------|----------|
| 0  1 |                 7  8 |        11 |

The exponent is biased (excess-8). What is the approximate relative error of representing the decimal value +0.4 on the Tomato Computer?

(A) 0.4%

(B) 2.2%

(C) 3.8%

(D) 5.1%

(E) 7.9%

28. Which of the following lists of nodes correspond to a postorder traversal of the binary tree in the figure shown?

(A)  *ABDEHCFIGJ*

(B)  *DHEBIFJGCA*

(C)  *DBEHAIFCJG*

(D)  *ABCDEFGHIJ*

(E)  *ACGJFIBEHD*

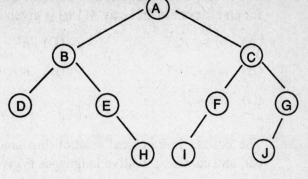

29.  A Fibonacci tree is an AVL tree with the minimum number of nodes. The depth of a node i in a binary tree is the length of the path from the root node to i. The depth of the root node is 0. If d is the depth of a Fibonacci tree, and $F_d$ is the dth number in the Fibonacci sequence, then the number of nodes in a Fibonacci tree is given by

$$|F_d| = |F_{d-1}| + |F_{d-2}| + 1.$$

$|F_d|$ is also given by the following relationship:

(A)  $|F_d| = F_{d+3} - 1$      (D)  $|F_d| = F_d$

(B)  $|F_d| = F_d + d$      (E)  $|F_d| = d * F_d$

(C)  $|F_d| = F_{d-1} + F_{d-2}$

30.  The hash function

        *hash : =key* **mod** *size*

and linear probing are used to insert the keys

        37, 38, 72, 48, 98, 11, 56

into the hash table with indices 0 … 6. The order of the keys in the array are given by

(A)  72, 11, 37, 38, 56, 98, 48

(B)  11, 48, 37, 38, 72, 98, 56

(C)  98, 11, 37, 38, 72, 56, 48

(D)  98, 56, 37, 38, 72, 11, 48

(E)  11, 37, 48, 38, 72, 98, 56

31. The average time required to perform a successful sequential search for an element in an array $A(1{:}n)$ is given by

    (A) $(n + 1)/2$                    (D) $n^2$

    (B) $n(n + 1)/2$                   (E) $n(n + 1)(2n + 1)/6$

    (C) $\log_2 n$

32. The correct hierarchical relationship among context-free, right-linear, and context-sensitive languages is given by

    (A) context-free $\subset$ right-linear $\subset$ context-sensitive

    (B) context-free $\subset$ context-sensitive $\subset$ right-linear

    (C) context-sensitive $\subset$ context-free $\subset$ right-linear

    (D) context-sensitive $\subset$ right-linear $\subset$ context-free

    (E) right-linear $\subset$ context-free $\subset$ context-sensitive

**QUESTIONS 33–34** are based upon the following code segment which is intended to sum the coefficients of any two non-empty polynomials where the terms of the polynomials are kept in a linked list.

```
type
        polynomial = ^term;
              term = record;
                        coeff: real;
                        exp: integer;
                        next: polynomial;
                   end;
     var
        summand1, summand2, result: polynomial;

     procedure add (summand1,summand2: polonomial;
                        var result: polynomial);

           var
                 p, q, t, current: polynomial;
     begin
           p:=summand1;
           q:=summand2;
           new(result);
```

```
       current:=result:
               while (p<>nil) and (q<>nil) do
                   begin
                               current ^.coeff:=p^.coeff + q^.coeff;
                               t:=current;
                               p:=p^.next;
                               q:=q^.next;
                               new(current);
                               t^.next:=current;
                   end;
       t^.next:=nil;                                                      (1)
           dispose(current);
   end;
```

33. Which of the following is (are) true?

    I.    The code segment produces the desired results only if the two polynomials are of the same length.

    II.    The code segment produces the desired results only if terms with matching exponents are located in the same relative nodes of the two link lists.

    III.    The code segment produces the desired results only if all coefficients are $\geq 0$.

    (A)  I only            (D)  II and III only

    (B)  I and II only     (E)  I, II, and III

    (C)  I and III only

34. What would be the effect on the outcome of the code segment if the line marked (1) is removed from the procedure add?

    (A)  the structure of all three link lists will be destroyed

    (B)  the values of the coefficients will be changed

    (C)  the next field in the last node of the link list result will be undefined

    (D)  the pointer to the result link list will be lost

    (E)  no effect

35. Two computers that communicate with each other use a simple parity check to detect errors for ASCII transmissions. Which of the following events will always lead to an *undetected* error?

    (A) one bit or any odd number of bits inverted in a byte during transmission

    (B) two bits or any even number of bits inverted in a byte during transmission

    (C) one bit or any odd number of bits inverted in a block of data during transmission

    (D) two bits or any even number of bits inverted in a block during transmission

    (E) data packets sent by one computer arrive out of sequence at the destination computer

36. Which of the following shows the correct relationship among some of the more common computing times for algirithms?

    (A) $O(\log n) < O(n) < O(n * \log n) < O(2^n) < O(n^2)$

    (B) $O(n) < O(\log n) < O(n * \log n) < O(2^n) < O(n^2)$

    (C) $O(n) < O(\log n) < O(n * \log n) < O(n^2) < O(2^n)$

    (D) $O(\log n) < O(n) < O(n * \log n) < O(n^2) < O(2^n)$

    (E) $O(\log n) < O(n * \log n) < O(n) < O(n^2) < O(2^n)$

37. In a multiprogramming system, a set of processes is deadlocked if each process in the set is waiting for an event to occur that can be initiated only by another process in the set. Which of the following is NOT one of the four conditions that are necessary for deadlock to occur?

    (A) mutual exclusion

    (B) partial assignment of resources

    (C) nonpreemption

    (D) process suspension

    (E) circular wait

38. Assume semaphore $S$ is used to manage the mutually exclusive use of a system resource and that only operations $P(S)$ and $V(S)$ may be performed on $S$. Which of the following is true of the $P$ and $V$ operations?

   I.   When the $P(S)$ operation is performed, if $S = 0$, then the executing process decrements $S$ and continues, using the system resource managed by $S$.

   II.  Only the test-and-set instruction $P$ needs special hardware allowing it to be performed in one instruction, while the $V$ operation can be performed in more than one instruction.

   III. When the $V(S)$ operation is performed, if $S$'s waiting queue is non-empty, then the process removes one waiting process.

   IV.  The $P$ and $V$ operations are used to manage software as well as hardware resources.

   (A) I only                      (D) III and IV

   (B) II only                     (E) All are true

   (C) II and III

39. Consider the following flow shop scheduling problem:

   |       | a  | b  |
   |-------|----|----|
   | J = 1 | 6  | 12 |
   | 2     | 9  | 3  |
   | 3     | 15 | 17 |
   | 4     | 20 | 26 |

   Which of the following is an optimal nonpreemptive schedule? Assume that each processor can perform one task at a time and a task $T_{a_i}$ must be completed before starting $T_{b_i}$.

   (A) $J_1 J_3 J_4 J_2$             (D) $J_4 J_2 J_1 J_3$

   (B) $J_3 J_4 J_1 J_2$             (E) $J_2 J_3 J_1 J_4$

   (C) $J_2 J_4 J_3 J_1$

40. For what values of $n$ is $10 * n * \log_2(n) > 2 * n^2$?

   (A) only $n \geq 32$            (D) only $n \geq 0$

   (B) only $2 \leq n \leq 22$     (E) only $n > 128$

   (C) only $20 \leq n \leq 32$

41. A computer with a 32-bit word size uses 2's complement to represent numbers. The range of integers that can be represented by this computer is

(A) $-2^{32}$ to $2^{32}$  (D) $-2^{32}$ to $2^{31}$

(B) $-2^{31}$ to $2^{32}$  (E) $-2^{32}-1$ to $2^{32}$

(C) $-2^{31}$ to $2^{31} - 1$

42. Consider the following Pascal function which is an implementation of Ackerman's function:

```
function ack(m,n: integer): integer;

begin
        if m=0 then
                ack:=n+1
        else if(m<>0) and (n=0) then
                ack:=ack(m-1, 1)
        else
                ack:=ack(m-1, ack(m,n-1))
end;
```

What value will be returned from the function when involved with the following call:

```
r:=ack(2,1);
```

(A) 1  (D) 4

(B) 2  (E) 5

(C) 3

43. In the following expression, **and** and **or** are arithmetic operators:

   (42 **or** 72) **and** 55

The value of this expression is

(A) 15  (D) 85

(B) 34  (E) 169

(C) 59

44. The black box in the following figure consists of a minimum complexity circuit that uses only AND, OR, and NOT gates:

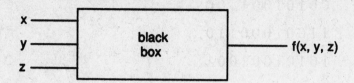

The function $f(x, y, z) = 1$ whenever $x$, $y$ are different and 0 otherwise. In addition the 3 inputs $x$, $y$, $z$ are never all the same value. Which of the following equations leads to the correct design for the minimum complexity circuit?

(A) $x'y + xy'$

(B) $x + y'z$

(C) $x'y'z' + xy'z$

(D) $xy + y'z + z'$

(E) $x'z + xy + y'z'$

**Questions 45–46** are based on the following information.

A one-dimensional cellular automaton consists of a line of sites or discrete variables, each with a value of 0 or 1. The state of a cellular automaton is completely specified by the values of the variables at each site. A cellular automaton evolves in discrete time steps, the value $a_i$ of a site at position $i$ is updated according to the rule:

$$a_i(t + 1) = \phi(a_{i-1}, a_i, a_{i+1})$$

The variables at each site are updated simultaneously. A rule is usually represented by a binary number. Each digit in the binary representation of the rule number gives the value of $\phi$ for a particular set of $(a_{i-1}, a_i, a_{i+1})$. The digit corresponding to the coefficient of $2^n$ in the rule number gives the value of $\phi(a_{i-1}, a_i, a_{i+1})$ where $n = 4a_{i-1} + 2a_i + a_{i+1}$. Thus the rightmost digit in the binary representation of the rule number gives $\phi(0,0,0)$, the next gives $\phi(0, 0, 1)$, right on up to $\phi(1, 1, 1)$.

45. A 1-dimensional cellular automaton is seeded (initialized) with the following values at time $t_0$

$$\ldots 0\,0\,0\,0\,1\,0\,1\,0\,0\,0\,0 \ldots$$

The automaton evolves according to the rule 01010110. What will the automaton look like at time $t_3$?

(A) ...00101001100...

(B) ...11001000110...

(C) ...10101001001...

(D) ...01101110110...

(E) ...00011011000...

46. Given the following rule for the evolution of a three-site cellular automaton which uses a Boolean function to give the digit corresponding to the coefficient of $2^n$ in the rule number:

$$(a_{-1}' a_1') + (a_0 a_1') \text{ where } n = 4a_{-1} + 2a_0 + a_1$$

which of the following is the binary representation of the rule?

(A) 01001010

(B) 00101100

(C) 00010000

(D) 11001110

(E) 01000101

47. Which of the following instances of the Post Correspondence Problem have a viable sequence?

I. $\{(ab, abb), (ba, aaa) (aa, a)\}$

II. $\{(ab, aba), (baa, aa), (aba, baa)\}$

III. $\{(b, bb), (bb, bab), (bab, abb), (abb, babb)\}$

(A) I only

(B) II only

(C) III only

(D) I and II only

(E) I, II, and III

48. A file server uses a form of locking as a concurrency control technique. When a file is locked by a client, all attempts to use or lock the file by other clients are prevented by the server. A potential problem exists if a client requests a lock on a file and then crashes. This situation could result in the file being locked indefinitely. To prevent this from occurring, the file server starts a timer whenever it sets a lock. If the timer runs out before the file is unlocked, the

server assumes that the client has crashed and releases the lock. Which of the following is (are) true of this strategy?

I. It provides a solution to the problem of preventing indefinite lockout.

II. It may result in interleaved access to a file by two or more clients.

III. It will guarantee mutual exclusion.

IV. It will fail to guarantee the prevention of indefinite lockout.

(A) I only          (D) II and IV

(B) I and II        (E) III and IV

(C) I and III

49. Assume that you have an algorithm that operates on a set of data with $n$ elements. If the recurrence formula that computes the time requirement for the algorithm is given by

$$T(n) = \begin{cases} 8T(n/2) + qn & \text{if } n > 1 \\ p & \text{if } n = 1 \end{cases}$$

where $p$ and $q$ are constants, which of the following gives the order of complexity, $0$, of the algorithm?

(A) $n*\log2n$       (D) $n^2$

(B) $n^3$           (E) $2^n$

(C) $\log2(n)$

50. A computer has **m** processors that are numbered $0 \leq k \leq (m-1)$. The following algorithm is executed on an array $x[0...(n-1)]$ where $n = 8$ and $n < m$.

```
for j:=1 to log₂(n) do
        for all k in parallel do
                if k ≥ 2ʲ⁻¹ then
                        x[k]:= x[k−2ʲ⁻¹] + x[k]
                endif
        endfor
    endfor
```

If the array $x$ is initialized with the following values, what will be the values of the elements in the array after the algorithm is executed?

| $x_0$ | $x_1$ | $x_2$ | $x_3$ | $x_4$ | $x_5$ | $x_6$ | $x_7$ |
|---|---|---|---|---|---|---|---|
| 2 | −3 | 4 | 5 | −6 | −1 | 1 | 3 |

| | $x_0$ | $x_1$ | $x_2$ | $x_3$ | $x_4$ | $x_5$ | $x_6$ | $x_7$ |
|---|---|---|---|---|---|---|---|---|
| (A) | 3 | 1 | −1 | −6 | 5 | 4 | −3 | 2 |
| (B) | −6 | −3 | −1 | 1 | 2 | 3 | 4 | 5 |
| (C) | 2 | −1 | 3 | 8 | 2 | 1 | 2 | 5 |
| (D) | 2 | −1 | 1 | 9 | −1 | −7 | 0 | 4 |
| (E) | 3 | 4 | 6 | −2 | 8 | −3 | 9 | 3 |

51. Let $\Sigma = \{0, 1, ..., \sigma-1\}$ be an alphabet of $\sigma$ symbols. A *de Bruijn* sequence is a circular sequence $a_0 a_1 ... a_{L-1}$ over $\Sigma$ such that for every string **w** of length $n$ over $\Sigma$ there exists a unique **i** such that

$$a_i a_{i+1} ... a_{i+n+1} = w$$

where $L = \sigma^n$ and the computation of the indices is modulo $L$. Which of the following is a *de Bruijn* sequence for $\Sigma = \{0, 1\}$ and $n = 3$?

(A)  01101010          (D)  00011101

(B)  01011010          (E)  10110100

(C)  10010110

52. The Pumpkin Computer uses a segmented addressing scheme in which individual bytes are accessed by combining a 16-bit segment paragraph and a 16-bit relative offset. SR is a 16-bit segment register that points to the beginning of a 16-byte paragraph that is evenly divisible by 16. The segment paragraph is treated as if it were shifted left by four bits. SI is a 16-bit segment index register that contains a relative offset from the segment paragraph specified in SR. What will be the actual memory address accessed if the contents of SR are 1234H and the contents of SI are 4392H?

(A)  55C6H          (D)  166D2

(B)  5626H          (E)  44B54

(C)  16732

53. Two matrices, *matrixa* and *matrixb* have the following record structure:

```
matrix = record
                cell: array[1..maxsize, 1..maxsize] of integer;
                row,
                col: maxsize;
          end;
```

The following code is designed to generate the product matrix of *matrixa* and *matrixb*:

```
for i:= 1 to matrixa.row do
        for j:= 1 to matrixb.col do
                begin
                        sum:= 0;
                        for k:= 1 to matrixa.col do
                                <statement–1>;
                        <statement–2>
                end;
```

What two statements are missing?

(A)   $sum := matrixa.cell[i, j] * matrixb.cell[k,j]$

     $prod[i,j] := sum$

(B)   $sum := sum + matrixa.cell[k, j] * matrixb.cell[i,k]$

     $prod[k,k] := sum$

(C)   $sum := sum + matrixa.cell[k,i] * matrixb.cell[j,k]$

     $prod[j,i] := sum$

(D)   $sum := sum + matrixa + matrixa.cell[k,k] * matrixb.cell[i,j]$

     $prod[j,i] := sum$

(E)   $sum := sum + matrixa.cell[i,k] * matrixb.cell[k,j]$

     $prod[i,j] := sum$

54. A language has the following two constructs

```
<assignment–statement>::= variable = expression
<do-loop>::= do label control-variable = initial-value,
                     final–value [, increment-value]
```

The language does not have reserved words and blank spaces are not significant. Consider the action of a compiler on the following two statements:

**do** 20 I = 1, 10                      (1)

**do** 20 I = 110                       (2)

Which of the following statements is/are true?

I.    The compiler will be able to distinguish statement (1) as a *<do-loop>* construct when it identifies the token **do**.

II.   The compiler will not be able to distinguish statement (1) from statement (2) until the ',' is reached in statement (1).

III.  The compiler will generate a syntax error for statement (2).

(A)  I only                    (D)  I and III only

(B)  II only                 (E)  II and III only

(C)  III only

55.  Consider the grammar G where the productions are numbered as shown:

(1)     $E \rightarrow E + T$
(2)     $E \rightarrow T$
(3)     $T \rightarrow T * F$
(4)     $T \rightarrow F$
(5)     $F \rightarrow (E)$
(6)     $F \rightarrow a$

If a shift-reduce (bottom-up) parser writes the production number used immediately after performing any reduction, what string will be printed if the parser input is $a + a * a$?

(A)  62461               (D)  64642331

(B)  6262441            (E)  64264631

(C)  6364231

56.  The **if .. then .. else** block

**if** (*grade* = 'A') **or** (*grade* = 'B') **then**

writeln('Good Work')
    **else if** (*grade* = 'C') **then**
        writeln('Average Work')
    **else if** (*grade* = 'D') **or** (*grade* = 'F') **then**
        writeln('Poor Work')

might be written as the **case** statement

```
case grade of
        'A', 'B' : writeln('Good Work');
        'C'     : writeln('Average Work');
        'D', 'F' : writeln('Poor Work');
end;
```

Which of the following is/are true of this translation?

I.    The translation is correct.

II.   A runtime error would be generated by the **case** statement if *grade* = 'E'.

III.  The **case** statement needs to be a part of the **if** statement

**if** *grade* **in** ['A', 'B', 'C', 'D', 'F'] **then**

in order to be a correct translation.

(A)  I only            (D)  I and II only

(B)  II only          (E)  II and III only

(C)  III only

57.  Consider the following query ( $\wedge$ = AND, $\vee$ = OR) for a random access file:

$$Q = (k_1 \wedge k_2 \wedge k_4) \vee (k_2 \wedge k_3) \vee (k_1 \wedge k_3 \wedge k_5) \vee$$

The number of records in the file which contain the corresponding key are listed by the directory as:

$k_1 = 12$
$k_2 = 24$
$k_3 = 18$
$k_4 = 40$
$k_5 = 32$
$k_6 = 56$

If $Q$ is optimized such that the number of records retrieved is minimized and the frequency of keywords in $Q$ is maximized, then the optimum set of keywords to be used for the retrieval is?

(A) $\{k_1, k_2, k_3\}$           (D) $\{k_1, k_3, k_4, k_6\}$

(B) $\{k_1, k_3, k_5\}$           (E) $\{k_2, k_3, k_5, k_6\}$

(C) $\{k_1, k_2, k_4\}$

58. Given the hash function:

$h = $ Data Item **mod** 60

If the chaining method is used, and if seven integer data items are stored in the hash table in the following order:

65   121   123   242   63   122   183

How many comparisons would it take to find integer data item 183?

(A) 1           (D) 3

(B) 7           (E) 8

(C) 4

59. Define $Q(I, J)$ for non-negative integers $I$, $J$ where $J$ is given and $I_n = I_{n-1} + J$.

$$Q(I,J) = \begin{cases} 0 & \text{if } I_n < J \\ Q(I_{n-1}, J) + 2 & \text{if } I_n \geq J \end{cases}$$

Then for all non-negative integers $I$ and $J = 3$, $Q(I, 3)$ is

(A) 4           (D) $2 * (I \textbf{ div } 3)$

(B) $J - 4$           (E) $2^I - 2^3$

(C) $I - 2$

60. A language $L$ is accepted by a finite automaton if and only if it is

(A) right-linear.           (D) primitive recursive.

(B) context-sensitive.           (E) recursive.

(C) context-free.

**QUESTIONS 61–62** are based upon the following program segment:

```
for item:=n downto 2 do
        begin
                large:=list[1];
                index:=1;
                for i:=2 to item do
                        if list[i] > large then
                                begin
                                        large:=list[i];
                                        index:=i;
                                end;
                list[index]:=list[item];
                list[item]:=large;
                {1}
        end;
```

61. The number of comparisons made by this algorithm is given by

(A) $O(n)$                    (B) $O(n^2)$

(C) $O(n^3)$                   (D) $O(n * \log_2 n)$

(E) $O(2^n)$

62. Which of the following assertions is most strongly satisfied at the point marked {1}?

(A) $list[j] < list[j + 1]$} for all $j$ such that $item \leq j < n$

(B) $list[j] < list[j + 1]$} for all $j$ such that $item < j \leq n$

(C) $list[j] \leq list[j + 1]$} for all $j$ such that $item \leq j < n$

(D) $list[j] < list[j - 1]$} for all $j$ such that $1 < j \leq item$

(E) $list[j] < list[j - 1]$} for all $j$ such that $item \leq j < n$

63. Consider the following control circuit which contains a 3-bit register and a black box with some combinational logic.

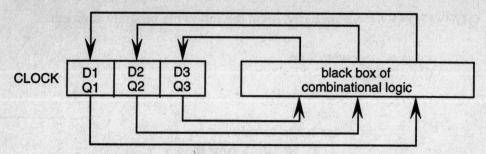

The initial state of the circuit is $Q_1Q_2Q_3 = 000$. The circuit generates the control sequence

$$(010) \to (110) \to (001) \to (001) \to \ldots \to (001)$$

on successive clock cycles. Which of the following sets of equations are implemented by the combinational logic in the black box?

(A) $D_1 = Q_1'Q_2'Q_3'$ , $D_2 = Q_1'$ , $D_3 = Q_2$

(B) $D_1 = Q_2Q_3'$ , $D_2 = Q_1Q_2'$ , $D_3 = Q_1Q_2Q_3'$

(C) $D_1 = Q_1 \vee Q_2$ , $D_2 = Q_1'$ , $D_3 = Q_1Q_2'$

(D) $D_1 = Q_1'Q_2$ , $D_2 = Q_1'Q_3'$ , $D_3 = Q_1 \vee Q_3$

(E) $D_1 = Q_2$ , $D_2 = Q_2Q_3$ , $D_3 = Q_1$

64. In the following program, which is written in Pascal syntax, parameters are passed by value-result.

```
program pass(input,output);

var x, y: integer;

procedure vr(value_result u, v: integer);

begin
        u:=2 * u;
        x:=u + v;
        u:=u − 1;
end;

begin
        x:=4;
        y:=2;
        vr(x,y);
```

*writeln(x);*
**end.**

The output for this program is

(A)  4                              (D)  8

(B)  5                              (E)  10

(C)  7

65.  Consider a problem in which you are given 5 objects with the weights

$$(W_1, W_2, W_3, W_4, W_5) = (6, 10, 9, 5, 12).$$

The following profits are associated with the objects:

$$(P_1, P_2, P_3, P_4, P_5) = (8, 5, 10, 15, 7)$$

In addition to the five objects, you are given a knapsack with a capacity of 30. The objective of the problem is to fill the knapsack while maximizing the total profit. Assuming that a fraction of an object may be placed in the knapsack in order to completely fill the knapsack, which of the following approximates the maximum profit that can be obtained by filling the knapsack with a combination of the five objects? Each object can be used only once.

(A)  12.2                           (D)  38.83

(B)  21.51                          (E)  43.1

(C)  30.34

66.  A two dimensional array $A\{1. . \text{row}, 1. . \text{col}]$ is stored in memory beginning at location $S$. Which of the following expressions points to the correct memory location of any arbitrary element $A[i, j]$?

(A)   $S + (i - 1) * col + j - 1$

(B)   $S + (j - 1) * row + i - 1$

(C)   $S + (i * j) + i$

(D)   $S + (i * j) + j$

(E)   $S + (row * col) - (i \bullet j)$

67. An operating system uses a Least Recently Used (LRU) page replacement algorithm for managing memory. Consider the following page reference string where each reference is made in one unit of time:

$$1, 8, 1, 7, 8, 2, 7, 2, 1, 8, 3, 8, 2, 1, 3, 1, 7, 1, 3, 7$$

Which of the following is the number of page faults that are generated for this particular LRU case assuming that the process has been allocated four page frames?

(A) 6                      (D) 3

(B) 5                      (E) 2

(C) 4

68. A Boolean function is a threshold function if and only if it can be realized by a single threshold gate — that is, there exists a set of real weights $w_1, w_2, \ldots, w_3$ and $T$ such that

$$\text{if } f(x_1, x_2, \ldots, x_n) = 1 \text{ then } (x_1 w_1 + x_2 w_2 + \ldots + x_n w_n) - T \geq 0$$

and

$$\text{if } f(x_1, x_2, \ldots, x_n) = 0 \text{ then } (x_1 w_1 + x_2 w_2 + \ldots + x_n w_n) - T < 0$$

Which of the following boolean functions are threshold functions?

I.    $f(x) = 0$

II.   $f(x) = 1$

III.  XOR

IV.  NOT

(A) I only              (D) II and IV only

(B) II only            (E) I, II, and IV only

(C) I and III only

69. Let $\Delta = \{X_1, X_2, X_3\}$, and let

$$X_1 = aX_2 + bX_1 + e$$
$$X_2 = aX_3 + bX_2$$
$$X_3 = aX_1 + bX_3$$

define the language L, where $\Sigma = \{a, b\}$ and $e$ is the empty string.

Which of the following set of regular expressions for $X_1$, $X_2$, $X_3$, provide a solution for the set of expression equations?

I.   $a * (b * (ab * (a + b) * b) + a *)$

II.  $b * (ab * a(ab * ab * a + b) * ab * + e)$

III. $(ab * ab * a + b) * ab *$

IV.  $(b * (ab * + a) * b)$

V.   $b * a (ab * ab * a + b) * ab *$

(A)  II, I, IV                    (D)  V, III, I

(B)  II, V, III                   (E)  IV, III, II

(C)  I, IV, V

70.  A circuit is designed to generate an even parity bit for a 3-bit register (3-Boolean variables). Which of the following equations generates a circuit to accomplish this task using a minimum number of AND, OR, and NOT gates?

(A)  $z = b_0b_1 + b_0'b_1'b_2'$

(B)  $z = b_0'b_1' + b_0b_1$

(C)  $z = b_0'b_1'b_2' + b_0'b_1 + b_0b_1'b_2$

(D)  $z = b_0'b_1'b_2 + b_0'b_1b_2' + b_0b_1'b_2' + b_0b_1b_2$

(E)  $z = b_0'b_1'b_2' + b_0'b_1b_2 + b_0b_1'b_2 + b_0b_1b_2'$

71.  A certain microprocessor requires 4.5 microseconds to respond to an interrupt. Assume that the three interrupts $I_1$, $I_2$, and $I_3$ require the following execution time after the interrupt is recognized:

(a)   $I_1$ requires 25 microseconds
(b)   $I_2$ requires 35 microseconds
(c)   $I_3$ requires 20 microseconds

$I_1$ has the highest priority and $I_3$ has the lowest. What is the possible range of time for $I_3$ to be executed assuming that it may or may not occur simultaneously with other interrupts?

(A)  24.5 microseconds to 93.5 microseconds

(B)  24.5 microseconds to 39.5 microseconds

    (C)   4.5 microseconds to 24.5 microseconds

    (D)   4.5 microseconds to 93.5 microseconds

    (E)   29.5 microseconds to 93.5 microseconds

72.   The combinational circuit given below is implemented with two NAND gates. To which of the following individual gates is it equivalent?

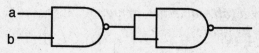

    (A)  NOT               (D)  XOR

    (B)  OR                  (E)  NOR

    (C)  AND

73.   A positive binary coded decimal (BCD) number may be represented as

$$N_1 = (D_{L-1}D_{1-2} \ldots D_0)$$

where $D_i$ is the four bit binary form of each digit. The binary value of $N_1$ may be written as

    (A)   $N_1 = (\ldots((D_{L-1} * 10_2 + D_{L-2}) * 10_2) + \ldots + D_1) * 10_2 + D_0$

    (B)   $N_1 = (\ldots((D_{L-1} * 1010_2 + D_{L-2}) * 1010_2 + \ldots + D_1)) * 1010_2 + D_0$

    (C)   $N_1 = (D_{L-1} D_{L-2} \ldots D_0) * 1010_2$

    (D)   $N_1 = (D_{L-1} D_{L-2} \ldots D_0) * 10_2$

    (E)   $N_1 = (\ldots((D_0 * 10_2 + D_1) * 10_2) + \ldots + D_{L-2}) * 10_2 + D_{L-1}$

74.   A character-interleaved time-division multiplexer is used to combine the data streams of a number of 600-bps asynchronous terminals for data transmission over a 9600-bps digital line. Each terminal sends characters consisting of a total of 10 bits. Assume that one synchronization character is sent every 29 characters and, in addition, at least 3% of the line capacity is reserved for pulse stuffing to accommodate speed variations from the various terminals. The number of terminals that can be accommodated by the multiplexer is

(A)  12

(D)  15

(B)  13

(E)  16

(C)  14

**QUESTIONS 75–76** are based on six files ($F_1$, $F_2$, $F_3$, $F_4$, $F_5$, $F_6$) which have corresponding sizes (100, 200, 70, 40, 250, 50) respectively.

75.  The files are to be stored on a sequential device (i.e., tape) in such a manner to optimize access time. In what order should the files be stored?

(A)  $F_1, F_2, F_3, F_4, F_5, F_6$

(B)  $F_5, F_2, F_1, F_3, F_6, F_4$

(C)  $F_4, F_6, F_3, F_1, F_2, F_5$

(D)  $F_6, F_5, F_4, F_3, F_2, F_1$

(E)  None of the above since the access time is independent of the order of storage.

76.  If the files are stored in such a manner to optimize access time, what will be the approximate average access time of a record from one of the six files on the sequential device?

(A)  131

(D)  352

(B)  198

(E)  433

(C)  286

77.  Consider the left-recursive grammar:

$$S \rightarrow Aa \mid b$$
$$A \rightarrow Ac \mid Sd$$

Which of the following grammars is equivalent to the grammar given above when the left-recursion is removed?

(A)  $S \rightarrow Aa \mid b$
     $A \rightarrow bdA'$
     $A' \rightarrow cA' \mid adA' \mid e$

(B)  $S \rightarrow Aa \mid b$
     $A \rightarrow ad \mid bd \mid cA$

(C) $S \rightarrow bA'$
$A' \rightarrow c \mid da$

(D) $S \rightarrow Aa \mid b$
$A \rightarrow Ac \mid Aad \mid bd$

(E) None of the above

78. Consider a job scheduling problem with four jobs, $J_1$, $J_2$, $J_3$, and $J_4$, with corresponding deadlines:

$$(d_1, d_2, d_3, d_4) = (4, 2, 4, 2)$$

Which of the following is not a feasible solution to the problem of scheduling the jobs without violating any job deadline?

(A) $J_2, J_4, J_1, J_3$        (D) $J_4, J_1, J_2, J_3$

(B) $J_4, J_2, J_1, J_3$        (E) $J_4, J_2, J_3, J_1$

(C) $J_2, J_4, J_3, J_1$

79. POS (Primitive disk Operating System) manages its disk files in contiguous blocks. A file is saved to the first available space that is large enough to hold the file. Assume that a disk has only 10 contiguous blocks of available free space. Which of the following set of file operations cannot be completed given the set of files and file sizes specified below?

$$fa = 1, \quad fb = 3, \quad fc = 5, \quad fd = 6$$

(A) $Save(fa)$, $Save(fb)$, $Save(fd)$, $Delete(fd)$, $Save(fc)$

(B) $Save(fb)$, $Save(fa)$, $Delete(fb)$, $Save(fd)$

(C) $Save(fd)$, $Save(fb)$, $Delete(fd)$, $Save(fc)$

(D) $Save(fc)$, $Save(fa)$, $Delete(fc)$, $Save(fd)$

(E) $Save(fb)$, $Save(fd)$, $Delete(fb)$, $Save(fa)$

80. The Mellon Computer can execute 1,000,000 instructions per second. A program running on this computer performs on average a one sector read and a one sector write for every 200 instructions that it executes. The disk drive handling the I/O transfers requires 0.0010 seconds each to perform the read and write operations. Assuming no

overlap of these operations, the percent of CPU time spent in the wait state, is

(A) 12%          (D) 78%

(B) 39%          (E) 91%

(C) 57%

# TEST 1

# ANSWER KEY

| | | | | | | | |
|---|---|---|---|---|---|---|---|
| 1. | (B) | 21. | (D) | 41. | (C) | 61. | (B) |
| 2. | (B) | 22. | (B) | 42. | (E) | 62. | (C) |
| 3. | (E) | 23. | (C) | 43. | (B) | 63. | (D) |
| 4. | (D) | 24. | (B) | 44. | (A) | 64. | (C) |
| 5. | (A) | 25. | (E) | 45. | (D) | 65. | (D) |
| 6. | (C) | 26. | (C) | 46. | (E) | 66. | (A) |
| 7. | (D) | 27. | (A) | 47. | (A) | 67. | (A) |
| 8. | (D) | 28. | (B) | 48. | (B) | 68. | (E) |
| 9. | (E) | 29. | (A) | 49. | (B) | 69. | (B) |
| 10. | (A) | 30. | (D) | 50. | (C) | 70. | (D) |
| 11. | (B) | 31. | (A) | 51. | (D) | 71. | (A) |
| 12. | (C) | 32. | (E) | 52. | (D) | 72. | (C) |
| 13. | (E) | 33. | (B) | 53. | (E) | 73. | (B) |
| 14. | (D) | 34. | (C) | 54. | (B) | 74. | (D) |
| 15. | (A) | 35. | (B) | 55. | (E) | 75. | (C) |
| 16. | (C) | 36. | (D) | 56. | (E) | 76. | (C) |
| 17. | (B) | 37. | (D) | 57. | (C) | 77. | (A) |
| 18. | (E) | 38. | (D) | 58. | (D) | 78. | (D) |
| 19. | (A) | 39. | (A) | 59. | (D) | 79. | (D) |
| 20. | (E) | 40. | (B) | 60. | (A) | 80. | (E) |

# DETAILED EXPLANATIONS
# OF ANSWERS

# TEST 1

1.   **(B)**

Hexidecimal digits run from 0 to F. A hexidecimal number can be converted directly to its binary equivalent by representing each hexidecimal digit in the number by four binary digits. Listed below is each hexidecimal digit in the hexidecimal system along with its binary equivalent:

| | | | |
|---|---|---|---|
| 0H = 0000B | 4H = 0100B | 8H = 1000B | CH = 1100B |
| 1H = 0001B | 5H = 0101B | 9H = 1001B | DH = 1101B |
| 2H = 0010B | 6H = 0110B | AH = 1010B | EH = 1110B |
| 3H = 0011B | 7H = 0111B | BH = 1011B | FH = 1111B |

Using this table it is easy to verify that

3B7F = 0011 1011 0111 1111

2.   **(B)**

Since the number of elements in the array is small, the easiest approach to solving problem 2 is to construct the corresponding search tree:

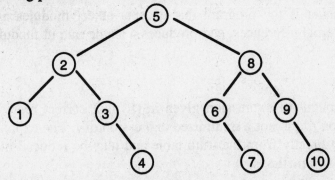

The values at each tree node represent the corresponding array index. Since the question asks for the average SUCCESSFUL time, $x$ must be present in $A$. If $x$ is located at $A[5]$, the time to find $x$ is 1 since only one comparison is required. If $x$ is located at $A[9]$, the time to find $x$ is 3 since three comparisons are required. Therefore, the average successful time for finding any arbitrary element $x$ is given by the following equation:

$$\text{Ave succ time} = (1 + 2 + 2 + 3 + 3 + 3 + 3 + 4 + 4 + 4)/10 = 2.9$$

3.  **(E)**

Variables whose types are exactly identical are called identical. Variables whose underlying type is the same are said to be compatible. Variable pairs, $a$ and $e$, $d$ and $e$, and $c$ and $f$ are not identical and are incompatible. Variables $b$ and $c$ are identical as well as being compatible. Variables $c$ and $d$ are compatible but are not identical. The variable $c$ is declared as type word and since word, which is not a reserved word in Pascal, is defined as an enumerated type from 0..15 and since 0..15 are integers, $c$ is compatible to $d$ which is declared as an integer.

4.  **(D)**

The three periods of delay involved in the physical transfer of information from moving head disks to memory are seek time, latency time, and transmission time. Seek time is the time required for the head to move to the track where information is to be read or written. Seek time is the slowest delay period when performing physical I/Os on moving head disks because of the physical movement of the disk head. Latency period is the time it takes the disk to rotate so that the head is located at the beginning of the sector where the information is to be read or written and is the next faster delay period. Unless the transfer (block) size is exceptionally large, transmission time is the fastest delay period for data transfer because this period does not involve any physical movement.

5.  **(A)**

A linker is the program that accepts object modules as input, resolves external references, and produces a single output module ready for loading.

6.  **(C)**

Although the expression given in (E) is a correct representation of the function $f$, it is not a minimized expression of $f$. The expression in (E) is derived directly from the truth table and may be reduced in one of the following two methods:

**Method 1:**
$$f = a'b'c'd' + a'b'cd' + a'bcd + ab'c'd' + ab'cd' + abcd$$
$$f = a'b'(c + c')d' + (a + a')bcd + ab'(c + c')d'$$

$$f = a'b'd' + bcd + ab'd'$$
$$f = (a + a')b'd' + bcd$$
$$f = b'd' + bcd$$

**Method 2:**

Construct the Karnaugh map for the function $f$:

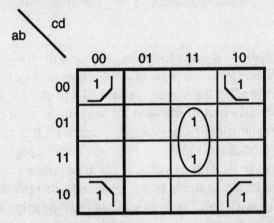

The minimized expression can be obtained directly from the two prime implicants (PIs) shown in the K-map.

7.  **(D)**
    The **var** that precedes the variable e in the procedure heading
    **procedure** *L2*(**var** *e*: *real*);

indicates that *e* is a variable parameter (actually a variable formal parameter) which means that *e* should be considered as a synonym for the actual parameter in the calling statement.

8.  **(D)**
    The scope of a variable is the range of the program in which that variable is known and can be used. This range includes the program block in which it is declared and all blocks internal to that block except for those blocks in which a variable is declared with the same identifier. Since new variables are defined in both *L2* and *L3* with the same identifier *b*, the scope of *b* declared in the statement {1} is all of *L1* except for *L2* and *L3*.

9.  **(E)**
    **Definition:**

    Let *R* be a binary relation on *A*. Then

    (a)  *R* is reflexive if *xRx* for every *x* in *A*.

(b)   $R$ is symmetric if $xRy$ implies $yRx$ for every $x,y$ in $A$.

(c)   $R$ is transitive if $xRy$ and $yRz$ together imply $x = y$ for every $x,y,z$ in $A$.

The relation given by the digraph in problem 9 has none of these properties. (Actually, the relation is irreflexive and antisymmetric.)

10.   **(A)**

A cache domain is always filled beginning with the start address of the read request. Therefore, subsequent read requests may begin with data that is partially located in the cache domain. Since the request cannot be completed because only part of the data for the request is in cache, another cache domain must be filled from disk. This can lead to redundant data in cache. Unpaged (read-ahead) caching requires a more sophisticated algorithm for managing I/Os. This is particularly true when a write request is made. The correct cache domain must be located to update the file, and then cache domains with "old" redundant data must be eliminated.

11.   **(B)**

Let $T_1$ = total processing time for local network workstation.

Let $T_2$ = total processing time for stand-alone workstation.

Let R = ratio of $T_1$ to $T_2$.

$T_1 = 300$ pages $* .09$ sec/page $+ 45$ sec $= 72$ sec

$T_2 = 300$ pages $* .03$ sec/page $+ 45$ sec $= 54$ sec

$R = 72$ sec/54 sec $= 4/3$

12.   **(C)**

The language that is generated by $S$ is the set of Fibonacci numbers. In this case, the axiom or start word is $ab1$. By applying the two rules we generate the first few Fibonacci numbers in base 1.

$ab1 \Rightarrow 0$

$ab1 \Rightarrow a1b1 \Rightarrow 1$

$ab1 \Rightarrow a1b1 \Rightarrow a11b111 \Rightarrow 11$

$ab1 \Rightarrow a1b1 \Rightarrow a11b111 \Rightarrow a111b11111 \Rightarrow 111$

$ab1 \Rightarrow a1b1 \Rightarrow a11b111 \Rightarrow a111b11111 \Rightarrow a11111b11111111 \Rightarrow 11111$

The first Fibonacci number (0) was arrived at by applying rule 2. The other Fibonacci numbers were arrived at by applying rule 1 one or more times followed by rule 2.

13. **(E)**

Typically, when memory is no longer required in Pascal, the memory is returned using the procedure *dispose*(**var** *p:pointer*) which makes use of the *dispose* statement. However, on some systems, this procedure does not do anything, and the space is actually lost and cannot be retrieved. On other systems, the overhead of memory management can cause the program to be inefficient. Therefore, one technique around these shortcomings is to add freed nodes to an available list until they are needed again. The fragment of code in question 13 adds the freed node pointed to by *p* to the available list of nodes pointed to by *availnode* provided that *p* is not *nil* in which case an error is encountered.

14. **(D)**

The number of strings of length 4 that can be formed from an alphabet of 6 symbols is the number of permutations of 6 objects taken 4 at a time since selection is without replacement. This is given by

$$P(6,4) = (6!)/(6-4)! = (6!)/(2!) = 6 * 5 * 4 * 3 = 360$$

15. **(A)**

*R* denotes the set of strings beginning with any combination of *ab* and/or *abb* and ending with *bbab*. The string *ababab* is not in this set because it does not terminate with *bbab*.

16. **(C)**

The function *calc* is recursive because of the statement

*calc*. = *n* + *calc*(*n*–1)

When *calc* is first called with *n* = 8, 8 will be pushed onto the stack and *calc* will be called recursively with the value 8 – 1 or 7. The process of pushing *n* onto the stack and recursively calling *calc* will continue until *n* = 0. At this point the stack will contain 8, 7, 6, 5, 4, 3, 2, 1. Now the values on the stack will be popped off and the statement above will be evaluated. This process is shown below:

| Value of n | Stack | Value of Calc |
|:---:|:---:|:---:|
| 8 | | |
| 7 | 8 | |
| 6 | 8,7 | |
| 5 | 8,7,6 | |

| 4 | 8,7,6,5 | |
| 3 | 8,7,6,5,4 | |
| 2 | 8,7,6,5,4,3 | |
| 1 | 8,7,6,5,4,3,2 | |
| 0 | 8,7,6,5,4,3,2,1 | 0 |
| 1 | 8,7,6,5,4,3,2 | 1 |
| 2 | 8,7,6,5,4,3 | 3 |
| 3 | 8,7,6,5,4 | 6 |
| 4 | 8,7,6,5 | 10 |
| 5 | 8,7,6 | 15 |
| 6 | 8,7 | 21 |
| 7 | 8 | 28 |
| 8 | | 36 |

17. **(B)**

The function can be found in the following manner:

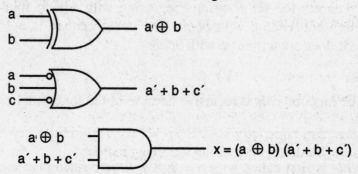

18. **(E)**

Choices (B) and (C) can be eliminated immediately since all words in the set of words accepted by $M$ must end with the digit '1'. The word in choice (A) 001 is accepted by $M$ but it does not describe the set of words accepted by $M$. Choice (D) 1 * 0 * 011 describes a subset of the words accepted by $M$. Only (E) describes the set of all words accepted by $M$.

19. **(A)**

The number of steps required to search a tree for a key is proportional to the number of symbols making up a key. It is not proportional to the logarithm of the number of keys, as is the case in other tree-based searches such as a binary search tree. For example, if $m = 5$ (keys consisting of all possible sequences of five numbers), then a tree search can locate any of almost 12 million keys in 5 iterations. A binary search would take $\log_2$ n or 23 iterations.

20. **(E)**

The regular expression may be derived in the following manner:

$S \rightarrow Ax \rightarrow Byx \rightarrow xyx$
$\rightarrow xw*yx$      (This term incorporates the term *xyx*.)
$\rightarrow Cwx \rightarrow ywx$
$\rightarrow By \rightarrow xy$
$\rightarrow xw*y$      (This term incorporates the term *xy*.)

21. **(D)**

A function $T: V \rightarrow W$ is a linear transformation if

$$T(v_1 + v_2) = T(v_1) + T(v_2), \text{ and } T(kv) = kT(v)$$

Two matrices $M$ and $N$ represent the same linear transformation with respect to different bases if and only if there exists two matrices $P$ and $Q$ such that $P$ and $Q$ have inverses and $N = P^{-1}MQ$. Since we are dealing with square matrices $P$ and $Q$ are the same. Therefore, $B = P^{-1}AP$.

22. **(B)**

The Shortest Seek First Algorithm will service the nearest request first. In this case, we have 7 requests that are queued. This is conceivable since these requests could come in while servicing a prior request. Assuming that the arm is initially at cylinder 20, the seek time to complete these requests can be determined in the following manner:

Requests = 5, 25, 18, 3, 39, 8, 35

$(20 - 18)$   cylinders * 5 msec/cylinder   =   10 msec
$(18 - 25)$   cylinders * 5 msec/cylinder   =   35 msec
$(25 - 35)$   cylinders * 5 msec/cylinder   =   50 msec
$(35 - 39)$   cylinders * 5 msec/cylinder   =   20 msec
$(39 - 8)$   cylinders * 5 msec/cylinder   = 155 msec
$(8 - 5)$   cylinders * 5 msec/cylinder   =   15 msec
$(5 - 3)$   cylinders * 5 msec/cylinder   =   10 msec

                                  295 msec

23. **(C)**

2 msec for clock/clock tick * 60 clock ticks/sec * 100% =

120 msec for clock/sec * 100% =

120 msec for clock/1000 msec * 100% =

.12 * 100% for clock =

12% for clock

24. **(B)**

A fixed number of floating-point numbers may be represented in a 32-bit word. Thus, when you change the sizes of the mantissa and the exponent, you must make a trade off between precision and range. Since, in this problem, the size of the exponent is increased, the range of numbers that can be represented is increased. The precision, however, is reduced since the number of bits being used has not been increased.

25. **(E)**

The first three micro-operations make up the fetch phase of the fetch/execute cycle. These operations include:

$t0$:   $MAR \leftarrow (PC)$     Load the contents of the Program Counter into the Memory Address Register

$t1$:   $IR \leftarrow (MDR)$     Contents of the location contained in the $MAR$ are loaded into the Instruction Register via the Memory Data Register

    $PC \leftarrow (PC) + 1$     Increment the $PC$ to the next instruction

$t2$:   $Decoder \leftarrow (IR)$     The op code of the instruction is determined at this point.

The operations at $t3$ begin the execute phase. At this point the contents of registers $R1$ and $R2$ are being moved to the ALU where they will be added.

26. **(C)**

Since there are 1024 words and $1024 = 2^{10}$, the address bus must have 10 lines.

27. **(A)**

The first step in calculating the relative error is to determine the floating-point representation of +0.4 that is used by the Tomato Computer.

$$+0.4_{10} + \overline{+0.0110011}_2$$

It is clear that the computer will not be able to represent 0.4 exactly. The next step is to normalize the binary value:

$$0.011001100 = 0.11001100 * 2^{-1}$$

Since the number is positive, the sign bit is zero. With four bits for the exponent biased, the value of the exponent is $8 - 1 = 7$ or $0111_2$.

The value of the mantissa is 1001100 because the first bit is always 1 in normalized form and therefore is simply assumed. Therefore, we have

0 0111 1001100

Now we determine the actual decimal value that has been represented by the computer. Working backwards we have

$$0111\,1001100 = 0.0110011_2 = \frac{1}{2^2} + \frac{1}{2^3} + \frac{1}{2^6} + \frac{1}{2^7} = 0.03984_{10}$$

If $N$ is a real number and $N'$ is the stored value approximating $N$, then the relative error, $r$, is given by the equation

$$r = \frac{N - N'}{N} * 100\%$$

Thus, the relative error of representing +0.4 on the Tomato Computer is

$$r = \frac{0.4 - 0.3984}{0.4} * 100\% = .4\%$$

28. **(B)**
The recursive definition for a postorder traversal of a binary tree is given by:

if the binary tree is not the null binary tree, then

    1. traverse its left subtree in postorder

    2. traverse its right subtree in postorder

    3. visit and process it root.

Applying this algorithm for the postorder traversal of the binary tree given in problem 28 results in the list of nodes given in (B).

29. **(A)**
Without deriving the equation formally, we can use the following approach. Write out the first several values for $F_4$ and $|F_4|$.

$$F_0 = 0 \qquad |F_0| = 1$$

$$F_1 = 1 \qquad |F_1| = 2$$

$$F_2 = 1 \qquad |F_2| = 4$$

$$F_3 = 2 \qquad |F_3| = 7$$

$$F_4 = 3 \qquad |F_4| = 12$$

$$F_5 = 5 \qquad |F_5| = 20$$

$$F_6 = 8 \qquad |F_6| = 33$$

$$F_7 = 13 \qquad |F_7| = 54$$

$$F_8 = 21 \qquad |F_8| = 88$$

From this list, we can see that $|F_d| = F_{d+3} - 1$ for $d > 1$. For example,

$$|F_4| = F_{4+3} - 1 = F_7 - 1 = 13 - 1 = 12$$

30. **(D)**

Since there are seven elements in the hash table, size = 7. If $E$ represents an empty element in the hash table, we can represent the table initially as

$$E, \ E, \ E, \ E, \ E, \ E, \ E$$

Applying the hashing algorithm, we can begin to insert the keys

$$37, \ 38, \ 72, \ 48, \ 98, \ 11, \ 56$$

into the hash table one at a time:

$$hash := 37 \bmod 7 = 2 \ \Rightarrow \ E, \ E, \ 37, \ E, \ E, \ E, \ E$$

$$hash := 38 \bmod 7 = 3 \ \Rightarrow \ E, \ E, \ 37, \ 38, \ E, \ E, \ E$$

$$hash := 72 \bmod 7 = 2 \ \Rightarrow \quad \text{collision}$$

The key 37 occupies the table element with index 2. Using linear probing, we find that the next available space in the table is at index 4

$$\Rightarrow \ E, \ E, \ 37, \ 38, \ 72, \ E, \ E$$

$$hash := 48 \bmod 7 = 6 \ \Rightarrow \ E, \ E, \ 37, \ 38, \ 72, \ E, \ 48$$

$$hash := 98 \bmod 7 = 0 \ \Rightarrow \ 98, \ E, \ 37, \ 38, \ 72, \ E, \ 48$$

$$hash := 11 \bmod 7 = 4 \ \Rightarrow \quad \text{collision} \ \Rightarrow$$

$$98, \ E, \ 37, \ 38, \ 72, \ 11, \ 48$$

$$hash:=56 \bmod 7 = 0 \quad \Rightarrow \qquad \text{collision} \quad \Rightarrow$$
$$98, \ 56, \ 37, \ 38, \ 72, \ 11, \ 48$$

### 31. **(A)**

The average number of comparisons is found by finding the number needed for all successful searches and dividing by $n$. This is

$$(1 + 2 + 3 + 4 + \ldots + n)/n. \tag{1}$$

The series

$$1 + 2 + 3 + 4 + \ldots + n = n(n + 1)/2. \tag{2}$$

Substituting into equation (1) we have

$$n(n + 1)/2n = (n + 1)/2.$$

### 32. **(E)**

A grammar is left-linear (right-linear) if only one nonterminal is found on the right side of each of its rules (i.e., $A \rightarrow Bx$ or $A \rightarrow y$). A grammar is context-free if each rule $x \rightarrow y$ satisfies length $(x) = 1$. A grammar is context-sensitive if each rule $x \rightarrow y$ has the property that $\text{length}(x) \leq \text{length}(y)$.

### 33. **(B)**

The procedure *add* assumes that the terms of the two polynomials are inserted into the link list in such a way that parallel nodes represent terms with the same exponents. The two polynomials must also be of the same length since the procedure terminates as soon as the end of the shortest polynomial is reached. There is no code to get the rest of the terms from the longer polynomial. The sign of the terms will have no effect upon the procedure, although a term with a coefficient of zero may be included in the result.

### 34. **(C)**

The next pointer in the last node, $t^\wedge.next$, is assigned to the current node at the end of the while loop. When the while loop terminates, there is an extra empty (current) node at the bottom of the list. If this node is disposed of while $t^\wedge.next$ is still pointing at it, $t^\wedge.next$ will become undefined (or lost).

### 35. **(B)**

Parity check involves appending a parity bit to the end of each byte in a frame of data that is transmitted. A common example is ASCII transmission, in which a parity bit is appended to each 7-bit ASCII character. Typically odd parity is used for synchronous transmission and even parity for asynchronous transmission. If even parity is being used, then the parity bit is set or cleared so that the number of set bits (including the parity bit) is even. When a packet of data is transmitted, the receiver checks the number of set bits in each byte with the value of the parity bit. If one or any odd number of bits is flipped in a byte, the parity check will detect an error. If two or any even number of bits is flipped, the parity check will miss the error.

Consider the following example for an ASCII *G* (1110001) where even parity is used. Since there is an even number of set bits, a 0 parity bit is appended giving 11100010.

| Example | Transmitted | Received | Error | Detected |
|---------|-------------|----------|-------|----------|
| 1 | 11100010 | 11100010 | No | No |
| 2 | 11100010 | 11000010 | Yes | Yes |
| 3 | 11100010 | 11110000 | Yes | No |

Since there is an even number of set bits in a 7-bit ASCII *G*, a 0 parity bit is appended giving 11100010 for the byte that is transmitted. In example 1, there is no transmission error so none is detected. In example 2, one bit is inverted during transmission resulting in an odd number of set bits in the byte that is received. As a result, the error is detected. Two bits are flipped in example 3. The number of set bits in the byte that is received is even, but the character is no longer a *G* and the error is undetected.

36. **(D)**

$$O(\log n) < O(n) < O(n * \log n) < O(n^2) < O(2n)$$

for $n > n_0$. The reader may plot graphs for values of n to demonstrate the rate of growth of these time functions.

37. **(D)**

In 1971, Coffman and associates described the four conditions for deadlock. They are

1. Mutual exclusion. Resources cannot be shared by processes.

2. Partial assignment of resources. Processes are assigned resources as they become available. A process does not have to wait for all required resources to become available before an available resource is assigned to the process.

3. Nonpreemption. Once resources have been assigned to a process they cannot be taken away until the completion of the process and the process releases them.

4. Circular wait queue. A circular wait queue must exist with two or more processes, each of which is waiting for a resource held by the next process in the queue.

Process suspension is not a condition since it can actually be used to avoid deadlock. If the operating system detects that allocating a resource to a process will lead to deadlock, the operating system may not grant the request for resources and instead suspend the process until it is safe.

38. **(D)**
I is false because when $S = 0$ the system resource is not available. If the $V(S)$ operation could not be performed in one instruction, another process could insert itself into $S$'s waiting queue without the process performing the $V$ operation knowing about it, so II is false. III is true because when the $V$ operation is performed, a process is relinquishing the resource. Software resources, such as a table in memory, may require mutually exclusive access, so IV is true. So the correct answer is (D).

39. **(A)**
The solution to problem 39 is to first sort the $a_1$'s and $b_1$'s together.

| $J_2$ | $J_1$ | $J_2$ | $J_1$ | $J_3$ | $J_3$ | $J_4$ | $J_4$ |
|-------|-------|-------|-------|-------|-------|-------|-------|
| 3 | 6 | 9 | 12 | 15 | 17 | 20 | 28 |
| $b_2$ | $a_1$ | $a_2$ | $b_1$ | $a_3$ | $b_3$ | $a_4$ | $b_4$ |

Begin scheduling jobs from the list. If the next number is an $a_i$ and job $J_i$ has not been scheduled, then schedule the job to the next spot from the left. If the next number is a $b_i$ and job $J_i$ has not been scheduled, then schedule the job to the next spot from the right. This will lead to the schedule given in choice (A). That this schedule is optimal is left to the reader to verify.

40. **(B)**

$$10 * n * \log_2 n > 2 * n^2$$
$$5 * \log_2 n > n$$
$$\log_2 n > n/5$$
$$n > 2^{(n/5)}$$
$$n - 2^{(n/5)} > 0$$

Assuming $n$ is an integer, substitute the following values into the equation to see if they yield a true statement:

     Try 20: True; Try 21: True; Try 22: True; Try 23: *False*

Thus, we find the upper limit to be 22. To find the lower limit, begin by testing 0 as a value:

     Try 0: False; Try 1: False; Try 2: *True*

So, if $n$ is an integer, $2 \leq n \leq 22$.

41.  **(C)**

The expression for the range of an integer $i$ that can be represented in the 2's complement format for the general case in which a computer has $n$ bit word size is given by

$$-2^{n-1} \leq i \leq 2^{n-1} - 1$$

Therefore, the range of integers that may be represented in 2's complement in a 32-bit word is

$$-2^{31} \text{ to } 2^{31} - 1$$

42.  **(E)**

The value of $r$ can be determined in the following manner:

$ack(2, 1) =$

$ack(1, a(2, 0)) =$

$ack(1, a(1, 1)) =$

$ack(1, a(0, a(1, 0))) =$

$ack(1, a(0, a(0, 1))) =$

$a(1, a(0, 2)) =$

$a(1, 3) =$

$a(0, a(1, 2)) =$

$a(0, a(0, a(1, 1))) =$

$a(0, a(0, a(0, a(1, 0)))) =$

$a(0, 1(0, a(0, a(0, 1)))) =$

$a(0, a(0, a(0, 2))) =$

$a(0, a(0, a(0, 2))) =$

$a(0, a(0, 3)) =$

$a(0, 4) =$

5

### 43. (B)

Since the arithmetic **and** and **or** are bit-wise operators, it is first necessary to convert the decimal values to their binary equivalent. This process is straightforward and therefore is not shown here. The next step is to perform the operations:

$$42 = 00101010$$
$$\text{or} \quad \underline{72 = 01001000}$$
$$106 = 01101010$$
$$\text{and} \quad \underline{55 = 00110111}$$
$$34 = 00100010$$

### 44. (A)

The equation leading to the design of the minimum complexity circuit for the inside of the black box can be obtained by constructing either a truth table or a Karnaugh map. The Karnaugh map technique is shown below:

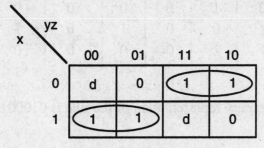

$$f(x, y, z) = x'y + xy'$$

### 45. (D)

The cellular automaton is seeded with the following values:

$$t_0 \ldots 0\,0\,0\,0\,1\,0\,1\,0\,0\,0\,0 \ldots$$

The automaton evolves according to the rule 01010110. This means that given some values for $(a_{i-1}, a_i, a_{i+1})$ such as (0, 1, 0) that the new value for $a_i$ or in our example, $a_2(t + 1)$, is given by the $n = 2$ digit of the rule which is 1 in this case. The automaton evolves in the following manner:

$$t_0 \quad \ldots 0\,0\,0\,0\,1\,0\,1\,0\,0\,0\,0 \ldots$$

$t_1$ ...00011011000...

$t_2$ ...00101001100...

$t_3$ ...01101110110...

46. **(E)**

The binary representation for the rule $(a_{-1}'a_1') + (a_0a_1')$ can be determined by setting up a truth table for the rule and finding values for all combinations of $a_{-1}, a_0, a_1$.

| $a_{-1}$ | $a_0$ | $a_1$ | $a_{-1}'$ | $a_1'$ | $a_{-1}'a_1'$ | $a_0a_1'$ | $a_{-1}'a_1' + a_0a_1'$ |
|---|---|---|---|---|---|---|---|
| 0 | 0 | 0 | 1 | 1 | 1 | 0 | 1 |
| 0 | 0 | 1 | 1 | 0 | 0 | 0 | 0 |
| 0 | 1 | 0 | 1 | 1 | 1 | 1 | 1 |
| 0 | 1 | 1 | 1 | 0 | 0 | 0 | 0 |
| 1 | 0 | 0 | 0 | 1 | 0 | 0 | 0 |
| 1 | 0 | 1 | 0 | 0 | 0 | 0 | 0 |
| 1 | 1 | 0 | 0 | 1 | 0 | 1 | 1 |
| 1 | 1 | 1 | 0 | 0 | 0 | 0 | 0 |

Therefore, the binary representation of the rule is 01000101.

47. **(A)**

The Post Correspondence Problem is one of the paradigm undecidable problems. An instance of the PCP over an alphabet $\Sigma$ is a finite set of pairs of strings over $\Sigma$. The problem is to determine whether there exists a viable sequence of pairs

$$(x_1, y_1), (x_2, y_2), ..., (x_n, y_n)$$

such that

$$(x_1x_2 ... x_n) = (y_1y_2 ... y_n)$$

I.   {$(ab, \text{abb}), (ab, aaa), (aa, a)$} has the following viable sequence:

$$(ab, abb), (ba, aaa), (aa, a), (aa, a) =$$
$$(ab, abb)\ (ba, aaa)\ (aa, a)\ (aa, a) =$$
$$abbaaaaa$$

II.    {(*ab, aba*), (*baa, aa*), (*aba, baa*)} does not have a viable sequence. Any possible solution must begin with the pair (*ab, aba*) since this is the only pair that begins with the same symbol. From this point on, however, the number of *a*'s in the second components of the pairs in the sequence will be greater than the number of *a*'s in the first components.

III.    {(*b,bb*), (*bb, bab*), (*bab, abb*), (*abb, babb*)} does not have a viable sequence. Any possible solution must begin with the either the pair (*b, bb*) or (*bb, bab*) since these are the only two pairs that begin with the symbol. However, (*bb, bab*) does not lead to a viable pair because the second symbol in *bb* is different than the second symbol in *bab*. This leaves (*b, bb*) as the only possible pair to begin the sequence. However, (*b, bb*) does not lead to a viable sequence because the second components in the sequence will have more *b*'s as well as more total symbols than the first components in the sequence.

## 48.    (B)

The strategy described in this problem to prevent indefinite lockout will work — but not without creating another problem. The file server may make an incorrect assumption when the timer runs out. Instead of the client crashing, it might be that the client is simply slow. Therefore, although this strategy will prevent indefinite lockout, it will allow, under certain circumstances, two or more clients to access a file simultaneously, thus compromising mutual exclusion.

## 49.    (B)

If $n$ is a power of two, then $n = 2^k$ for some positive integer $k$ and we can obtain the order of complexity in the following manner:

$$
\begin{aligned}
T(q) &= 8T(n/2) + qn \\
&= 8[8T(n/2^2) + qn/2] + qn \\
&= 8^2T(n/2^2) + qn/2 + qn \\
&= 8^2[8T(n/2^3) + qn/2^2] + 8qn/2 + qn \\
&= 8^3T(n/2^3) + 8^2qn/2^2 + 8qn/2 + qn \\
&= \qquad \bullet \\
&= \qquad \bullet \\
&= \qquad \bullet \\
&= 8^k(n/2^k) + 8^{(k-1)}qn/2^{(k-1)} + \dots 8^1qn/2^1 + 8^0qn/2^0
\end{aligned}
$$

Since $n = 2^k$ then $p$ may be substituted into the first term since $n/2^k = n/n = 1$,

$$T(n) = 8^k p + 4^{(k-1)} qn + 4^{(k-2)} qn + \ldots + 4^1 qn + 4^0 qn$$

Solving for $k$ we have $k = \log_2(n)$ and substituting into the first term once again we obtain

$$T(n) = 8^{(\log 2n)} p + 4^{(k-1)} qn + 4^{(k-2)} qn + \ldots + 4^1 qn + 4^0 qn$$

$$T(n) = pn^{(\log 2\ 8)} + 4^{(k-1)} qn + 4^{(k-2)} qn + \ldots + 4^1 qn + 4^0 qn$$

$$T(n) = pn^3 + 4^{(k-1)} qn + 4^{(k-2)} qn + \ldots + 4^1 qn + 4^0 qn$$

Recognizing that this a geometric expression, we may make an educated deduction at this point as to the order of complexity of the algorithm. However, we complete the evaluation of the expression below by removing the geometric progression with the appropriate substitution:

$$T(n) = pn^3 + qn(4^{(k-1)} * 4 - 1)/(4 - 1)$$

$$= pn^3 + qn(4^k - 1)/3$$

$$= pn^3 + qn(4^{(\log 2(n))})/3$$

$$= pn^3 + qn(n^{(\log 2(4))} - 1)/3$$

$$= pn^3 + qn(n^2 - 1)/3$$

$$= pn^3 + qn^3/3 - qn/3$$

Therefore, the order of complexity is $n^3$.

50. **(C)**

The algorithm given in Question 50 will compute all partial sums of the array. The following diagram illustrates how the partial sums are computed:

| $x_0$ | $x_1$ | $x_2$ | $x_3$ | $x_4$ | $x_5$ | $x_6$ | $x_7$ |
|---|---|---|---|---|---|---|---|
| 2 | −3 | 4 | 5 | −6 | −1 | 1 | 3 |

| $\Sigma_0^0$ | $\Sigma_0^1$ | $\Sigma_1^2$ | $\Sigma_2^3$ | $\Sigma_3^4$ | $\Sigma_4^5$ | $\Sigma_5^6$ | $\Sigma_6^7$ |
|---|---|---|---|---|---|---|---|
| 2 | −1 | 1 | 9 | −1 | −7 | 0 | 4 |

| $\Sigma_0^0$ | $\Sigma_0^1$ | $\Sigma_0^2$ | $\Sigma_1^3$ | $\Sigma_2^4$ | $\Sigma_3^5$ | $\Sigma_4^6$ | $\Sigma_5^7$ |
|---|---|---|---|---|---|---|---|
| 2 | −1 | 3 | 8 | 0 | 2 | −1 | −3 |

| $\Sigma_0^0$ | $\Sigma_0^1$ | $\Sigma_1^2$ | $\Sigma_1^3$ | $\Sigma_0^4$ | $\Sigma_1^5$ | $\Sigma_2^6$ | $\Sigma_3^7$ |
|---|---|---|---|---|---|---|---|
| 2 | −1 | 3 | 8 | 2 | 1 | 2 | 5 |

51. **(D)**

For $\Sigma = \{0, 1\}$ and $n = 3$, 00011101 is a *de Bruijn* sequence. This is easily demonstrated by beginning with $a_0$ and identify the 3 symbol string beginning at this position. Repeat this process for strings beginning at $a_1$ through $a_7$. Remember to use modular arithmetic for strings beginning at $a_6$ and $a_7$. The strings generated from this process are

000, 001, 011, 111, 110, 101, 010, 100

52. **(D)**

Since the segment paragraph is treated as if it were shifted left by four bits, we must shift 1234H left by four bits. This is comparable to multiplying the segment paragraph by 16 or adding a zero to the right of the segment paragraph to generate the 20-bit segment paragraph of 12340H. To this the relative offset of 4392H is added to generate the actual byte in memory that is accessed which is 166D2H.

53. **(E)**
   Multiplication of two matrices can be defined by

$$c_{ij} = \sum_{k=1}^{n} a_{ik} * b_{kj}$$

where  $i$ is the $i$th row of $a$
   $j$ is the $j$th column of $b$
   $c_{ij}$ is the $i$th, $j$th cell of the product matrix
   $n$ is the number of columns of matrix $A$ and the number of rows of matrix $B$

54. **(B)**
   The constructs described are similar to those found in FORTRAN. Since the language does not have reserved words, the compiler will not be able to distinguish the first statement as a <do-loop> until the ',' is reached. Likewise, the compiler will not be able to distinguish the second statement as an <assignment-statement> until it reaches the end of the statement. Furthermore, since blank spaces are not significant, the second statement is legal. **do** 20 $I$ will be identified as a variable name.

55. **(E)**
   The action of the shift-reduce parser is shown below. Whenever the parser performs a reduction, the production used is shown to the left. The production rules are listed as well. A '$' is used to indicate the bottom of the stack as well as the end of the input string.

   (1)   $E \rightarrow E + T$
   (2)   $E \rightarrow T$
   (3)   $T \rightarrow T * F$
   (4)   $T \rightarrow F$
   (5)   $F \rightarrow (E)$
   (6)   $F \rightarrow a$

| | stack | expression |
|---|---|---|
| | $ | $a + a * a\,$$ |
| | $ $a$ | $+ a * a\,$$ |
| 6 | $ $T$ | $+ a * a\,$$ |
| 4 | $ $T$ | $+ a * a\,$$ |
| 2 | $ $E$ | $+ a * a\,$$ |
| | $ $E +$ | $a * a\,$$ |

|   | | |
|---|---|---|
|   | $\$\,E\ a$ | $*\,a\,\$$ |
| 6 | $\$\,E + T$ | $*\,a\,\$$ |
| 4 | $\$\,E + T$ | $*\,a\,\$$ |
|   | $\$\,E + T *$ | $a\,\$$ |
|   | $\$\,E + T * a$ | $\$$ |
| 6 | $\$\,E + T * T$ | $\$$ |
| 3 | $\$\,E + T$ | $\$$ |
| 1 | $\$\,E$ | $\$$ |

56. **(E)**

Although not all compilers will generate a runtime error, the ISO standard for Pascal states that grade = 'E' is an error condition since 'E' is an invalid **case** selector value. By making the **case** statement subject to the **if** statement

**if** *grade* **in** ['A', 'B', 'C', 'D', 'F'] **then**

will ensure that an invalid **case** selector value does not occur.

57. **(C)**

The query

$$Q = (k_1 \wedge k_2 \wedge k_4) \vee (k_2 \wedge k_3) \vee (k_1 \wedge k_3 \wedge k_5) \vee (k_4 \wedge k_6)$$

can be optimized in the following manner.

Let $n_1$ = the number of records in the file with key $k_1$, and $f_1$ = the frequency or number of terms in $Q$ with key $k_1$.

Find $n_1/f_1$ for all $i$. Select key $k_j$ such that $n_j/f_j$ is minimized. Add $k_j$ to the set of keys to be used. Eliminate all terms in $Q$ that contain $k_j$. Repeat the process until all terms have been covered.

| | | Step 1 | | Step 2 | | Step 3 | |
|---|---|---|---|---|---|---|---|
| $n_i$ | $f_i$ | $n_i/f_i$ | | $f_i$ | $n_i/f_i$ | $f_i$ | $n_i/f_i$ |
| $k_{11} = 12$ | 2 | 6 | | – | – | – | – |
| $k_{12} = 24$ | 3 | 8 | | 2 | 12 | – | – |
| $k_{13} = 18$ | 2 | 9 | | 1 | 18 | – | – |
| $k_{14} = 40$ | 2 | 20 | | 1 | 40 | 1 | 40 |
| $k_{15} = 32$ | 2 | 16 | | 1 | 32 | – | – |
| $k_{16} = 56$ | 2 | 28 | | 2 | 28 | 1 | 56 |

At step 1, $k_1$ is added to the set of keys to be used and terms 1 and 3, which contain $k_1$, are covered. At step 2, $k_2$ is added to the set of keys and terms 2 and 5 are covered. The only term not yet covered is term 4 with keys $k_4$ and $k_6$. Step 3 determines that key $k_4$ should be added to the set of keys and now all the terms are covered.

58. **(D)**
   If the chaining method was used the hash table would look like this

   | Index | Data |
   |-------|------|
   | 0 | |
   | 1 | 121 |
   | 2 | 242 $\longrightarrow$ 122 |
   | 3 | 123 $\longrightarrow$ 63 $\longrightarrow$ 183 |
   | 4 | |
   | 5 | 65 |

   The hash function would be applied to 183 and since 183 **mod** $60 = 3$ the index would be 3. After that it would take 3 comparisons so the answer is (D).

59. **(D)**
   Assume that for any $I_n = I_{n-1} + 3$
   $$Q(I_0, 3) = 0$$
   $$Q(I_1, 3) = Q(I_0, 3) + 2$$
   $$\vdots \qquad \vdots$$
   $$\vdots \qquad \vdots$$
   $$\vdots \qquad \vdots$$
   $$Q(I_{n-1}, 3) = Q(I_{n-2}, 3) + 2$$
   $$Q(I_n, 3) = Q(I_{n-1}, 3) + 2$$

   From this
   $$Q(I_n, 3) = \sum_{i=1}^{n} 2 = 2 * n,$$

   where $n$ is the number of steps that generates a '+ 2' term.
   $$I_n = n * 3 + I_0 \quad \text{where } I_0 < 3$$
   $$n = (I_n - I_0)/3$$

$$n = I_n \text{ div } 3$$

Substituting into equation (1)

$$Q(I_n, 3) = 2 * (I_n \text{ div } 3)$$

60. **(A)**
    If $L = L(M)$ for a finite automaton $M$, then $L = L(G)$ for some right-linear grammar $G$. We may start by letting $M = (Q, \Sigma, \delta, q_0, F)$ $G' = (Q, \Sigma, P, q_0)$, where we define $P$ as

 

   (1)   If $\delta (q, a) = r$, then $P$ contains the production $q \to ar$
   (2)   If $P$ is in $F$, then $P \to e$ is a production of $P$.

 

The proof is left to the reader. Proceed by showing that each step of a derivation in $G$ mimics a move by $M$.

61. **(B)**
    Analysis of the sort algorithm is straightforward. On the first pass $n - 1$ comparisons are made, on the second $n - 2$, and so on. The total number of comparisons is given by

$$(n - 1) + (n - 2) + (n - 3) + \ldots + 1 = n(n - 1)/2$$

which is $O(n^2)$.

62. **(C)**
    The algorithm in this question sorts the array *list*[1:$n$] in non-decreasing order. Furthermore, the array is sorted from bottom to top. At the point in the algorithm marked {1} *list*[*item*] is the last item to be placed in the sorted subarray. At this point the array has been sorted in non-decreasing order from *list*[*item*] through *list*[$n$]. Therefore,

    *list*[$j$] $\leq$ *list*[$j + 1$] for all $j$ such that *item* $\leq j < n$

63. **(D)**

The correct set of equations may be obtained by constructing Karnaugh maps for $D_1$, $D_2$, and $D_3$. These are shown here:

$D_1 = Q_1'Q_2$

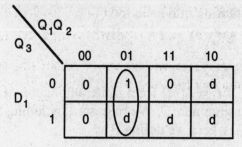

$D_2 = Q_1'Q_3'$

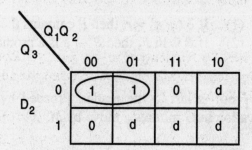

$D_3 = Q \vee Q_3$

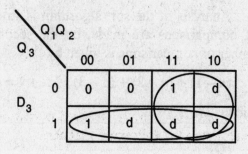

64. **(C)**

Ada supports pass by value-result. The values of $x$ and $y$ are stored in a local storage area for $u$ and $v$ at the beginning of the invocation. The final values for $u$ and $v$ are copied back to the variables $x$ and $y$ at the end of the invocation.

$u \leftarrow x = 4$

$v \leftarrow y = 2$

$u \leftarrow 2 * u = 2 * 4 = 8$

$x \leftarrow u + v = 8 + 2 = 10$

$u \leftarrow u - 1 = 8 - 1 = 7$

$x \leftarrow u = 7$

$y \leftarrow v = 2$

65. **(D)**
Given five objects with the following corresponding weights and profits:

$$(W_1, W_2, W_3, W_4, W_5) = (6, 10, 9, 5, 12)$$
$$(P_1, \quad P_2, \ P_3, \ P_4, \ P_5) = (8, 5, 10, 15, 7)$$

and a knapsack with capacity 30, the objective is to fill the knapsack while maximizing the total profit. This can be done easily by maximizing

$$(P_1/W_1, P_2/W_2, P_3/W_3, P_4/W_4, P_5/W_5) \quad = \quad (8/6, 5/10, 10/9, 15/5, 7/12)$$
$$= \quad (.75, .5, 1.1, 3.0, .58)$$

The order of selection for inserting objects into the knapsack is

$$C = (4, 3, 1, 5, 2)$$

The set $S$ of objects inserted into the knapsack can be arrived at in a straightforward manner. Let $M$ equal the amount of weight yet to be filled in the knapsack.

| | |
|---|---|
| $S = \{0, 0, 0, 1, 0\}$ | $M = 30 - 5 = 25$ |
| $S = \{0, 0, 1, 1, 0\}$ | $M = 25 - 9 = 16$ |
| $S = \{1, 0, 1, 1, 0\}$ | $M = 16 - 6 = 10$ |
| $S = \{1, 0, 1, 1, 10/12\}$ | $M = 10 - 10 = 0$ |

The total profit $= 8 + 10 + 15 + 7 * 10/12 = 38.83$.

66. **(A)**
Since the array $A$ is stored in row dominant form, the elements of $A$ are stored in the following manner:

$S \rightarrow A [1, 1]$

$A [1, 2]$

•

•

$A [1, col]$

$A[2, 1]$

$A [2, 2]$

•

•

•

$A[row, col]$

$A[m, n]$ m rows, n columns Since $A[1, 1]$ is stored in $S$, we obviously must begin here. For any arbitrary element $A[i, j]$, all elements in rows $1 \le k \le i$ must be stored in memory below $A[i, j]$. And since there are n elements per row, we have $S + (i - 1) * n$. To locate a specific element in a row, we add $j - 1$ resulting in $S + (i - 1) * n + j - 1$.

67. **(A)**
    When the Least Recently Used (LRU) algorithm for memory management is employed, the least recently used page is replaced by the new page when a page fault occurs. Since four page frames have been allocated to the process, the number of page faults can be determined by simulating the LRU algorithm with the particular case in the problem. Remember that a page fault occurs whenever the process needs to access a page that is not currently in memory. An 'F' is placed next to each page frame set whenever a page fault occurs.

$$1, \, 8, \, 1, \, 7, \, 8, \, 2, \, 7, \, 2, \, 1, \, 8, \, 3, \, 8, \, 2, \, 1, \, 3, \, 1, \, 7, \, 1, \, 3, \, 7$$

|   |   |   |   |   |
|---|---|---|---|---|
|   | $-$, | $-$, | $-$, | $-$ |
| F | 1, | $-$, | $-$, | $-$ |
| F | 8, | 1, | $-$, | $-$ |
|   | 1, | 8, | $-$, | $-$ |
| F | 7, | 1, | 8, | $-$ |
|   | 8, | 7, | 1, |   |
| F | 2, | 8, | 7, | 1 |
|   | 7, | 2, | 8, | 1 |
|   | 2, | 7, | 8, | 1 |
|   | 1, | 2, | 7, | 8 |
|   | 8, | 1, | 2, | 7 |
| F | 3, | 8, | 1, | 2 |
|   | 8, | 3, | 1, | 2 |
|   | 2, | 8, | 3, | 1 |
|   | 1, | 2, | 8, | 3 |
|   | 3, | 1, | 2, | 8 |
|   | 1, | 3, | 2, | 8 |
| F | 7, | 1, | 3, | 2 |
|   | 1, | 7, | 3, | 2 |
|   | 3, | 1, | 7, | 2 |
|   | 7, | 3, | 1, | 2 |

Counting the number of F's gives us 6 page faults.

68. **(E)**

I. $f(x) = 0$ is a threshold function as shown below:

| $x$ | $f(x)$ |
|-----|--------|
| 0   | 0      |
| 1   | 0      |

$w * 0 - T < 0 \Rightarrow T > 0$

$w * 1 - T < 0 \Rightarrow w < T$

Let $T = 5$ and $w = 3$.

Then $\quad 3 * 0 - 5 < 0 \qquad 3 * 1 - 5 < 0$

$\qquad\qquad\quad -5 < 0 \qquad\qquad 3 - 5 < 0$

$\qquad\qquad\qquad\qquad\qquad\qquad -2 < 0$

II. $f(x) = 1$ is a threshold function:

| $x$ | $f(x)$ |
|-----|--------|
| 0   | 1      |
| 1   | 1      |

$w * 0 - T \geq 0 \Rightarrow T < 0$

$w * 1 - T \geq 0 \Rightarrow w \geq T$

Let $T = -5$ and $w = -2$.

Then $\quad -2 * 0 - (-5) \geq 0 \quad -2 * (1) - (-5) \geq 0$

$\qquad\qquad\qquad 5 \geq 0 \qquad\qquad\quad -2 + 5 \geq 0$

$\qquad\qquad\qquad\qquad\qquad\qquad\qquad 3 \geq 0$

III. XOR is not a threshold function:

| $x_1$ | $x_2$ | XOR |
|-------|-------|-----|
| 0     | 0     | 0   |
| 0     | 1     | 1   |
| 1     | 0     | 1   |
| 1     | 1     | 0   |

$w_1 * 0 + w_2 * 0 - T < 0 \Rightarrow T > 0$

$w_1 * 0 + w_2 * 1 - T \geq 0 \Rightarrow w_2 \geq T$

$w_1 * 1 + w_2 * 0 - T \geq 0 \Rightarrow w_1 \geq T$

$w_1 * 1 + w_2 * 1 - T < 0 \Rightarrow w_1 + w_2 < T$

It is not difficult to show from these inequalities that a contradiction exists.

IV. NOT is a threshold function

| $x$ | NOT |
|-----|-----|
| 0   | 1   |
| 1   | 0   |

$w * 0 - T \geq 0 \Rightarrow T < 0$

$w * 1 - T < 0 \Rightarrow w < T$

Let $T = -3$ and $w = -5$.

Then $\quad -5 * 0 - (-3) \geq 0 \quad -5 * 1 - (-3) < 0$

$\qquad\qquad\qquad 3 \geq 0 \qquad\qquad\quad -5 + 3 < 0$

$\qquad\qquad\qquad\qquad\qquad\qquad\quad -2 < 0$

69. **(B)**

Given $\Delta = \{X_1, X_2, X_3\}$ and the set of equations

$$X_1 = aX_2 + bX_1 + e \tag{1}$$
$$X_2 = aX_3 + bX_2 \tag{2}$$
$$X_3 = aX_1 + bX_3 \tag{3}$$

where $\Sigma = \{a, b\}$ and $e$ is the empty string, we can solve these equations by first writing the equations in the form

$$X_1 = \alpha X_i + \beta$$

$\beta$ is a regular expression over $\Sigma$ and $\beta$ is a regular expression of the form $\beta = \beta_0 + \beta_1 X_{i+1} + \ldots + \beta_m X_n$. Next, we replace all $X_i$ in equations $X_{i+1} \ldots X_n$ with $\alpha * \beta$. Repeat this process for all $1 \le i < n$. At this point, begin with $X_n$ which will be of the form

$$X_1 = \alpha X_i + \beta$$

Generate $X_i = \alpha * \beta$ and substitute this for $X_i$ in all statements $X_j$ where $1 \le j \le i$. Decrement $i$ and repeat until $i = 1$. Beginning with equation (1) we have

$$X_1 = bX_1 + (aX_2 + e) \tag{4}$$

Replacing $X_1$ with $b * (aX_2 + e)$ in equation (3),

$$X_3 = ab * aX_2 + ab * + bX_3 \tag{5}$$

Changing equation (2)

$$X_2 = bX_2 + aX_3 \tag{6}$$

Replacing $X_2$ with $b * aX_3$ in equation (5),

$$X_3 = (ab * ab * a + b)X_3 + ab * \tag{7}$$

At this point we replace any $X_i = \alpha X_i + \beta$ with $X_1 = \alpha * \beta$.
Applying this rule to equation (7) results in

$$X_3 = (ab * ab * a + b) * ab * \tag{8}$$

Substituting for $X_3$ in equation (6) gives

$$X_2 = bX_2 + a(ab * ab * a + b) * ab * \tag{9}$$

Solving equation (9) we have

$$X_2 = b * a(ab * ab * a + b) * ab * \tag{10}$$

Substituting into equation (4) we have

$$X_1 = bX_1 + ab * a(ab * ab * a + b) * ab * +e \qquad (11)$$

Solving this equation, we obtain

$$X_1 = b * (ab * a(ab * ab * a + b) * ab * +e) \qquad (12)$$

The solution to this set of expression equations are the equations (12), (10), and (8).

70. **(D)**

The value of the parity bit is set such that the sum of the three bits in the register and the parity bit is an even number. The equation for designing the circuit to accomplish this can be determined by first setting up a truth table that shows the value of the parity bit, $z$, for all combinations of the register's bits.

| $b_2$ | $b_1$ | $b_0$ | $z$ |
|---|---|---|---|
| 1 | 1 | 1 | 1 |
| 1 | 1 | 0 | 0 |
| 1 | 0 | 1 | 0 |
| 1 | 0 | 0 | 1 |
| 0 | 1 | 1 | 0 |
| 0 | 1 | 0 | 1 |
| 0 | 0 | 1 | 1 |
| 0 | 0 | 0 | 0 |

Using the truth table, the following Karnaugh Map can be constructed:

$$z = b_0'b_1'b_2 + b_0'b_1b_2' + b_0b_1'b_2' + b_0b_1b_2$$

71. **(A)**

The time to execute $I_1$ if the interrupt occurs alone is given by

$$T_{I_1} = 4.5 \text{ microseconds} + 25 \text{ microseconds} = 29.5 \text{ microseconds}$$

For $I_2$, the time is

$$T_{I_2} = 4.5 \text{ microseconds} + 35 \text{ microseconds} = 39.5 \text{ microseconds}$$

The time to execute $I_3$, if the interrupt occurs alone is

$$T_{I_3} = 4.5 \text{ microseconds} + 20 \text{ microseconds} = 24.5 \text{ microseconds}$$

Therefore, the minimum time to execute $I_3$ is 24.5 microseconds. Should all three interrupts occur simultaneously, $I_1$ and $I_2$ would be acknowledged first because they have higher priority. Therefore the maximum time to execute $I_3$ is

$$T_{I_3} = 29.5 \text{ microseconds} + 39.5 \text{ microseconds} + 24.5 \text{ microseconds}$$

$$T_{I_3} = 93.5 \text{ microseconds}$$

72. **(C)**

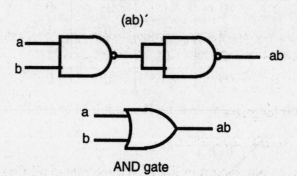

AND gate

73. **(B)**

The binary representation of a BDC $N_1$ can be found by taking the most significant digit $D_{L-1}$ and multiplying it by $1010_2$ ($10_{10}$) and then adding the next most significant digit and multiplying by $1010_2$ and repeat the process until the last digit, $D_0$, is added.

74. **(D)**

Since 3% of the line capacity is reserved for other uses this leaves

$$9600 - 9600 * .03 = 9600 - 288 = 9312 \text{ bps}$$

Also, a synchronization character is sent every 29 characters resulting in

$$9312 - 9312 * 1/30 = 9312 - 311 = 9001 \text{ bps}$$

available to the terminals. Dividing by 600 bps/terminal gives

$$9001 \text{ bps} / 600 \text{ bps/terminal} = 15 \text{ terminals.}$$

75. **(C)**

To optimize access time, the files should be stored according to their lengths from smallest to largest. Therefore, the files would be stored in the order of

$$F_4, F_6, F_3, F_1, F_2, F_5$$

76. **(C)**

If the files are stored on a sequential device to optimize record access time to the six files, they will be stored in the order

$$F_4, F_6, F_3, F_1, F_2, F_5$$

which gives file lengths of

$$(40, 50, 70, 100, 200, 250).$$

In order to access any record in file $F_i$, the records in all files stored before $F_i$ must be processed. Therefore, the average access time is given by

$$
\begin{aligned}
T_{ave} = {} & ((40) + (40 + 50) + (40 + 50 + 70) + (40 + 50 + 70 + 100) + \\
& (40 + 50 + 70 + 100 + 200) + (40 + 50 + 70 + 100 + 200 + \\
& 250)/6 \\
= {} & 1720/6 \\
\approx {} & 286
\end{aligned}
$$

77. **(A)**
Given the left-recursive grammar

$S \rightarrow Aa \mid b$

$A \rightarrow Ac \mid Sd$

the left-recursion may be removed by first substituting for $S$ in the second production giving

$A \rightarrow Ac \mid Aad \mid bd$

Next we replace the $A$ production with $A \rightarrow A\alpha_i \mid \beta_i$ with $A \rightarrow \beta A'$ and $A' \rightarrow \alpha A' \mid e$. In our example this becomes

$A \rightarrow bdA'$

$A' \rightarrow cA' \mid adA' \mid e$

78. **(D)**
Both jobs $J_2$ and $J_4$ must be scheduled by time 2. Choice (D) has job sequence $J_4, J_1, J_2, J_3$ which violates the deadline for job $J_2$ since it is not scheduled until time 3.

79. **(D)**
Given file sizes of $fa = 1, fb = 3, fc = 5, fd = 6$, the set of operations

*Save (fc), Save (fa), Delete (fc), Save (fd)*

is not possible as shown below:

| | | | | | blocks | | | | | |
|---|---|---|---|---|---|---|---|---|---|---|
| | 1 | 2 | 3 | 4 | 5 | 6 | 7 | 8 | 9 | 10 |
| *Save (fc)* | *fc* | *fc* | *fc* | *fc* | *fc* | | | | | |
| *Save (fa)* | *fc* | *fc* | *fc* | *fc* | *fc* | *fa* | | | | |
| *Delete(fc)* | | | | | | *fa* | | | | |
| *Save (fd)* | This operation cannot be performed since there are not 6 blocks of free contiguous space. | | | | | | | | | |

80. **(E)**
The wait time can be calculated in the following manner:

| | |
|---|---|
| Time to read 1 sector | 0.0010 |
| Time to write 1 sector | 0.0010 |
| Time to execute 200 instructions | 0.0002 |
| Total program cycle time | 0.0022 |

Wait time = 0.0020/0.0022 * 100% ≈ 91%

# The Graduate Record Examination in

# COMPUTER SCIENCE

# Test 2

# THE GRADUATE RECORD EXAMINATION IN
# COMPUTER SCIENCE
# TEST 2
## ANSWER SHEET

1. Ⓐ Ⓑ Ⓒ Ⓓ Ⓔ
2. Ⓐ Ⓑ Ⓒ Ⓓ Ⓔ
3. Ⓐ Ⓑ Ⓒ Ⓓ Ⓔ
4. Ⓐ Ⓑ Ⓒ Ⓓ Ⓔ
5. Ⓐ Ⓑ Ⓒ Ⓓ Ⓔ
6. Ⓐ Ⓑ Ⓒ Ⓓ Ⓔ
7. Ⓐ Ⓑ Ⓒ Ⓓ Ⓔ
8. Ⓐ Ⓑ Ⓒ Ⓓ Ⓔ
9. Ⓐ Ⓑ Ⓒ Ⓓ Ⓔ
10. Ⓐ Ⓑ Ⓒ Ⓓ Ⓔ
11. Ⓐ Ⓑ Ⓒ Ⓓ Ⓔ
12. Ⓐ Ⓑ Ⓒ Ⓓ Ⓔ
13. Ⓐ Ⓑ Ⓒ Ⓓ Ⓔ
14. Ⓐ Ⓑ Ⓒ Ⓓ Ⓔ
15. Ⓐ Ⓑ Ⓒ Ⓓ Ⓔ
16. Ⓐ Ⓑ Ⓒ Ⓓ Ⓔ
17. Ⓐ Ⓑ Ⓒ Ⓓ Ⓔ
18. Ⓐ Ⓑ Ⓒ Ⓓ Ⓔ
19. Ⓐ Ⓑ Ⓒ Ⓓ Ⓔ
20. Ⓐ Ⓑ Ⓒ Ⓓ Ⓔ
21. Ⓐ Ⓑ Ⓒ Ⓓ Ⓔ
22. Ⓐ Ⓑ Ⓒ Ⓓ Ⓔ
23. Ⓐ Ⓑ Ⓒ Ⓓ Ⓔ
24. Ⓐ Ⓑ Ⓒ Ⓓ Ⓔ
25. Ⓐ Ⓑ Ⓒ Ⓓ Ⓔ
26. Ⓐ Ⓑ Ⓒ Ⓓ Ⓔ
27. Ⓐ Ⓑ Ⓒ Ⓓ Ⓔ

28. Ⓐ Ⓑ Ⓒ Ⓓ Ⓔ
29. Ⓐ Ⓑ Ⓒ Ⓓ Ⓔ
30. Ⓐ Ⓑ Ⓒ Ⓓ Ⓔ
31. Ⓐ Ⓑ Ⓒ Ⓓ Ⓔ
32. Ⓐ Ⓑ Ⓒ Ⓓ Ⓔ
33. Ⓐ Ⓑ Ⓒ Ⓓ Ⓔ
34. Ⓐ Ⓑ Ⓒ Ⓓ Ⓔ
35. Ⓐ Ⓑ Ⓒ Ⓓ Ⓔ
36. Ⓐ Ⓑ Ⓒ Ⓓ Ⓔ
37. Ⓐ Ⓑ Ⓒ Ⓓ Ⓔ
38. Ⓐ Ⓑ Ⓒ Ⓓ Ⓔ
39. Ⓐ Ⓑ Ⓒ Ⓓ Ⓔ
40. Ⓐ Ⓑ Ⓒ Ⓓ Ⓔ
41. Ⓐ Ⓑ Ⓒ Ⓓ Ⓔ
42. Ⓐ Ⓑ Ⓒ Ⓓ Ⓔ
43. Ⓐ Ⓑ Ⓒ Ⓓ Ⓔ
44. Ⓐ Ⓑ Ⓒ Ⓓ Ⓔ
45. Ⓐ Ⓑ Ⓒ Ⓓ Ⓔ
46. Ⓐ Ⓑ Ⓒ Ⓓ Ⓔ
47. Ⓐ Ⓑ Ⓒ Ⓓ Ⓔ
48. Ⓐ Ⓑ Ⓒ Ⓓ Ⓔ
49. Ⓐ Ⓑ Ⓒ Ⓓ Ⓔ
50. Ⓐ Ⓑ Ⓒ Ⓓ Ⓔ
51. Ⓐ Ⓑ Ⓒ Ⓓ Ⓔ
52. Ⓐ Ⓑ Ⓒ Ⓓ Ⓔ
53. Ⓐ Ⓑ Ⓒ Ⓓ Ⓔ

54. Ⓐ Ⓑ Ⓒ Ⓓ Ⓔ
55. Ⓐ Ⓑ Ⓒ Ⓓ Ⓔ
56. Ⓐ Ⓑ Ⓒ Ⓓ Ⓔ
57. Ⓐ Ⓑ Ⓒ Ⓓ Ⓔ
58. Ⓐ Ⓑ Ⓒ Ⓓ Ⓔ
59. Ⓐ Ⓑ Ⓒ Ⓓ Ⓔ
60. Ⓐ Ⓑ Ⓒ Ⓓ Ⓔ
61. Ⓐ Ⓑ Ⓒ Ⓓ Ⓔ
62. Ⓐ Ⓑ Ⓒ Ⓓ Ⓔ
63. Ⓐ Ⓑ Ⓒ Ⓓ Ⓔ
64. Ⓐ Ⓑ Ⓒ Ⓓ Ⓔ
65. Ⓐ Ⓑ Ⓒ Ⓓ Ⓔ
66. Ⓐ Ⓑ Ⓒ Ⓓ Ⓔ
67. Ⓐ Ⓑ Ⓒ Ⓓ Ⓔ
68. Ⓐ Ⓑ Ⓒ Ⓓ Ⓔ
69. Ⓐ Ⓑ Ⓒ Ⓓ Ⓔ
70. Ⓐ Ⓑ Ⓒ Ⓓ Ⓔ
71. Ⓐ Ⓑ Ⓒ Ⓓ Ⓔ
72. Ⓐ Ⓑ Ⓒ Ⓓ Ⓔ
73. Ⓐ Ⓑ Ⓒ Ⓓ Ⓔ
74. Ⓐ Ⓑ Ⓒ Ⓓ Ⓔ
75. Ⓐ Ⓑ Ⓒ Ⓓ Ⓔ
76. Ⓐ Ⓑ Ⓒ Ⓓ Ⓔ
77. Ⓐ Ⓑ Ⓒ Ⓓ Ⓔ
78. Ⓐ Ⓑ Ⓒ Ⓓ Ⓔ
79. Ⓐ Ⓑ Ⓒ Ⓓ Ⓔ
80. Ⓐ Ⓑ Ⓒ Ⓓ Ⓔ

# GRE COMPUTER SCIENCE
## TEST 2

**TIME:** 170 Minutes
80 Questions

---

**DIRECTIONS:** Each of the questions or incomplete statements below is followed by five suggested answers or completions. Select the one that is best in each case. Refer to Pages vii – ix for *Notations and Conventions.*

---

1. The corresponding binary tree of the expression

   $(A + B * C) / (A - C)$ is:

(A)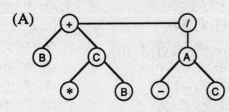

(D)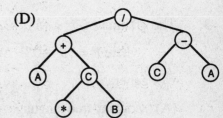

(B)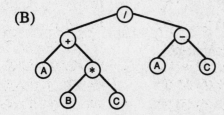

(E)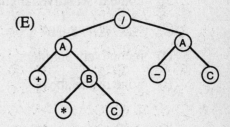

(C)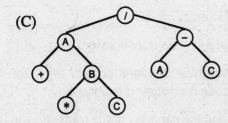

2. Determine which sum of minterms corresponds to the following Boolean function:

| x | y | z | f(x, y, z) |
|---|---|---|---|
| 0 | 0 | 0 | 0 |
| 0 | 0 | 1 | 1 |
| 0 | 1 | 0 | 1 |
| 0 | 1 | 1 | 0 |
| 1 | 0 | 0 | 1 |
| 1 | 0 | 1 | 0 |
| 1 | 1 | 0 | 0 |
| 1 | 1 | 1 | 0 |

(A) $z + y + x$

(B) $xyz' + xy'z + x'yz$

(C) $x'y'z + x'yz' + xy'z'$

(D) $x'y'z + x'yz + xy'z + xyz' + xyz$

(E) $x'y'z' + xyz' + xy'z$

3. The grammar $G = <\{S\}, \{0,1\}, P, S>$

   where $P = \{S \rightarrow 0S1, S \rightarrow 0S, S \rightarrow S1, S \rightarrow 0\}$

   will generate a:

   (A) context-free language

   (B) context-sensitive language

   (C) regular language

   (D) recursively enumerable language

   (E) none of the above

4. When is the baud rate always equal to the bit rate (bps)?

   (A) When phase code modulation is used.

   (B) When a twisted pair is used for the transmission.

   (C) When two levels of amplitude modulation are used for the transmission and phase code modulation is not used.

   (D) When the bit rate is less than the capacity of the transmission line as computed by Shannon's Law.

   (E) The baud rate and the bit rate are never equal.

5.   In a PASCAL–like programming language, the following program segment constitutes a function to find the maximum value of a given set of real numbers, *A*, if the missing statement as indicated in {missing statement} is given as:

   (A)   **if** *maxval* = *A*[1] **then** *A*[*range*] : = *maxval*

   (B)   **if** *maxval* = *A*[*limit*] **then** *maxval* : = *A*[*range*]

   (C)   **if** *maxval* < *A*[*range*] **then** *maxval* : =*A*[*range*]

   (D)   **if** *maxval* > *A*[*range*] **then** *maxval* : = *A*[*range*]

   (E)   **if** *maxval* <> *A*[*A*] **then** *maxval* : = *A*[*range*]

   Program segment:

```
type
        indexp = 1..limit;
        vector = array [indexp] of REAL;

function max (A : vector, N : indexp) : real;
var
        maxval : real;
        range : indexp;
begin
        maxval : = A[1];
        for range : = 2 to N do
                begin
                        {missing statement}
                end;
        max : = maxval
end;
```

6.   Let *L* be a language recognizable by a finite automaton. The language *REVERSE* (*L*) = {*W* such that *W* is the reverse of *V* where *V* ∈ *L*} is a:

   (A)   context-free language

   (B)   context-sensitive language

(C)  regular language

(D)  recursively enumerable language

(E)  none of the above

7.  A decimal number has 30 digits. Approximately, how many digits would the binary representation have?

(A)  30

(B)  60

(C)  90

(D)  120

(E)  150

8.  What is false about the record type?

(A)  Two different "templates" can be used to decompose a record into different fields (by using variant records).

(B)  Variant records can be expressed by the case of clause.

(C)  The with clause is absolutely necessary for record-processing.

(D)  Arrays of records can hold a complete customer file in memory with 50 records (each with a prod. name field and price).

(E)  All of the above are true.

9.  Let $E$ be a shifting operation applied to a function $f$, such that $E(f) = f(x + h)$. Then

(A)  $E(\alpha f + \beta g) = \alpha E(f) + \beta E(g)$

(B)  $E(\alpha f + \beta g) = (\alpha + \beta) E(f + g)$

(C)  $E(\alpha f + \beta g) = \alpha E(f + \beta g)$

(D)  $E(\alpha f + \beta g) = \alpha \beta E(f + g)$

(E)  $E(\alpha f + \beta g) = \alpha + \beta E(f + g)$

Where $\alpha$ and $\beta$ are non-zero constants.

10.  Let the incidence matrix of a graph be:

$$M = \begin{bmatrix} 1 & 0 & 0 \\ 1 & 0 & 1 \\ 1 & 1 & 0 \end{bmatrix}$$

The corresponding graph is given as:

(A)

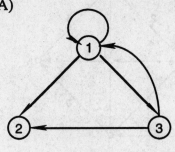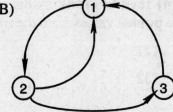

(D)

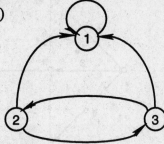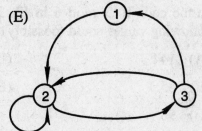

(B)

(E)

(C)

11. How many Boolean functions of 3 variables are there?

(A) 16          (D) 512

(B) 64          (E) 1024

(C) 256

12. Given the digraph (shown on the following page) whose edges are labelled by flow capacities, compute the maximum flow for this system from source $A$ to sink $K$. All flows are left to right or vertical (as shown).

(A) max flow < 9          (D) 11

(B) 9          (E) max flow > 11

(C) 10

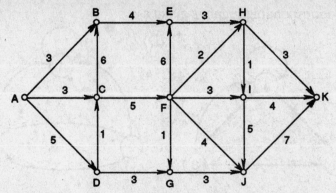

13. In the code if ($x$ mod 6 in [2, 3, 4] then *writeln*($x$); which of the following values could (possibly) be printed values from the *writeln*?

(A) 144           (D) 121

(B) 85            (E) 732

(C) 98

14. The language recognized by the following finite automaton is:

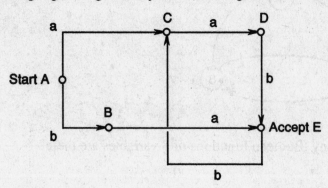

(A) *aabb* + *bab**

(B) (*aab*) (*empty* + (*bab*)*)*

(C) (*aa* + *empty*) (*b* + *ba*) (*bab*)*

(D) (*aab*) (*bab*)* + (*bab*)*

(E) (*aab* + *ba*) (*bab*)*

15. If Julius Caesar wanted *Power* (ie. $x^y$) in PASCAL, but he didn't want to write a function or procedure or loop for it, then

(A) The situation is hopeless; it is impossible.

(B) He should write $x$**$y$.

(C)  He should write *exp* (*ln* (*x\*y*)).

(D)  He should write *exp* (*x\*ln*(*y*)).

(E)  He should write *exp* (*y\*ln*(*x*)).

16.  In solving a system of linear equations $Ax = b$; the $L$ and $U$ matrices of the matrix,

$$A = \begin{bmatrix} 1 & -1 & 1 \\ 0 & -1 & -1 \\ 1 & 2 & 0 \end{bmatrix}.$$

using $L\,U$ decomposition method are given as

(A)  $L = \begin{bmatrix} 1 & 0 & 0 \\ 0 & -1 & 0 \\ 1 & 3 & -4 \end{bmatrix}$ and $U = \begin{bmatrix} 1 & -1 & 1 \\ 0 & 1 & 1 \\ 0 & 0 & 1 \end{bmatrix}$

(B)  $L = \begin{bmatrix} 1 & -1 & 0 \\ 0 & 1 & -1 \\ 1 & 0 & 2 \end{bmatrix}$ and $U = \begin{bmatrix} 1 & -1 & -1 \\ 0 & 1 & 1 \\ 0 & 0 & 2 \end{bmatrix}$

(C)  $L = \begin{bmatrix} 1 & 0 & 1 \\ 1 & 1 & -1 \\ -1 & 0 & 3 \end{bmatrix}$ and $U = \begin{bmatrix} 1 & 0 & 0 \\ -1 & 1 & 0 \\ 0 & 0 & 1 \end{bmatrix}$

(D)  $L = \begin{bmatrix} 1 & 0 & 0 \\ 0 & -1 & 0 \\ -1 & 2 & 3 \end{bmatrix}$ and $U = \begin{bmatrix} 1 & 2 & 1 \\ 0 & 1 & 1 \\ 0 & 0 & 1 \end{bmatrix}$

(E)  $L = \begin{bmatrix} 1 & 0 & 0 \\ 0 & -1 & 0 \\ 1 & 3 & -2 \end{bmatrix}$ and $U = \begin{bmatrix} 1 & -1 & 3 \\ 0 & 1 & 2 \\ 0 & 0 & 1 \end{bmatrix}$

17.  An array has an hour by hour observation of a slow pulsing pulsar. Every few hours, the observations reach a peak intensity and then go back down. At hour $J$, the observation is stored in $A[J]$. Compute and print each local peak value as they occur. Let $A$ have 5000 values.

Examples: 2, 2, 2, 7, 3, 2, 3, 4, 1, 5, 1 will print 7, 4, 5.

Assume that the $A[1]$ amd $A[N]$ cannot be acceptable as peaks.

(A)  **for** $J := 2$ **to** 4999 **do**
     **if** $(A[J] > A[J + 1])$
     **then write** $(A[J])$;

(B)  **for** $J := 2$ **to** 4999 **do**
     **if** $(A[J] > A[J - 1])$
     **then write** $(A[J])$;

(C)  $MAX := A[1]$;
     **for** $J := 2$ **to** 4999 **do**
     **if** $(A[J] > MAX)$ **then begin**;
     **write** $(A[J])$; $MAX: + A[J]$;
     **end**;

(D)  **for** $J := 2$ **to** 4999 **do**
     **if** $((A[J] > A[J + 1])$
     **and** $(A[J] < A[J - 1]))$
     **then write** $(A[J])$;

(E)  **for** $J := 2$ **to** 4999 **do**
     **if** $((A[J] > A[J + 1])$
     **and** $((A[J - 1] < A[J]))$
     **then write** $(A[J])$;

18.  Remove all hazards from: $xy + zx'$

(A)  $xy + zx'$ (ie. no hazard)

(B)  $xy + zx' + yz$

(C)  $xy + zx' + wyz$

(D)  $xy + zx' + w'yz$

(E)  $xy + zx' + wz$

19.  The productions

$$E \rightarrow E+E, \quad E \rightarrow E-E, \quad E \rightarrow E*E, \quad E \rightarrow E/E, \quad E \rightarrow id$$

(A)  generate an inherently ambiguous language.

(B)  generate an ambiguous language but not inherently so.

(C)  are unambiguous.

(D)  can generate all possible fixed length valid computations for carrying out addition, subtraction, multiplication, and division which can be expressed in one expression.

(E)   None of the above.

20.   What can we correctly say about proposition *P*1:

$$P1: (p \lor \text{not } q) \land (q \rightarrow r) \land (r \lor p)$$

(A)   *P*1 is a tautology

(B)   *P*1 is a contradiction

(C)   if *p* is true and *q* is false and *r* is false, then *P*1 is true

(D)   if *p* is true and *q* is true and *r* if false, then *P*1 is true

(E)   the statement "*P*1 and **not** *P*1" is a tautology

21.   Compute the average of heights (of people) stored in array A declared by:

**var** *A* : **array** [1..50 ] **of** *real*;

Assume that a zero entry marks the end of the valid heights (ie. there
are less than 50 actual people.) Heights are positive numbers. Assume we already wrote: *Sum*: = 0;

(A)   *K*:=1;
**repeat**;
*Sum*:=*Sum*+*A*[*K*];
*K*:=*K*+1;
**until** (*A*[*K*]=0);
*A*:*Sum*/*K*;

(B)   *K*:=1;
**repeat**;
*K*:=*K*+1;
*Sum*:=*Sum*+*A*[*K*];
**until** (*A*[*K*]=0);
*A*:*Sum*/*K*;

(C)   *K*:=0;
**repeat**;
*K*:=*K*+1;
*Sum*:=*Sum*+*A*[*K*];
**until** (*A*[*K*]=0);
*A*:=*Sum*/*K*;

(D)   *K*:=0;
**repeat**;
*K*:=*K*+1;
*Sum*:=*Sum*+*A*[*K*];
**until** (*A*[*K*+1]=0;
*A*:=*Sum*/*K*;

(E)   *K*:=1;
**repeat**;
*Sum*:=*Sum*+*A*[*K*];
*K*:=*K*+1;
**until** (*A*[*K*+1] = 0);
*A*:= *Sum*/*K*;

22. The class of context-free languages is not closed under:

    (A) union.

    (B) concatenation.

    (C) repeated concatenation (i.e., *-closure).

    (D) intersection.

    (E) none of the above (i.e., they are closed under operations a–d).

23. At a single terminal CPU, if 40% of all users have no wait to use the terminal and the average wait time for all users is 50 minutes, then what is the average wait time for those who wait? Round-off to the closest answer.

    (A)  60                      (D)  90

    (B)  70                      (E)  100

    (C)  80

24. Which of the following WILL NOT compute the polynomial:

    $$P := a[n]x^n + a[n-1]x^{(n-1)} + \ldots$$

    $$+ a[2]x^2 + a[1]x + a_0;$$

    Note: Not all polynomial-computing programs have to use the exact same operations in the same order as above. Choose the one which will NOT compute the correct value for $P$.

    (A) $P:=a[0]$; $m:=1$; **for** $j=1$ **to** $n$ **do**
        **begin**; $m: = m*x$; $P:=P+a[j]*m$
        **end**;

    (B) $P:=a[0]$; **for** $j:=1$ **to** $n$ **do**
        **begin**; $m:=1$;
            **for** $k:=1$ **to** $j$ **do** $m:=m*x$;
            $P:=P + a[j]*m$
        **end**;

    (C) $P:=a[0]$; **for** $j:=1$ **to** $n$ **do**
        **begin**; $m:=1$; $k:=1$;
            **repeat**; $m:= m*x$; $k:= \text{succ}(K)$;
            **until** $(k=j+1)$; $P:=P+a[j]*m$
        **end**;

(D)  $P:=0$; **for** $j:= n$ **downto** 1 **do**
   $P:=(P + a[j]) * x$;
   $P:=P + a[0]$;

(E)  $P:= 0$; **for** $j: = 1$ **to** $n$ **do**
   $P:= (P + a[j]) *x$;
   $P:= P + a[0]$;

25.  What function exactly satisfies:

   $$T(n) = T(n/2) + 2T(n-1) - 2^n$$

   Assume the $k$'s are constants.

   (A)  Logarithmic function $k_1 \log(n)$

   (B)  Linear function $k_1{}^n + k_0$

   (C)  Quadratic function $k_2 n^2 + k_1 n + k_0$

   (D)  Exponential function $k_1 n^{k0}$

   (E)  None of the above

26.  Which of the following will determine if $N$ is a prime or not?

   (A)  **for** $k := 2$ **to** $n-1$ **do**
      **if** ($n$ **mod** k $<>0$ )
         **then** *writeln* ($n$, 'is prime')
         **else** *writeln* ($n$, 'is not a prime');

   (B)  $PR:= True$;
      **for** $k : = 2$ **to** $n-1$ **do**
      **if** ($n$ **mod** $k = 0$)
      **then** $PR: =$ False;
      **if** ($PR$)
         **then** *writeln* ($n$, 'is prime')
         **else** *writeln* ($n$, 'not prime')')'

   (C)  $PR:= False$;
      **for** $k : = 2$ **to** $n-1$ **do**
      **if** ($n$ **mod** $k <> 0$)
         **then** $PR:= True$;
         **if** ($PR$)
         **then** *writeln* ($n$, 'is prime')
         **else** *writeln* ($n$, 'not prime');

(D)  *PR:= True;*
      **for** $k := 2$ **to** $n-1$ **do**
      **if** $(n \bmod k = 0)$
          **then** *PR:* = False
          **else** *PR:* = *True*;
      **if** *(PR)*
          **then** *writeln* $(n,$ 'is prime')
          **else** *writeln* $(n,$ 'not prime');

(E)  *PR:* = *False*;
      **for** $k := 2$ **to** $n-1$ **do**
      **if** $(n \bmod k = 0)$
          **then** *PR:* = *True*;
      **if** *(PR)*
          **then** *writeln* $(n,$ 'is prime')
          **else** *writeln* $(n,$ 'not prime');

27. In a microprogrammed control unit the microinstructions $M_j$ and the control signals $(a,b,c,...)$ they generate are:

$M_1: a,b,e,f$

$M_2: b,c,d,e$

$M_3: a,c,e,g$

Determine the total number of maximal compatibility classes (MCCs) for the control signals.

(A)  2                          (D)  5

(B)  3                          (E)  6

(C)  4

28. Which function solves the recurrence relation:

$$r(n) = r(n-1) + r(n-2) - r(n-3)$$

$$r(1) = 1, \quad r(2) = 2, \quad r(3) = 3$$

(A)  a quadratic function        (D)  a constant function

(B)  a cubic function            (E)  a linear function

(C)  an exponential function

29. Which statements will pick the largest value in an array:

> var *Item* : **array**[1..100] **of** *integer*;

(A)  *MaxY := MaxInt*;
    **for** *j* := 1 **to** 100 **do**
    **if** (*Item*[*j*] < *MaxY*) **then** *MaxY* := *Item*[*j*];

(B)  *MaxY = MaxInt*;
    **for** *j* := 1 **to** 100 **do**
    **if** (*Item*[*j*] > *MaxY*) **then** *MaxY* := *Item*[*j*];

(C)  *MaxY* := − *MaxInt*;
    **for** *j* := 1 **to** 100 **do**
    **if** (*Item*[*j*] < *MaxY*) **then** *MaxY* := *Item*[*j*];

(D)  *MaxY* := − *MaxInt*;
    **for** *j* := 1 **to** 100 **do**
    **if** (*Item*[*j*] > *MaxY*) **then** *MaxY* := *Item*[*j*];

(E)  *MaxY := MaxInt*;
    **for** *j* := 1 **to** 100 **do**
    **if** (*Item*[*j*] < *MaxY*) **then** *Item*[*j*] := *MaxY*;

30. The Ackermann function

$$A(0, y) = y + 1$$

$$A(x + 1, 0) = A(x, 1)$$

$$A(x + 1, y + 1) = A(x, A (x + 1, y))$$

is an example of a function that:

(A)  operates in cubic time (in $x$ and $y$).

(B)  operates in quartic time (in $x$ and $y$, e.g., $O(x^4 y^4)$).

(C)  requires exponential time to be computed (i.e., $O(k^{xy})$) for some constant $k$.

(D)  cannot be computed by a fixed number of iterative loops with bounds of $x$ or $y$ and using only + and * for arithmetic.

(E)  is not computable.

31. Horace Debussy Jones grades his class numerically, from 0–100. Write some of the code for computing the frequencies of the letter grades A and B from those numeric grades.

(A) **case** *G* **of**
90 .. 100 : *CA*:=*CA*+1;
80..89 : *CB*:=*CB*+1;
**end**;

(B) **case** *G* **of**
90, 100 : *CA*:=*CA*+1;
80, 89 : *CB*:=*CB* + 1;
**end**;

(C) **case** *G* **of**
'A' : *CA*:=*CA*+1;
'B' : *CB*:=*CB*+1;
**end**;

(D) **case** *G* **of**
A : *CA*:=*CA*+1;
B : *CB*:=*CB*+1;
**end**;

(E) **if** (*G* > 90)
**then** *writeln* ('A') **else** *writeln* ('B');

32. A small machine shop manufactures two items, Product *A* and Product *B*, by utilizing a grinder and a polisher according to the following schedule.

|           | Grinder | Polisher | Profit |
|-----------|---------|----------|--------|
| Product *A* | 4 hrs. | 1 hr. | $4 |
| Product *B* | 3 hrs. | 3 hrs. | $6 |

The shop works a 36-hour week, and it contains 4 grinders and 3 polishers. Assuming that they sell all they produce, how many of each item should be manufactured in order to maximize the profit? Let *x* and *y* be the number of items for product *A* and *B* respectively.

(A) $x = 10, y = 12$

(B) $x = 12, y = 32$

(C) $x = 5, y = 14$

(D) $x = 32, y = 12$

(E) $x = 120, y = 5$

33. Flavius Maximus of the Roman Empire needed a program as his namesake. Which of the following will compute the maximum of *A*, *B*, and *C* and return it in *M*?

(A)  *procedure Max  (a,b,c,m: real);* ·
     **begin;**
          **if** *(a>b)* **then if** *(b>c)* **then** *m:=b* **else** *m:=a*
          **else if** *(b>c)* **then** m:=c **else** *m:=b;*
     **end;**

(B)  *procedure Max  (**var** a,b,c,m: real);*
     **begin;**
          **if** *(a>b)* **then if** *(b>c)* **then** *m:=a*
          **else if** *(a>c)* **then** *m:=a* **else** *m:=c*
     **else if** *(b>c)* **then** *m:=c* **else** *m:=b;*
     **end;**

(C)  *procedure Max  (**var** a,b,c,m: real);*
     **begin;**
          **if** *(a>b)* **then if** *(a>c)* **then** *m:=a* **else** *m:=c*
          **else if** *(b>c)* **then** *m:=b* **else** *m:=c;*
     **end;**

(D)  *procedure Max  (**var** a,b,c,m: real);*
     **begin;**
          **if** *(a>b)* **then if** *(a<c)* **then** *m:=b* **else** *m:=a*
          **else if** *(b>c)* **then** *m:=b* **else** *m:=c;*
     **end;**

(E)  *procedure Max  (a,b,c,m: real);*
     **begin;**
          **if** *(a>b* **and** *a>c)* **then** *m:=a*
          **else if** *(b>c)* **then** *m:=b* **else** *m:=c;*
     **end;**

34. Which application is best handled in ROM?

    (A)  storage for temporay variables

    (B)  storage for protected passwords

    (C)  storage for microprograms

    (D)  storage for information on cabling of terminals, such as which
         ports have terminals on them

    (E)  storage of the operating system's boot sector

35. The best algorithms for determining if an arbitrary Boolean function
    of $N$ variables produces a 1 value require:

(A) logarithmic time.

(B) linear time.

(C) quadratic time.

(D) exponential time.

(E) this is an unsolvable problem

36. Which one of the following functions (over real numbers) is invertible?

(A) $Y = \sin(X)$

(D) $Y = X^3 - 2X^2 - 5X + 6$

(B) $Y = X^2$

(E) $Y = X^3$

(C) $Y = X^2 - 90$

37. How many dimensions is KENNEL?

```
type    DOG       =    (Doberman, Pitbull, Bulldog, GermanShepherd,
                        Labrador, Husky, RobotPitBull, Boxer);
        DOGCAGE  =     array [1..10] of DOG;
var     KENNEL   :     array [1..10, 'a'..'z'] of DOGCAGE;
```

(A) 1

(D) 4

(B) 2

(E) 5

(C) 3

38. Which assertion would be the best for the position in the program marked by {zzz} in:

```
if (J*J - 4 > 0) then
      begin
            {zzz}
      end;
```

(A) $J > 4$

(D) $-2 < J$ or $J < 2$

(B) $-4 <= J <= 4$

(E) $-2 > J$ or $J > 2$

(C) $J*J - 4 <= 0$

39. Which of the following is false?

    (A)  Segmentation suffers from external fragmentation.

    (B)  Paging suffers from internal fragmentation.

    (C)  Virtual memory is used only in multi-user systems.

    (D)  Segmented memory can be paged.

    (E)  Thrashing may occur due to too many users on a system.

40. What will the following program do:

    ```
    program x (input, output);
    var j, k, z : integer;
    begin;
         z : = 0;
         for j : = 1 to10 do
              begin;
                  z:=z+1; for k := 1 to 10 do z := z + 1;
              end;
         writeln (z);
    end.
    ```

    (A)  compute 10          (D)  compute 1000

    (B)  compute 100         (E)  compute 20

    (C)  compute 110

41. What set-theoretic expression is equal to: $A - (B \cap C)$

    (A)  $(A - B) \cap (A - C)$          (D)  $(A \cup B) - (A \cup C)$

    (B)  $(A \cap B) - (A \cap C)$          (E)  $(A \cup B) \cap (A \cup C)$

    (C)  $(A - B) \cup (A - C)$

42. Array $X[10]$ is unsorted; to sort it in ascending order (ie. $X[1]$ smallest, $X[10]$ largest), which code inside subprocedure *FixaPair* will do best as the sort routine below:

    ```
    {j loop will repeatedly make passes over the array}
         for j : = 1 to 10 do
    {k loop will make one pass over the array}
         for k : = 1 to 9 do FixaPair (j,k,X);
    ```

Hint: you may assume Switch $(l,m,X)$ will switch $X[l]$ and $X[m]$.

(A)  if $(X[j] > X[k]$ then *Switch* $(j + 1,k,X)$;

(B)  if $(X[j] > X[k \ div \ 2])$ then *Switch* $(j,k, div \ 2, X)$;

(C)  if $(X[k] > X[k + 1])$ then *Switch* $(k,k + 1,X)$;

(D)  if $(X[k] > X[k-1])$ then *Switch* $(k,k-1,X)$;

(E)  if $(X[j] > X[k * 2])$ then *Switch* $(j,k * 2,X)$;

43.  Cached and interleaved memories are ways of speeding up memory access between CPUs and slower RAM. Which memory models are best suited (improves performance the most) for which programs?

1) Cached memory is best suited for small loops.

2) Interleaved memory is best suited for small loops.

3) Interleaved memory is best suited for large sequential code.

4) Cached memory is best suited for large sequential code.

(A)  1 and 2 are true          (D)  4 and 3 are true

(B)  1 and 3 are true          (E)  all of the above are true

(C)  4 and 2 are true

44.  What is the minimal number of edges which must be removed from a complete bipartite graph of six nodes $K(6)$ so that the remaining graph is planar?

(A)  2          (D)  5

(B)  3          (E)  6

(C)  4

45.  Top-Down design does not require:

(A)  flowcharting          (D)  loop invariants

(B)  step-wise refinement          (E)  hierarchical organization

(C)  modularity

46. A time complexity function *G* was formulated for a program. What term asymptotically dominates *G*:

$$G(x) = 9999999x - .0001x^2 + x \log(\log(x))$$

$$+ x^2/(x - 99) + 0.9^x$$

(A) linear term $9999999x$

(B) quadratic term $-.0001x^2$

(C) $x \log(\log x))$

(D) $x^2/(x-99)$

(E) exponential function $0.9^x$

47. Using *Pop (S1, Item)*, *Push (S1, Item)*, *Read (Item)*, *Print (Item)*, the variables *S1* (stack) and *Item*, and given the input file:

    *A, B, C, D, E, F* <EOF>

which stacks are possible:

(A)

| 5 | A |
|---|---|
| 4 | B |
| 3 | C |
| 2 | D |
| 1 | E |

(D)

| 5 |   |
|---|---|
| 4 |   |
| 3 | F |
| 2 | D |
| 1 | B |

(B)

| 5 |   |
|---|---|
| 4 |   |
| 3 | D |
| 2 | A |
| 1 | F |

(E)

| 5 |   |
|---|---|
| 4 |   |
| 3 | C |
| 2 | E |
| 1 | B |

(C)

| 5 |   |
|---|---|
| 4 |   |
| 3 | B |
| 2 | D |
| 1 | F |

48. Using the same funcations and files in Problem 47, which of the below stacks are impossible:

(A)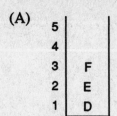

| 5 | |
| 4 | |
| 3 | F |
| 2 | E |
| 1 | D |

(D)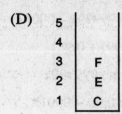

| 5 | |
| 4 | |
| 3 | F |
| 2 | E |
| 1 | C |

(B)

| 5 | |
| 4 | D |
| 3 | C |
| 2 | F |
| 1 | A |

(E)

| 5 | |
| 4 | |
| 3 | F |
| 2 | D |
| 1 | B |

(C)

| 5 | |
| 4 | |
| 3 | E |
| 2 | D |
| 1 | C |

49. Which PROLOG list unifies with

$L1$: $[f,r,e,d,d,i,e]$

and with

$L2$: $[f,r,e,e,b,i,e]$

(A) $[f,r,e,\_,\_,i,e]$      (D) $[f,r,e.e,b,i,e]$

(B) $[f,r,e,d,\_,i,e]$      (E) $[\_]$

(C) $[j,a,s,o,n,\_,\_]$

50. Using *Pop* (*S1, Item*), *Push* (*S1, Item*), *Getlist* (*Item*), *Putlist* (*Item*), *Pop* (*S2, Item*), Push (*S2, Item*), and the variables *S1, S2* (stacks with *Tops1* and *Tops2*) and *Item* and given the input file:

*A, B, C, D, E, F* <EOF>

which stacks are possible:

(A) all possible stacks with A, B, C, D, E, and F.

(B) no possible stacks with A, B, C, D, E, and F.

(C) exactly and only those stacks which can be produced with S1 alone.

(D) twice as many stacks as can be produced with S1 alone.

(E) half of all possible stacks with A, B, C, D, E, and F.

51. Suppose a computer has three types of instructions, each with the following opcode lengths and assuming opcodes occur at the front of each machine instruction:

　　6 bit opcode

　　8 bit opcode

　　12 bit opcode

Now determine the number of possible commands that can be represented in the 6 bit opcode.

(A) 32　　　　　　　　　　(D) 4

(B) 16　　　　　　　　　　(E) 64

(C) 8

52. Super-Jarvis said "I can write a super-merge sort which splits an array into 4 components (unlike regular merge sort which splits in two) and then recursively sorts the 4 subarrays and then merges them. Though similar to merge sort, it is faster and called SJ4." What is true?

(A) SJ4 cannot possibly work; a four-way split and then later merge is preposterous

(B) SJ4 works and SJ4 operates in O(Merger-Sort)

(C) SJ4 works and SJ4 is greater than (slower than) O(Merge-Sort)

(D) SJ4 works and SJ4 is less than (faster than) O(Merge-Sort)

(E) None of the above

53. What is the shortest distance for a path from *A* to *K*?

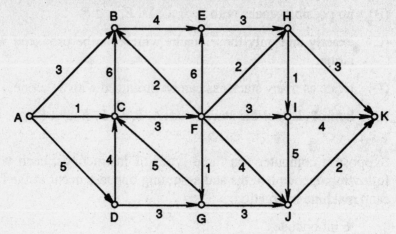

| | |
|---|---|
| (A) 8 | (D) 11 |
| (B) 9 | (E) 12 |
| (C) 10 | |

54. What is the weight of the minimal spanning tree for the graph in problem 53?

| | |
|---|---|
| (A) 17 | (D) 20 |
| (B) 18 | (E) 21 |
| (C) 19 | |

55. In evaluating the infix expression $4 - (3 + 5)$, which stack is impossible:

(A)
```
5
4
3
2
1   4
```

(D)
```
5
4   3
3   (
2   –
1   4
```

(B)
```
5
4
3   8
2   –
1   4
```

(E)
```
5
4
3   (
2   –
1   4
```

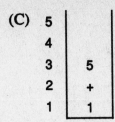

(C)

56. Which of the below is operator precedence? These are segments of bigger grammars, so don't worry about completeness.

(A)  $E \rightarrow E + T \mid T$
     $T \rightarrow E$

(B)  $E \rightarrow E + E$

(C)  $E \rightarrow T$
     $T \rightarrow T + T \mid E$

(D)  $E \rightarrow E + T \mid T$
     $T \rightarrow (E) \mid id$

(E)  $E \rightarrow E + T \mid T$
     $T \rightarrow E \mid (E) \mid id$

57. How many gates (minimum) are needed for a 3-bit up-counter using standard binary and using $T$ flip-flops? Assume unlimited fan-in.

(A)  4

(B)  3

(C)  2

(D)  1

(E)  0

58. Represent the forest (below) as a binary tree:

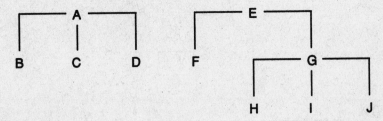

(A)

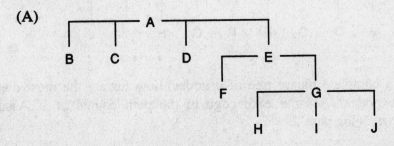

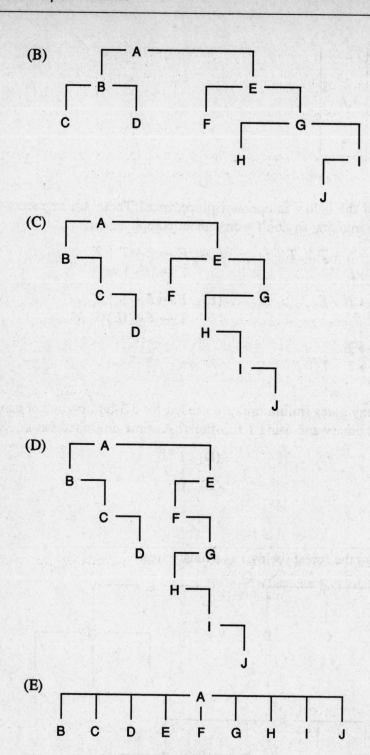

59. In a complete binary tree of *n* nodes, how far are the most distant two nodes? Assume each edge in the path counts as 1. Assume log(*n*) is log base 2.

(A)  about log($n$)        (D)  about 4 log($n$)

(B)  about 2 log($n$)      (E)  about 5 log($n$)

(C)  about 3 log($n$)

60.  After constructing a "sorted" binary insertion tree, to produce a sorted array of numbers (for printing purposes), what must be done?

(A)  pre-order traversal      (D)  top-down traversal

(B)  in-order traversal       (E)  print as is

(C)  post-order traversal

61.  In a parallel processing system with $k$ processors, each processor makes a request at most every 2 microseconds and each request can ask for a maximum of 64 bits. These requests are made over a high-speed shared bus with a maximum throughput of 100 megabits. Assume that with each request, 40 bits are required for transmission of the data-address and protocol. Approximately, what is the maximum value of $k$ for which the system can operate without any delays at peak load?

(A)  1        (D)  4

(B)  2        (E)  5

(C)  3

62.  How many nodes are in the largest maximal independent set of the complete bipartite graph $K(4,2)$?

(A)  2        (D)  5

(B)  3        (E)  6

(C)  4

63.  Rutherford traversed the following binary tree in pre-order. What did his tour brochure say?

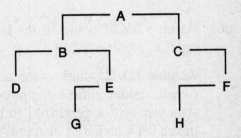

(A) None of the below

(D) $A D G E B C H F$

(B) $A B C D E F G H$

(E) $D G E B C H F A$

(C) $A B D E G C F H$

64. Determining (exactly) that a number $n$ is prime requires (according to the standard algorithm):

(A) logarithmic time (in terms of $n$).

(B) linear time.

(C) quadratic time.

(D) exponential time.

(E) constant time.

65. The annual profit of a company during a 10-year period is given as in Table 1:

**Table 1: Annual profit of a company during a 10-year period.**

| Year | 1 | 2 | 3 | 4 | 5 | 6 | 7 | 8 | 9 | 10 |
|---|---|---|---|---|---|---|---|---|---|---|
| Profit in millions of $ | 1.87 | 2.19 | 2.06 | 2.31 | 2.26 | 2.39 | 2.61 | 2.56 | 2.82 | 2.96 |

Using the least square error approximation, find a regression line:

$$y = a + bx,$$

which closely represents the data. The values of $a$ and $b$ for this line are

(A) $a = 1.811, b = 0.108$

(D) $a = 3.0, b = 2.0$

(B) $a = 1.5, b = 1.8$

(E) $a = -1.5, b = 2.6$

(C) $a = 2.7, b = 2.1$

66. Assume *ILAST* points to the last node in a singly linked list whose top (i.e., front) is *TOP*1.

Assume *TOP*2 points to the first node in another singly linked list (which resides in the same physical arrays *DATA* and *LINK*.) Which statement will append *list*2 to the end of *list*1 (i.e., make them one linked list with *list*1's elements before *list*2)?

(A)  *ILAST := ILAST + TOP2;*

(B)  *TOP2 := ILAST* ;

(C)  *ILAST := TOP2;*

(D)  LINK[*TOP2*] := *ILAST* ;

(E)  LINK[*ILAST* ] := *TOP2;*

67.  How many real links are needed to store a sparse matrix (or LOTUS spreasdsheet) of 10 rows, 10 columns, and 15 non-zero entries? (Pick the closest answer.)

(A)  100          (D)  35

(B)  15           (E)  20

(C)  50

68.  What is the distance of the following code?

00011000    11000111    01010010    11111111

(A)  6           (D)  3

(B)  5           (E)  2

(C)  4

69.  In complexity theory of specific problems, lower bounds are most often shown by _____ 1 and upper bounds are shown by _____ 2.

(A)  1. constructing an algorithm;
     2. proving a property restricts efficient algorithm design

(B)  1. proving a property restricts efficient algorithm design;
     2. constructing an algorithm

(C)  1. constructing an algorithm;
     2. constructing an algorithm

(D)  1. proving a property restricts efficient algorithm design;
     2. proving a property restricts efficient algorithm design

(E)  none of the above (i.e., neither method is useful)

70. The DAG shown here represents:

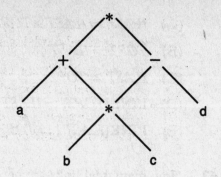

    (A) $a + (b * c) - d$

    (B) $a + b * c * b * c - d$

    (C) $(a + b) * (c - d)$

    (D) $(a + b * c) * (b * c - d)$

    (E) $a + (b * c) * (b * c) - d$

71. How many colors are needed (minimally) to color the following graph?

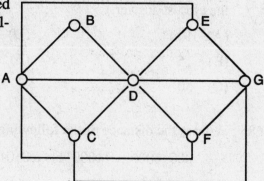

    (A) 3

    (B) 4

    (C) 5

    (D) 6

    (E) 7

72. The set $S=\{0,1,2,3,4,5,6,7\}$ and the operation $X \Theta Y = (X + Y) \bmod 8$ constitutes a:

    (A) binary operation with none of the needed properties for the choices below.

    (B) semigroup.

    (C) monoid.

    (D) group.

    (E) abelian group.

73. Pick one:

    (A) network models are complicated by physical keys (spaghetti) but the relational model is faster because it uses logical keys.

    (B) network models are complicated by logical keys (spaghetti) but the relational model is faster because it uses physical keys.

(C) network models are complicated by logical keys (spaghetti) but the relational model is slower because it uses physical keys.

(D) network models are complicated by physical keys (spaghetti) but the relational model is slower because it uses logical keys.

(E) network models are higher level implementations than relational models, and network model programs are shorter.

74. In the following code, which assertion would be the best to place after the code executes?

```
x: = z;
for j : = 1 to m do
        begin
            x : = x - 1;
        end;
```

(A) $j=0$ and $x=z-1$     (D) $x=z-m$

(B) $x=j+m$     (E) $x=x-j$

(C) $x=j-z$

75. A small microprocessor's microinstructions has 6 control fields, each one triggering the following number of control lines:

control field:          1 2 3 4 5 6

number of control lines: 7 4 5 2 1 3

What is the fewest number of control bits required to describe all the control fields?

(A) 6     (D) 14

(B) 7     (E) 22

(C) 12

76. To reduce storage space and avoid bloated (giant redundant) intermediate relations, we can cross reference many fields in a query efficiently by: (Note: Assume all *Projects* have no *Where* clause in them.)

(A) write many *Join* operations together, then do *Select*.

(B)  write many *Join* operations together, then do *Project*.

(C)  write many *Join* operations but put only *Select* in between them.

(D)  write many *Join* operations but put *Select* and *Project* in between them as early as possible.

(E)  write many *Join* operations but *Project* in between; the order of *Select* has no effect on the space issue but *Join*s and *Project*s do. We leave *Select* for the end.

77.  Elmer Fudd hunts wabbits for three hours. If the probability of catching a wabbit (profit = 1) in one hour is 1/3, then what is the expected profit of a three-hour hunt if:

    1.  Elmer quits after 2 successive hours of no-wabbit.

    2.  Elmer quits after 2 successful hours (i.e., 2 wabbits in 2 sequential hours).

Use decision trees to compute expected profits. This is a decision analysis problem.

(A)  22/27          (D)  27/27

(B)  24/27          (E)  None of above

(C)  26/27

78.  If 2 lines go into an $X$ address decoder and 2 lines go into a $Y$ address decoder, then a 2-dimensional addressing scheme can access at most _____ values?

(A)  2          (D)  16

(B)  4          (E)  64

(C)  8

79.  If a virtual memory system has 4 pages in real memory and the rest must be swapped to disk, determine the hit ratio for the following page address stream. Assume memory starts empty. Use the First In First Out (FIFO) algorithm. Choose the closest answer.

PAGE REQUESTS: 2 5 3 4 1 4 7 2 1 3 1 7 4 5 4 6

(A)  10%          (D)  31%

(B)   15%                          (E)   50%

(C)   25%

80.   In the following loop, determine which is a loop invariant:

```
j: = 3;
read (k);
x. = + 4.7;
while (k * sine(x) < j) do
        begin
                j: = j − 1;
                k: = − k;
        end;
```

(A)  $j > 3$                          (D)  $j < 0$

(B)  $k > 0$                          (E)  $x > 0$

(C)  $k < 0$

# TEST 2

# ANSWER KEY

| | | | | | | | |
|---|---|---|---|---|---|---|---|
| 1. | (B) | 21. | (D) | 41. | (C) | 61. | (B) |
| 2. | (C) | 22. | (D) | 42. | (C) | 62. | (C) |
| 3. | (C) | 23. | (C) | 43. | (B) | 63. | (C) |
| 4. | (A) | 24. | (E) | 44. | (E) | 64. | (B) |
| 5. | (C) | 25. | (E) | 45. | (D) | 65. | (A) |
| 6. | (C) | 26. | (B) | 46. | (B) | 66. | (E) |
| 7. | (C) | 27. | (D) | 47. | (D) | 67. | (C) |
| 8. | (C) | 28. | (D) | 48. | (B) | 68. | (D) |
| 9. | (A) | 29. | (D) | 49. | (A) | 69. | (B) |
| 10. | (D) | 30. | (D) | 50. | (A) | 70. | (D) |
| 11. | (C) | 31. | (A) | 51. | (B) | 71. | (A) |
| 12. | (C) | 32. | (B) | 52. | (B) | 72. | (E) |
| 13. | (C) | 33. | (C) | 53. | (B) | 73. | (D) |
| 14. | (E) | 34. | (C) | 54. | (E) | 74. | (D) |
| 15. | (E) | 35. | (D) | 55. | (C) | 75. | (D) |
| 16. | (A) | 36. | (E) | 56. | (D) | 76. | (D) |
| 17. | (E) | 37. | (C) | 57. | (C) | 77. | (A) |
| 18. | (B) | 38. | (E) | 58. | (D) | 78. | (D) |
| 19. | (B) | 39. | (C) | 59. | (B) | 79. | (D) |
| 20. | (C) | 40. | (C) | 60. | (B) | 80. | (E) |

# DETAILED EXPLANATIONS OF ANSWERS

# TEST 2

1.  **(B)**
    Using the LNR (Left-Node-Right) scan technique of a binary tree, we have the scanning order:

    $(A + B * C) / (A - C)$

2.  **(C)**
    Each row of the table can be represented by a minterm. The three rows of the table with an $f$ value of 1 are:

    | $x$ | $y$ | $z$ | | |
    |---|---|---|---|---|
    | 0 | 0 | 1 | | $x'y'z$ |
    | 0 | 1 | 0 | with corresponding minterms: | $x'yz'$ |
    | 1 | 0 | 0 | | $xy'z'$ |

    Each minterm is computed by taking the complement of each variable that has a 0 and the variable itself for each 1. Summing them produces answer (C). Note choice (A) is not a sum of minterms. Choices (B), (D), and (E) are the sum of the wrong minterms.

3.  **(C)**
    The grammar looks like it will generate the language $\{0^n1^n \mid n>0\}$ but productions $S{\to}0S$ and $S{\to}S1$ will generate 0's and 1's in unequal numbers. So the language is really $\{0^m1^k \mid m >= 1, k >= 0\}$, which is clearly a regular language with productions = $\{S{\to}0S, S{\to}S1, S{\to}9\}$.

4.  **(C)**
    (A) is wrong because phase code modulation can have more than two phases. (B) looks good because early modems, transmitting data on twisted pairs usually had identical bit and baud rates, but multiple phases, or multiple levels of voltage, can be transmitted on twisted pairs. (C) is correct because only two values are possible corresponding to the 0 and 1 of a bit. The bit rate (bps) must always fall within the bounds of Shannon's Law, but that has

nothing to do with the bit rate and the baud rate being equal, so (D) is wrong. (E) is illogical because the baud rate and bit rate are often equal.

5.   **(C)**
Since we are looking for the largest value of $A$, if variable *maxval* is smaller than any element in the array $A$, then their positions need to be exchanged by the statement following **then**.

6.   **(C)**
*Reverse*($L$) can be generated by a finite automaton $F$ for language $L$ if we essentially:

1.   change every accept state of $F$ to a start state.

2.   change every start state of $F$ to an accept state.

3.   reverse the direction of each edge.

Though it may be non-deterministic, we can reduce out the non-determinism since this is a finite automaton. Since we have a finite automaton to recognize it, the language must be regular.

7.   **(C)**
The decimal number $N$ has 30 digits, so roughly $\log_{10}(N) = 30$. The value of $\log_{10}(N)$ is approximately $\log_8(N)$ which is $\log_2(N) / 3$, since $8 = 2^3$. So, $\log_2(N) = 3*30 = 90$. Hence, the answer is (C).

8.   **(C)**
(C) is false since the WITH clause is only for notational convenience but is not necessary and is often troublesome in debugging. (A) and (B) are standard features of variant records. (D) refers to the ability of arrays to have multiple records.

9.   **(A)**
$$E(\alpha f + \beta g) \quad = \alpha f(x + h) + \beta g\,(x + h)$$
$$= \alpha E(f) + \beta E(g)$$

(A)   $\therefore E\,(\alpha f + \beta g) \quad = \alpha E(f) + \beta E(g)$

(B)   $(\alpha + \beta\,)E\,(f + g) = (\alpha + \beta)\,[f(x + h) + g(x + h)]$
$$\neq \alpha E(f) + \beta E(g)$$

(C)   $\alpha E(f + \beta g) \quad = \alpha((f + h) + \beta(g + h))$
$$\neq \alpha Ef(f) + \beta E(g)$$

(D)    $\alpha\,\beta E(f + g)$      $= \alpha\beta(f(x + h) + g(x + h))$

                                 $= \alpha E(f) + \beta E(g)$

(E)    $\alpha + \beta E(f + g)$      $= \alpha + \beta(f(x + h) + g(x + h))$

                                 $\neq \alpha E(f) + \beta E(g)$

10.   **(D)**

     The directed graph (D) had a path of length one between the following nodes

        ① to ① $\rightarrow m_{11} = 1$

        ② to ① $\rightarrow m_{21} = 1$

        ③ to ① $\rightarrow m_{31} = 1$

        ③ to ② $\rightarrow m_{32} = 1$

        ② to ③ $\rightarrow m_{23} = 1$

There are no directed edges connecting nodes:

        ① to ②

        ② to ②

        ① to ③    $\rightarrow m_{12} = m_{22} = m_{13} = m_{33} = 0$

        ② to ③

11.   **(C)**

     There are $2^3 = 8$ input variable cases for a Boolean function of 3 variables. Each case can have either a 0 or 1. So there are $2^8$ patterns (or functions). Answer (C) is $256 = 2^8$.

12.   **(C)**

     Choose a path to send a flow from source to sink (like path $A\ B\ E\ H\ K$ which has a maximum flow of 3.) Now relabel all edges on that path, subtracting 3 from each edge. Note: 3 is the smallest flow on $A\ B\ E\ H\ K$. So, $AB = 3 - 3 = 0$, $BE = 4 - 3 = 1$, $EH = 3 - 3 = 0$, and $HK = 3 - 3 = 0$.

This gives the following graph:

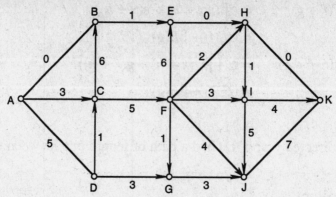

Repeat this for path $A\ C\ F\ I\ K$ with flow = 3. So, $AC = 3 - 3 = 0$, $CF$ = $5 - 3 = 2$, $FI = 3 - 3 = 0$, and $IK = 4 - 3 = 1$.

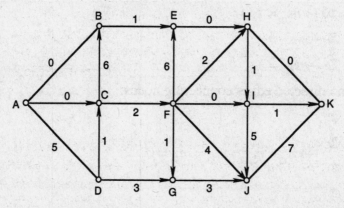

Repeat the process for path $A\ D\ G\ J\ K$ with flow = 3. So $AD = 5 - 3$ = 2, $DG = 3 - 3 = 0$, $GJ = 3 - 3 = 0$, and $JK = 7 - 3 = 4$.

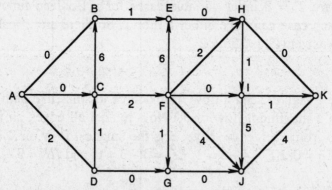

At this point, note that we still have some flow capacity from the source (i.e., $AD = 2$) so take path $A\ D\ C\ F\ J\ K$ with flow = 1 (note the bottleneck in this path is $DC = 1$), so subtract one from each edge on this path. So $AD = 2 - 1 = 1$, $DC = 1 - 1 = 0$, $CF = 2 - 1 = 1$, $FJ = 4 - 1 = 3$, and $JK = 4 - 1 = 3$. The resulting graph of remaining flow capacities is:

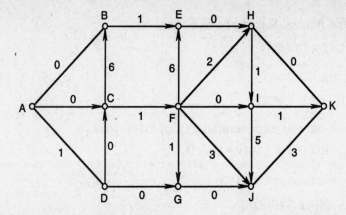

Note that this is a terminal case because we can construct a cutset with no flow capacity left (i.e., a set of edges whose flow capacities are fully utilized (labelled 0).) For this final graph, the cutset is (*AB, AC, DC, DG*). Note that the cutset is a set of bottlenecks and that those four edges effectively "block" any possible path from source *A* to sink *K*. No further flow can be added. In military intuition, there are no other supply lines left from *A* to *K*. Hence, the optimal flow is $3 + 3 + 3 + 1 = 10$.

13. **(C)**

This problem involves the concept of the set-type and the concept of precondition-postcondition. For the "**then** *writeln(x)*" to execute, the **if** condition must be true. The condition "(*x* **mod** 6 **in** [2,3,4])" says that "division of *x* by 6 gives a remainder of either 2 or 3 or 4". We now test the five answers: 144 **mod** 6 = 0, 85 **mod** 6 = 1, 98 **mod** 6 = 2, 121 **mod** 6 = 1, 732 **mod** 6 = 0. So only 98 **mod** 6 satisfies the condition.

14. **(E)**

To convert a finite automaton to a regular expression, take paths to the accept state, namely ACDE and ABE giving strings *aab* and *ba* respectively. Now take the cycle ECDE which generates *bab*. The two paths to reach the loop state E gives the term (*aab* + *ba*) which is then followed by the *bab* – loop, giving (*aab* + *ba*) (*bab*)*. We could quickly reject Choice (A) since it generates *babbbbbb*, Choice (B) since it can't generate *babab*, Choice (C) since it generates *aaba*, and Choice (D) since it generates *babbab*.

15. **(E)**

(B) is false since ** is not allowed in PASCAL. So, we need to derive:

$$x^y = x^y$$

Taking the natural logarithm of both sides.

$\ln (x^y) = \ln (x^y)$.

Simplifying,

$\ln (x^y) = y * \ln x$.

Taking the natural exponentian exp of both sides,

$\exp (\ln (x^y)) = \exp(y * \ln(x))$.

The left side then reduces to

$x^y = \exp(y * \ln(x))$,

which is answer choice (E).

Among the wrong answers, $exp(ln(x*y)) = x*y$, so (C) is just multiplication. Likewise, $exp(x*ln(y)) = exp(ln(y**x)) = y**x$, so (D) is wrong.

16. **(A)**

$$A = \begin{bmatrix} a_{11} & a_{12} & a_{13} \\ a_{21} & a_{22} & a_{23} \\ a_{31} & a_{32} & a_{33} \end{bmatrix}, \text{ and } LU = \begin{bmatrix} l_{11} & 0 & 0 \\ l_{21} & l_{22} & 0 \\ l_{31} & l_{32} & l_{33} \end{bmatrix} \begin{bmatrix} 1 & u_{12} & u_{13} \\ 0 & 1 & u_{23} \\ 0 & 0 & 1 \end{bmatrix}$$

(1) $l_{11} = a_{11}, \ l_{21} = a_{21}, \ l_{31} = a_{31}$

(2) $l_{11} u_{12} = -1 \rightarrow u_{12} = -1$
    $l_{11} u_{13} = 1 \rightarrow u_{13} = 1$

(3) $l_{21} u_{12} + l_{22} = -1 \rightarrow l_{22} = -1$
    $l_{31} u_{12} + l_{32} = 2 \rightarrow l_{32} = 3$

(4) $l_{21} u_{13} + l_{22} u_{23} = -1 \rightarrow u_{23} = 1$

(5) $l_{31} u_{13} + l_{32} u_{23} + l_{33} = 0 \rightarrow l_{33} = -4$

17. **(E)**
    (A) is wrong since every increasing value of $A[J + 1]$ causes the lower value $A[J]$ to print. (B) is wrong because since every increasing value of $A[J]$ will print but an increasing value is not always a peak. (C) only finds the maximum value, which will be a peak, but ignores all the other peaks (i.e., local peaks.) (D) is wrong since it checks for $A[J + 1] < A[J] < A[J - 1]$, which means $A[J]$ is neither peak nor trough, but an intermediate value. (E) is correct since it tests that $A[J]$ is bigger than both

$A[J + 1]$ and $A[J - 1]$, which is a true peak; without both conditions, $A[J]$ would just be larger than one neighbor but may be smaller than the other (i.e., an intermediate value).

18. **(B)**

Using Karnaugh maps, we have:

|        |    | 00 | 01 | 11 | 10 | $= x, y$ |
|--------|----|----|----|----|----|----------|
| $z, w =$ | 00 | 0  | 0  | 1  | 0  |          |
|        | 01 | 0  | 0  | 1  | 0  |          |
|        | 11 | 1  | 1  | 1  | 0  |          |
|        | 10 | 1  | 1  | 1  | 0  |          |

The $xy$ and $zx'$ 4-cubes have a hazard, so we cover the adjacent boundaries with the 4-cube $yz$. This removes the hazard. (A) is false. (C) removes only the upper half of the hazard. (D) removes only the lower half. (E) is not the same function.

19. **(B)**

The productions are ambiguous since $E + E + E$ has two distinct derivations

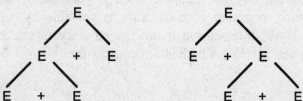

It is not inherently ambiguous since we can introduce new variables and modify the productions (for example, $E \rightarrow E + E$ can be replaced by $E \rightarrow E + P$, $E \rightarrow P$, etc.), ultimately ending in an unambiguous grammar. So (A) and (C) are false while (B) is true. (D) is false since the sequence of computations for $(3 + 4) / (7 + 9)$ is not expressible with these productions alone.

20. **(C)**

One approach is to build a full truth table; however, there are faster approaches. Choice (A) means the truth table has all $T$ (true); it is wrong because we can force $P1$ to be false by setting $p = F$ and $q = T$. Choice (B) requires the truth table to be all false; by setting $p = T$ and $q = F$, we can easily force $P1$ to be true. Choice (E) is always false, since $P1$ and not $P1$ is never true. Choice (E) is always false since $P1$ and not $P1$ is never true. By plugging in the respective values, we can test choices (C) and (D).

(C)  $(T \lor \text{not } F) \land (F \to F \land (F \lor T)$ becomes true

(D)  $(T \lor \text{not } T) \land (T \to F) \land (F \lor T)$ becomes false

21.  **(D)**
  (A) looks fine at first, but the $K:=K+1$ occurs just before the **until** condition, in this case resulting in an overcount for $K$ by 1. (B) starts summing from $A[2]$, another error. (C) looks like (B) but starts summing from $A[1]$ and keeps summing, but it sums the $A[K]=0$ case as if it was valid, so $K$ will overcount. (D) does the same as (C) but avoids summing $A[K]=0$ and the overcount by testing $A[K+1]$ (i.e., it catches the 0-value one loop before it causes the error). So (D) is best. (E) is bad since $K$ is incremented at the end of the loop and $A[K+1]$ is tested, resulting in a test of $A[K+2]$ for a 0-value. (E) would leave the loop prematurely and not sum the last valid height.

22.  **(D)**
  Let $L1$ and $L2$ be two context-free languages with start symbols $T$ and $V$, respectively. We can add the production $S \to T$ and $S \to V$ and we have the productions for the unions of $L1$ and $L2$ (provided we rename any similar nonterminal names). Concatenation is possible by adding $S \to TV$ instead. Likewise, repeated concatenation is possible by adding $S \to TS$, $S \to T$, $S \to VS$, $S \to V$. Intersection is not closed since intersecting $\{0^k 1^k 2^n\}$ and $\{0^n 1^k 2^k\}$ gives $\{2^k 1^k 2^k\}$ which is not context-free.

23.  **(C)**
  We know that 100% - 40% = 60% of all users have a wait time > 0. Let average wait time for group $X = AWT(X)$. Then,
  $AWT$ (all people) = (% of waiters) * $AWT$ (waiters)
  + (% of nonwaiters) * $AWT$ (nonwaiters).
So,  $50 = .60 * AWT$ (waiters) + $.40 * (0)$
  $AWT$ (waiters) = $50 / .60 = 83.33$.

So the answer is (C)

24.  **(E)**
  (A) will compute $x^n$ in $m$ and sum $a[j]x^n$ in $P$, so it is fine. (B) is just a slow version of (A), wasting time recomputing $m$ but otherwise fine. (C) is an expanded version of (A) where $m$ is recomputed every time $x^j$ is needed. (D) is a more efficient way of computing polynomials (classical synthetic division):

$$a_0 + ((\ldots+a[2])x = a_0+a[1]x+a[2]x^2+\ldots$$

(E) will not compute the polynomial since it computes the $a[1]$ term first, then $a[2]$, then $a[3]$, ... , giving

$$a_0+((\ldots((a[1]x+a[2])\ldots)x+a[n]x=a)$$
$$+a[1]x^n+a[2]x^{(n-1)}+\ldots$$

So, (E) gives a totally wrong polynomial.

25. **(E)**
    A logarithmic function would have an equation like $T(n) = T(n/k)$; if $k$ is 2, then it would be log-base 2. So choice (A) is false. Note: functions of this type are relevant in divide-and-conquer methods. A linear function would have a recurrence relation like $T(n) = T(n - 1) + k$, so choice (B) is false. Choice (C) requires a form like $T(n) = T(n - 1) - 2*n - 1$ (ie. a sum of linear terms). Choice (D) requires a form like $T(n) = k*T(n - 1)$, so exponential is false. Therefore, this bizarre function doesn't belong in any nice category.

26. **(B)**
    (B) will assume a number is print until (in the loop) a number is encountered (between 2 and $n - 1$) that divides $n$, in which case the flag is set to False. When the loop finishes, it prints the result correctly. (A) will loop and print every time $n$ is not divisible by a number. For example, $n = 15$ will print *is prime* because 2 doesn't divide $n$. (C) will set flag $PR$ to false and then in the loop, if one number doesn't divide $N$, will eventually print *is prime*, as in (A). (D) looks like (B) but the **if** statement has a fatal **else** clause; if n is not prime at one time through the loop, then a later loop can "reinstate" $n$ as a prime. For example, $n = 15$ divides by $k = 5$, but on the $k = 6$ loop, it won't divide, setting $n$ back to $PR$ = True. So (D) is wrong. (E) is a joke, since it says $n$ is not prime until something divides it.

27. **(D)**
    Starting with $\{a,b,c,d,e,f,g\}$, compute all pairs which don't occur on the $M_j$ rows above. For example, $a$ and $d$ don't occur on the same row, so $ad$ is a valid pair. The pairs are: $\{ad, bg, cf, df, dg, fg\}$. Similarly form triples, getting $\{dfg\}$. Note: $e$ had no pair, so it remains. Also, $\{df, dg, fg\}$ are subsets of $\{dfg\}$ and may be deleted. So, MCCs = $\{e, ad, bg, cf, dfg\}$.

28. **(D)**
    The standard approach of solving the difference equation is too time consuming. In fact, those familiar with fibonnacci series might incorrectly

guess this as exponential. A better approach is to look at the growth behavior.

$$r(1) = 1, \; r(2) = 2, \; r(3) = 3,$$
$$r(4) = 3 + 2 - 1 = 4,$$
$$r(5) = 4 + 3 - 2 = 5.$$

It seems $r(n) = n$. Doing a quick induction test, we have

$$r(n) \; = \; r(n - 1) + r(n - 2) - r(n - 3)$$

which becomes

$$n = (n - 1) + (n - 2) - (n - 3)$$

reducing to $n = n$, an identity; so $r(n) = n$ is true. For amusement, note that initial values $r(1) = 1, r(2) = 1, r(3) = 1$ will give a constant function.

## 29. **(D)**

Choices (A), (B), and (E) start off with *MaxInt* as an initial approximation to the maximum. Since no value can ever exceed that, it is a poor choice. (C) starts off with $-$ *MaxInt* (fine) but then replaces it with a lower value (impossible). (D) starts like (C) but replaces each *MaxY* value as it encounters larger values in the *Item* array.

## 30. **(D)**

The Ackermann function is an example of a function which is recursive but not primitive recursive. (A) and (B) are false since the Ackermann function cannot be computed in primitive recursive time. (C) seems tempting but suffers similarly. (D) is true since the operations mentioned are primitive recursive constructs. (E) is totally (pun intended) false, since Ackermann will halt (i.e., the recursion is well behaved, not resulting in an infinite recursion tree.) In fact, the real fame of this function is that it is computable despite its not being primitive recursive.

## 31. **(A)**

(A) splits into subrange categories 90..100 and 80..89 which match the letter grades 'A' and 'B.' In each category, a different counter is incremented correctly. (B) assumes only two numbers (namely 90 and 100) are in the 'A' grade, neglecting 91 through 99. (C) is wrong because it assumes the grades are letter, whereas the problem states they are numeric. (D) is even worse than (C) because 'A' and 'B' would be wrong here, being misinterpreted as variable names or worse. The only way 'A' and 'B' can be in that position is if they are values (in an enumerated type) or a name of a subrange type (which was not mentioned). (E) looks great but neglects that $G = 90$ should be an 'A' and that any value below (such as 0) should be a 'B.'

32. **(B)**

Mathematical model of this optimization problem is constructed as

Maximize :  $4x + 6y$

Subject to constraints:  $4x + 3y < = 144$

$x + 3y < = 108$

$x, y > = 0$

Using the graphic method to solve this system, first construct the feasibility region (shaded area in the following figure) and then move the equation $4x + 3y = k$ from the inside of the feasibility region toward the outside region. The last corner point of the feasibility region which meets the line: $4x + 3y = k$ gives the solution.

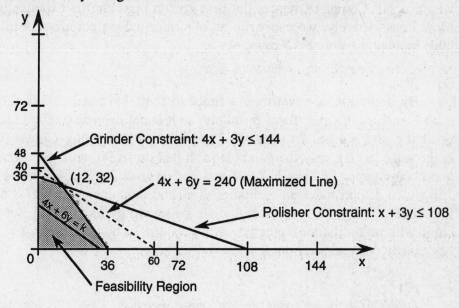

33. **(C)**

(A) and (E) are wrong because they use *call-by-value*, which loses the values of $m$ when control returns from the procedure to the calling program. (B) works fine if $m:=a$ since $a>b>c$ but note that in the statement **if** $(b>c)$ the program choses $c$ even though $b>c$. Likewise, (D) is wrong since **if** $(a>b)$ results in a choice of $m:=b$ which is wrong.

Looking at (C):

if $(a>b)$ and $(a>c)$ then $a$ is the max.

if $(a>b)$ and $(a<=c)$ then $c$ is largest.

(else) if $(a<=b)$ and $(b>c)$ then $b$ is largest.

(else) if $(a<=b)$ and (else) $(b<+c)$ then $c$ is largest.

In this manner, we have informally gone through all assertions needed to verify the code for (C).

### 34. **(C)**

(C) is correct since microprograms generally don't change and that condition makes ROM usage feasible. Temporary variables (A) disappear after a job executes. Passwords (B) and the cabling of ports (D) change seasonally. By definition, boot sectors (E) are on disk.

### 35. **(D)**

This problem is really a rephrasing of the satisfiability problem which is NP Complete; hence, the best known algorithm is exponential. More constructively, we can write an algorithm which computes a truth table but that requires $2**N$ rows.

### 36. **(E)**

By definition of invertible, a function must have one $X$ value for each $Y$ value. $\sin(X)$ oscillates infinitely, so it is not invertible. $Y = X^2$ is a quadratic, so $Y = 4$ has $X$ values of $+2$ and $-2$, so (B) is wrong. Choice (C) is the same as (B), only the parabola is shifted down 90 steps. (D) seems good but plugging in $X = -1$, $X = 0$, and $X = 10$ gives $Y = 8$, $Y = 6$, and $Y = 756$ which demonstrates an oscillation (i.e., non-monotonic), so (D) is not invertible. Finally, (E)'s invertibility can be shown by its familiar plot (a cubic with no oscillation), plugging a few values, or by noting that $Y = X^3$ has exactly one real solution, $X = Y^{(1/3)}$.

### 37. **(C)**

*DOGCAGE* is an array-type of one dimension. *KENNEL* is a two dimensional array, each element of which is of type *DOGCAGE*, so we have three dimensions.

### 38. **(E)**

The **if** condition must be true for us to reach {zzz}, so $J*J - 4 > 0$ and $J*J > 4$ and finally $J > 2$ or $J < -2$. This example can be verfied graphically, since the parabola $J*J - 4$ goes above the $x$-axis (really the $J$-axis) when $J > 2$ or $J < -2$.

39. **(C)**
Virtual memory could be used on a single user system when running a very large program, so (C) is the answer (i.e., false.) (A) is true since variable size segments produce fragmentation between segments when a big segment is replaced by a smaller one. (B) is true since the last page of a program might not be full. (D) is true since CPU's can use a two step address translation. (E) is true since too many users may result in too many pages being demanded in memory so one user "bumps" the other out of RAM and on to disk.

40. **(C)**
The $K$-loop computes $z:=z+10$; just preceding it is a $z:=z+1$.
So the inner **begin-end** computes $z:=z+11$.
That **begin-end** executes 10 times, so $z=10*11=110$.

41. **(C)**
This problem could be attacked by a Venn Diagram very quickly, but that requires diagramming all five choices and the original expression. A little algebra often works better.

$$A - (B \cap C) = A \cap (B \cap C)' = A \cap (B' \cup C')$$
$$= (A \cap B') \cup (A \cap C') = (A - B) \cup (A - C) \quad \text{(Choice (C))}$$

To negate the other choices, Choice (B) gives sets $B$ and $C$ asymmetric roles, so it is wrong. Choice (C) is really $A - (B \cup C)$. Choice (D) gives sets $B$ and $C$ asymmetric roles. In Choice (E), we expand to $A \cup (A \cap C)$ $\cup \ldots$ which is bigger than $A$, while the original is smaller than $A$. Venn diagrams may prove quicker.

42. **(C)**
(A) is wrong since a comparison of $X[j]$ and $X[k]$ will cause a switch in $X[j+1]$ and $X[k]$ but the $j+1$st element's value is totally independent of the $j$th value, resulting in total chaos. In (B), $k$ **div** 2 will never exceed the half-way mark in array $X$, so at best it can sort half of the array. On the other extreme, (E) has $X[k*2]$ but $k*2$ exceeds the array bound. (D) has $X[K-1]$, also out of array bounds when $k = 1$. So (C) remains. (C) makes 10 passes through the array and each pass switches all adjacent elements that are out of order. (C) is really a very inefficient bubble-sort with no flag to stop the process (i.e., the worst case and best case behaviors are the same). Very slow.

43. **(B)**

1. Caches are small relative to the size of memory and a small loop would fit within it, reuslting in few accesses to slower RAM.

3. Interleaved memory accesses RAM in sequential memory addresses in parallel (i.e., multiple banks). With large sequential code, branching is rare and so each sequential chunk read from slow RAM is completely utilized. So the answer is (B).

Choices (A), (C), (D), and (E) are false since:

2. A small loop would cause branching often, which forces interleaved memory to reaccess RAM without using all it read from RAM at the previous read.

4. Large sequential code results in new addresses being accessed resulting in more RAM read and cache performance diminishes.

44. **(E)**

$K(5)$ is not planar (Kuratowski's theorem or a quick visual test will confirm this.) Deleting one node from $K(5)$ will make it planar (again confirmable by Kuratowski or visual test). To reduce $K(6)$ to $K(5)$, we may think of $K(6)$ as $K(5)$ with 1 more node and 5 more edges (to connect with new node to $K(5)$'s nodes). So 1 edge reduces $K(5)$ to a planar graph and 5 edges reduces $K(6)$ to $K(5)$, totalling to 6 (Choice (E).) Since the nodes of $K(6)$ are symmetrical, deleting fewer edges from $K(6)$ will leave a "copy" of $K(5)$ in the graph and prevent planarity.

45. **(D)**

Loop invariants have no relevance to top-down design. Flowcharting is a standard representation for top-down code design. Step-wise refinement involves the process of repeatedly replacing short high-level pseudocode descriptions with repeatedly more detailed and less abstract code. Modularity refers to the process of breaking down large tasks into modules, a complementary aspect of step-wise refinement. Together with hierarchical organization, they constitute the major tools of top-down design methodology.

46. **(B)**

$$G(x) = 9999999x - .0001x^2 + x \log(\log(x)) + x^2/(x-99) + 0.9^x$$

$$O(x) - O(x^2) + x \log(\log(x)) + O(x^2)/O(x) + 0.9^x$$

Since $O(x)$ is dominated by $O(x^2)$ and we an divide $O(x^2)/O(x)$, we have

$$O(x^2) + x \log(\log(x)) + O(x) + 0.9^x$$

Since $x$ dominates $\log(\log(x))$ the $O(x^2)$ dominates the term and the $O(n)$ term too, giving $O(x^2) + 0.9^x$.

At first, a hasty decision would state that exponentials dominate quadratics but this is false here since $0.9^x$ is less than one for large $x$ (tending toward 0 as $n$ goes to infinity.) So the quadratic term dominates.

47. **(D)**
(A) is not possible since $E$ is the fifth item read but ends up the first in the stack. (B) and (C) put $F$, the final item read, at the bottom of the stack and previous items above, so they are impossible. Similarly, (E) is not possible since $E$ is deeper than $C$. (D) is possible because we can: *Read*(A), *Read*(B), *Push*(B), *Read*(C), *Read*(D), *Push*(D), *Read*(E), *Read*(F), *Push*(F), giving the above.

48. **(B)**
A simpler way to attack these problems is to note that the order of input is the order of the stack (i.e., first input is at the bottom.) Pushing keeps the order. Popping only deletes nodes in the order but retains the order. Choices (A), (C), (D), and (E) all retain the order (notably alphabetic here). (B) has $F$ below $C$, thereby violating the order and becoming impossible.

49. **(A)**
Don't care conditions are required where the two lists differ, so positions 4 and 5 require don't cares while the rest can be the same list elements (or even don't cares). (A) is fine. (B) has the element $d$ which doesn't unify with $L2$. (C) is totally wrong. (D) is fine for $L2$ but not with $L1$. Finally, (E) has only one element to unify.

50. **(A)**
All stacks are possible because each time we are about to read an item from the input, we can first pop off one stack and pop on to the other until we find the desired position of the next input. Also, because we can write back to file immediately after reading from it, we can read the same item again and repeat the process with the other stack. So, since we can put any input in any position, all patterns are possible.

51. **(B)**
Two bits are needed to represent which of four opcode lengths a command uses. This leaves $6 - 2 = 4$ bits for the actual opcode description, giving $2^4 = 16$ possible commands, answer (B).

## 52. (B)

Clearly, a four-way merge sort is possible, though it requires more code than a standard merge sort. A standard merge sort operates in time $N \log_2(N)$ by making $\log_2(N)$ "passes" over the $N$ elements and the log base 2 is due to the recursive partitionings (followed by mergings) conducted during those "passes." If we partition by 4, then the array can be sorted/merged in log base 4 "passes," giving a total time of $N \log_4(N)$. Since $\log_2(N) = 2 \log_4(N)$, we know that it appears to be twice as fast, but requires careful coding to be so. Either way, it is $O$ (Merge-Sort).

## 53. (B)

We can compute first the shortest distance for nodes near the source. $B = \min (3, 1 + 6, 5 + 4 + 6) = 3$. Similarly, $C = 1$ and $D = 5$. Now that we solved the problem for nodes adjacent to the source, compute distances for the next frontier spreading outward (i.e., $E, F, G$). $E = \min (4 + B, 6 + 2 + B, 6 + 3 + C, \ldots = 4 + B = 7$. Likewise, $F = 3 + 1 = 4$ and $G = 1 + 3 + C = 5$. At the next frontier, we have $H, I, J$. $J = 4 + F = 8$. $I = 3 + F = 7$. $H = 2 + F = 6$. Lastly, $K = \min (3 + H, 4 + I, 2 + J) = \min (9, 11, 10) = 9$. The shortest path is $A\,C\,F\,H\,K$. These computations are handled most quickly by labelling the graph and computing by inspection.

## 54. (E)

First pick the lightest edges (weight $= 1$) and keep those edges that connect new nodes (or subtrees). Then add all edges of weight 2. Add all the edges of weight 3 except for edges $AB$, $FI$, and $GJ$ since they don't add any new nodes to the tree (i.e., adding them would be "wasteful" (non-minimal) and would create a cycle, which is not tree-like. No further edges need be added since all nodes are connected.

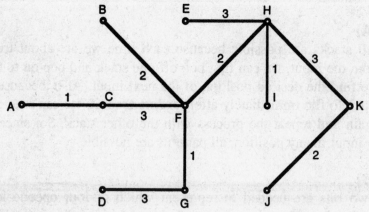

This sums to 21.

55. **(C)**

(C) is impossible since $4 - 3 = 1$ ignores the parentheses (i.e., invalid evaluation). (A) is the first step of a valid evaluation while (B) is near the last step. (E) is an intermediate phase between (A) and (B). (D) is one valid push after (E).

56. **(D)**

Clearly (B) is ambiguous and therefore not operator precedence (O.P.). Note: in (B), $E + E + E$ has two derivations. Choice (A) has a precedence problem since $E \rightarrow E + T \rightarrow E + E$ can be used to give two derivations for $E + E + E$, giving two conflicting precedence values (just like choice (B)). Choice (C) has the same problem but now $T \rightarrow T + T$ is causing the same problem. Choice (E) has the productions of choice (A) as a subset, so (E) has the same trouble. Choice (D) avoids these problems by having $E \rightarrow E + T \rightarrow E + T + T \rightarrow T + T + T$ (note that T's "grow" on one side of the E's and likewise with +). Note also that rather than let $T \rightarrow E$, we have $T \rightarrow (E)$, so the indirect ambiguity is avoided.

57. **(C)**

Rather than build a full Karnaugh map, note that $X_3(t + 1)$ always differs from $X_3(t)$, so the clock pulse can trigger it: $T_3$ = clock pulse. $X_2(t + 1)$ differs from $X_2(t)$ when $X_3(t)$ is 1, so $T_2$ = AND ($X_3$, clock pulse). Lastly, a change to $X_1$ occurs when $X_2$ and $X_3$ are both 1, so $T_3$ = AND ($X_3$, $X_2$, clock pulse).

| Present State | | | Next State | | |
|---|---|---|---|---|---|
| $X_1$ | $X_2$ | $X_3$ | $X_1$ | $X_2$ | $X_3$ |
| 0 | 0 | 0 | 0 | 0 | 1 |
| 0 | 0 | 1 | 0 | 1 | 0 |
| 0 | 1 | 0 | 0 | 1 | 1 |
| 0 | 1 | 1 | 1 | 0 | 0 |
| 1 | 0 | 0 | 1 | 0 | 1 |
| 1 | 0 | 1 | 1 | 1 | 0 |
| 1 | 1 | 0 | 1 | 1 | 1 |
| 1 | 1 | 1 | 0 | 0 | 0 |

So exactly two AND gates were needed (answer (C)).

58. **(D)**

The first tree's top node becomes the root. In the binary tree, every left link means "son of" while every right link means "brother of". (D) adheres to these standards (e.g., nodes *B, C,* and *D* are brothers in the old trees, but right linked in a row in the binary tree). Of the other choices, (A) is not even a binary tree. (B) is a senseless encoding which is not even consistent. (C)'s left subtree is correct but the right subtree "uses" part of the original (which is wrong and inconsistent). (E) loses all the original structure.

59. **(B)**

The distance from root to leaf node (the farthest from the root) in a complete binary tree is $\log(n)$. The greatest distance is between two leaves ($L_1$ and $L_2$) whose connecting path is via the root. Therefore, the distance from $L_1$ to root is $\log(n)$ and from root to $L_2$ is also $\log(n)$, so the total is $2 \log(n)$.

60. **(B)**

(B) is correct since in-order means "visit the left, then the root, then the right," while the binary insertion tree has a number in the root, smaller numbers on the left, and bigger on the right. So, the in-order tour will visit the smaller numbers, then the number, then higher numbers, giving us a sorted order. (E) is totally wrong since linked lists dumped in memory order are in random order. (D) is meaningless but sounds real. (C) would recursively visit lower, higher, and then intermediate numbers which is not sorted. Likewise, (A) will hit the intermediate, then smaller, then larger numbers, giving as bad results as (C).

61. **(B)**

Inter-request time per processor *IRTP* = 2 microseconds.
Rate of requests per processor *RRP* = 1/*IRTP* = 500,000.
Rate of requests (system-wide) 500,000 * *k*.
Each request is for 64 bits + 40 bits = 104 bits.
Bus capacity = 100,000,000. Since total load must equal bus capacity, we have: 100,000,000 = 104 * 500,000 * *k*.
So the system can support approximately *k* = 2 processors.

62. **(C)**

The maximal independent set of a graph is the largest set of nodes in the graph which are mutually disjoint. *K*(4,2) has two disjoint sets (by definition of complete bipartite), specifically of size 2 and 4. Clearly, 4 is the largest and by completeness, no further nodes can be added.

63. **(C)**

Pre-order means "hit the root first, then the left, then the right." Trouble occurs because this must be done recursively. So, hit root *A*, then its left subtree. Now hit root *B* (of the subtree), then left *D*, then right subtree (where we hit root *E* and then left node *G* and no right node). Now that the left subtree of $A$ is finished, we proceed to the right subtree of $A$ which starts at root $C$; then no left of $C$ exists, so go to the right subtree (where root $F$ and left son $H$ are encountered). Two recursive returns later (i.e., $F$ to $C$ and then $C$ to $A$) and the task is over. The itinerary was *ABDEGCFH*. The pre-order traversals are unique, so the other choices are bad.

64. **(B)**

Determining exact primality of $N$ (by the standard algorithm) requires linear time since a single loop is used to test divisibility by all numbers less than $N$.

65. **(A)**

Apply the least square error approximation.
Technique: We have

$$E = \sum_{i=1}^{10} \{y_i = -(a + bx_i)\}^2. \tag{1}$$

Where $E$ is the square of errors at each sampling point $(x_i, y_i)$, $i = 1, 2, \ldots 10$
Differentiate with respect to $a$ and $b$ in equation (1) we have

$$an + b \sum x_i = \sum y_i \tag{2}$$

$$a \sum x_i + b \sum x_i^2 = \sum x_i y_i \tag{3}$$

Solve for $a$ and $b$ from equations (2) and (3), we have

$$a = \frac{\sum y_i \sum x_i^2 - \sum x_i y_i \sum x_i}{n \sum x^2 - (\sum x_i)^2} = 1.811$$

$$b = \frac{n \sum x_i y_i - \sum x_i \sum y_i}{n \sum x_i^2 - (\sum x_i)^2} = 0.108$$

66. **(E)**

(A), (B), and (C) will not modify the array of links; they only modify the temporary "pointers" that are outside. Note that (A) is a meaningless operation, (B) will destroy the topmost pointer to the second linked list (fatal, since we lose that list), and (C) just loses track of where the end of the first list is. (D) looks good but actually kills the second linked list by chopping off all nodes after the first node and then pointing the first node to the last node of the first list. (E) is correct since it asks us to fill the link field of the last node in list #1 with the pointer to the first node in list #2.

67. **(C)**

10 links are needed to point to the first node in each row, 10 links are

needed to point to the first node in each column, and 30 links are part of the 15 non-zero nodes (each data field needs a link to the next element in its columnn and its row). Total = 50 + plus a few links for administration (TOPs).

68. **(D)**

The distance between any two code words is the number of bits that differ between them. For instance, dist (00011000, 11111111) = 6. The distance of a code is the minimum distance of all pairs of code words. The distance between 11000111 and 11111111 is 3, which is the minimum (D).

69. **(B)**

Lower bounds prove that a problem can't be solved in less time; a construction of an algorithm cannot show that an algorithm cannot be constructed (at least not often.) Lower bounds generally use a property of a problem to show that there is intrinsic difficulty. On the dual side, upper bounds are most often shown by constructing an algorithm which essentially gives the lowest upper bound so far. A faster algorithm will lower that bound. Far more rare (if there are any at all) is a non-constructive proof that a faster algorithm could exist but is not given or described (provided we ignore the speed-up theorem, which is not the issue here).

70. **(D)**

The DAG represents common subexpressions by linking two occurrences into one copy. So, $a + b * c$ is multiplied by $b * c - d$. Choice (A) ignores the topmost *. Choice (B) has lost the order of the operations. Choice (C) totally ignores most operations. Choice (E) multiplies the two occurrences first, which is the wrong operator order.

71. **(A)**

One possible approach is the Welch-Powell algorithm. First sort nodes by arity and then assign colors while checking adjacency constraints. So we get:

| node | *D* | *A* | *G* | *C* | *E* | *F* | *B* |
|------|-----|-----|-----|-----|-----|-----|-----|
| arity | 6 | 5 | 4 | 3 | 3 | 3 | 2 |

Now color 1 may be applied to node *D* and no other. Use color 2 on nodes *A* and *G*. Finally, nodes *C*, *E*, *F*, and *B* can be colored with 3. This shows 3 colors are sufficient (i.e., a valid coloring). Since there is a triangle *ABD*, we know 3 colors are necessary (i.e., minimal). In a trickier graph, minimality is harder to show. Welch-Powell and other quick algorithms don't guarantee minimality.

72. **(E)**

Θ is a semigroup because Θ is associative (since addition is associative.) More restrictively, Θ is a monoid since it has an identity element (namely 0) which satisfies $X \Theta 0 = 0 \Theta X = X$ for all $X$ in S. Θ is a group since each element $X$ has an inverse $X'$ such that $X \Theta X' = X' \Theta X = 0$; they are:

| Element | 0 | 1 | 2 | 3 | 4 | 5 | 6 | 7 |
|---------|---|---|---|---|---|---|---|---|
| Inverse | 0 | 7 | 6 | 5 | 4 | 3 | 2 | 1 |

For example, $3 \Theta 5 = (3 + 5) \bmod 8 = 8 \bmod 8 = 0$. Θ is abelian since addition is commutative.

73. **(D)**

Network models are physical key (not logical key) models. They use actual pointers rather than more abstract keys. They are fast because of that close association to the hardware. So (A), (B), (C) and (E) are false. (D) is correct.

74. **(D)**

Before the loop, $x = z$. Each time through the loop, we decrease $x$ by 1. Since we loop m times, $x$ decreases by $m$, giving condition $x = z - m$. Clearly (A) is false since $j <> 0$. (B) is totally absurd. (C) looks good but is close to negative of the answer. (E) makes no sense since this is not an assignment but a logical condition (i.e., if $x = x - j$ then $j = 0$).

75. **(D)**

If each control field has $k$ lines, then ceil($\log_2(k + 1)$) bits are needed. For 1, 7 lines exist. The closest power of 2 equal to or larger than $7 + 1$ is $2^3 = 8$. So 3 control bits are needed to describe those 7 lines. Note: $7 + 1$ is needed since No activity is one more alternative besides selecting one of seven lines. Likewise, $4 + 1$ requires 3 bits, $5 + 1$ requires 3 bits, $2 + 1$ requires 2 bit, $1 + 1$ requires 1 bit and $3 + 1$ requires 2 bits, so the total number of bits needed is: $3 + 3 + 3 + 2 + 1 + 2 = 14$.

76. **(D)**

(D) is correct since *Joins* produce huge tables but this waste can be reduced by *Projecting* irrelevant fields out and Selecting the relevant records for the queries. (A) and (B) will waste memory and CPU time and then finally trim. (C) is only a half-way measure. (E) is also a half-way measure.

77. **(A)**

Let $W$ = wabbit, $N$ = no wabbit.

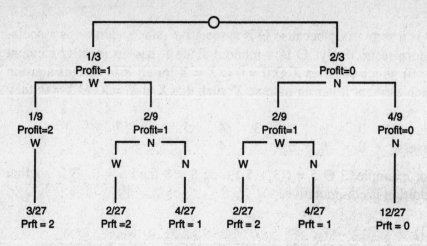

Expected Value = $\Sigma$ (Profit*Probability)

= 6/27 + 4/27 + 4/27 + 4/27 + 4/27 + 0

= 22/27 (Choice (A))

**78. (D)**

Each decoder generates 4 signals. By using 16 AND-gates (with 2 inputs for each gate coming from each possible $X$ and $Y$ pair), we can access 16 possible positions.

**79. (D)**

| TIME: | 1 | 2 | 3 | 4 | 5 | 6 | 7 | 8 | 9 | 10 | 11 | 12 | 13 | 14 | 15 | 16 |
|---|---|---|---|---|---|---|---|---|---|---|---|---|---|---|---|---|
| P.R.: | 2 | 5 | 3 | 4 | 1 | 4 | 7 | 2 | 1 | 3 | 1 | 7 | 4 | 5 | 4 | 6 |
| MEMORY | | | | | | | | | | | | | | | | |
| PAGE 1: | 2 | 5 | 3 | 4 | 1 | 1 | 7 | 2 | 2 | 3 | 3 | 3 | 4 | 5 | 5 | 6 |
| PAGE 2: | | 2 | 5 | 3 | 4 | 4 | 1 | 7 | 7 | 2 | 2 | 2 | 3 | 4 | 4 | 5 |
| PAGE 3: | | | 2 | 5 | 3 | 3 | 4 | 1 | 1 | 7 | 7 | 7 | 2 | 3 | 3 | 4 |
| PAGE 4: | | | | 2 | 5 | 5 | 3 | 4 | 4 | 1 | 1 | 1 | 7 | 2 | 2 | 3 |
| HIT CASE: | | | | | H | | | H | | H | H | | | | H | |

A hit occurs when a page request occurs for a page in real memory at the moment. Hit Ratio = Hit Requests / Total Requests = 5/16 = 31%

**80. (E)**

Clearly (A) is false since $j$ is never greater than 3. Since $k$ is read in, we can't determine if it is positive or negative prior to the loop and it changes inside it. So (B) and (C) are too conditional and make for risky assertions. (D) is also absurd. So, (E) remains. (E) is true since $x = 4.7$ before the loop and after.

# The Graduate Record Examination in

# COMPUTER SCIENCE

## Test 3

# THE GRADUATE RECORD EXAMINATION IN
# COMPUTER SCIENCE
# TEST 3
# ANSWER SHEET

1. Ⓐ Ⓑ Ⓒ Ⓓ Ⓔ
2. Ⓐ Ⓑ Ⓒ Ⓓ Ⓔ
3. Ⓐ Ⓑ Ⓒ Ⓓ Ⓔ
4. Ⓐ Ⓑ Ⓒ Ⓓ Ⓔ
5. Ⓐ Ⓑ Ⓒ Ⓓ Ⓔ
6. Ⓐ Ⓑ Ⓒ Ⓓ Ⓔ
7. Ⓐ Ⓑ Ⓒ Ⓓ Ⓔ
8. Ⓐ Ⓑ Ⓒ Ⓓ Ⓔ
9. Ⓐ Ⓑ Ⓒ Ⓓ Ⓔ
10. Ⓐ Ⓑ Ⓒ Ⓓ Ⓔ
11. Ⓐ Ⓑ Ⓒ Ⓓ Ⓔ
12. Ⓐ Ⓑ Ⓒ Ⓓ Ⓔ
13. Ⓐ Ⓑ Ⓒ Ⓓ Ⓔ
14. Ⓐ Ⓑ Ⓒ Ⓓ Ⓔ
15. Ⓐ Ⓑ Ⓒ Ⓓ Ⓔ
16. Ⓐ Ⓑ Ⓒ Ⓓ Ⓔ
17. Ⓐ Ⓑ Ⓒ Ⓓ Ⓔ
18. Ⓐ Ⓑ Ⓒ Ⓓ Ⓔ
19. Ⓐ Ⓑ Ⓒ Ⓓ Ⓔ
20. Ⓐ Ⓑ Ⓒ Ⓓ Ⓔ
21. Ⓐ Ⓑ Ⓒ Ⓓ Ⓔ
22. Ⓐ Ⓑ Ⓒ Ⓓ Ⓔ
23. Ⓐ Ⓑ Ⓒ Ⓓ Ⓔ
24. Ⓐ Ⓑ Ⓒ Ⓓ Ⓔ
25. Ⓐ Ⓑ Ⓒ Ⓓ Ⓔ
26. Ⓐ Ⓑ Ⓒ Ⓓ Ⓔ
27. Ⓐ Ⓑ Ⓒ Ⓓ Ⓔ

28. Ⓐ Ⓑ Ⓒ Ⓓ Ⓔ
29. Ⓐ Ⓑ Ⓒ Ⓓ Ⓔ
30. Ⓐ Ⓑ Ⓒ Ⓓ Ⓔ
31. Ⓐ Ⓑ Ⓒ Ⓓ Ⓔ
32. Ⓐ Ⓑ Ⓒ Ⓓ Ⓔ
33. Ⓐ Ⓑ Ⓒ Ⓓ Ⓔ
34. Ⓐ Ⓑ Ⓒ Ⓓ Ⓔ
35. Ⓐ Ⓑ Ⓒ Ⓓ Ⓔ
36. Ⓐ Ⓑ Ⓒ Ⓓ Ⓔ
37. Ⓐ Ⓑ Ⓒ Ⓓ Ⓔ
38. Ⓐ Ⓑ Ⓒ Ⓓ Ⓔ
39. Ⓐ Ⓑ Ⓒ Ⓓ Ⓔ
40. Ⓐ Ⓑ Ⓒ Ⓓ Ⓔ
41. Ⓐ Ⓑ Ⓒ Ⓓ Ⓔ
42. Ⓐ Ⓑ Ⓒ Ⓓ Ⓔ
43. Ⓐ Ⓑ Ⓒ Ⓓ Ⓔ
44. Ⓐ Ⓑ Ⓒ Ⓓ Ⓔ
45. Ⓐ Ⓑ Ⓒ Ⓓ Ⓔ
46. Ⓐ Ⓑ Ⓒ Ⓓ Ⓔ
47. Ⓐ Ⓑ Ⓒ Ⓓ Ⓔ
48. Ⓐ Ⓑ Ⓒ Ⓓ Ⓔ
49. Ⓐ Ⓑ Ⓒ Ⓓ Ⓔ
50. Ⓐ Ⓑ Ⓒ Ⓓ Ⓔ
51. Ⓐ Ⓑ Ⓒ Ⓓ Ⓔ
52. Ⓐ Ⓑ Ⓒ Ⓓ Ⓔ
53. Ⓐ Ⓑ Ⓒ Ⓓ Ⓔ

54. Ⓐ Ⓑ Ⓒ Ⓓ Ⓔ
55. Ⓐ Ⓑ Ⓒ Ⓓ Ⓔ
56. Ⓐ Ⓑ Ⓒ Ⓓ Ⓔ
57. Ⓐ Ⓑ Ⓒ Ⓓ Ⓔ
58. Ⓐ Ⓑ Ⓒ Ⓓ Ⓔ
59. Ⓐ Ⓑ Ⓒ Ⓓ Ⓔ
60. Ⓐ Ⓑ Ⓒ Ⓓ Ⓔ
61. Ⓐ Ⓑ Ⓒ Ⓓ Ⓔ
62. Ⓐ Ⓑ Ⓒ Ⓓ Ⓔ
63. Ⓐ Ⓑ Ⓒ Ⓓ Ⓔ
64. Ⓐ Ⓑ Ⓒ Ⓓ Ⓔ
65. Ⓐ Ⓑ Ⓒ Ⓓ Ⓔ
66. Ⓐ Ⓑ Ⓒ Ⓓ Ⓔ
67. Ⓐ Ⓑ Ⓒ Ⓓ Ⓔ
68. Ⓐ Ⓑ Ⓒ Ⓓ Ⓔ
69. Ⓐ Ⓑ Ⓒ Ⓓ Ⓔ
70. Ⓐ Ⓑ Ⓒ Ⓓ Ⓔ
71. Ⓐ Ⓑ Ⓒ Ⓓ Ⓔ
72. Ⓐ Ⓑ Ⓒ Ⓓ Ⓔ
73. Ⓐ Ⓑ Ⓒ Ⓓ Ⓔ
74. Ⓐ Ⓑ Ⓒ Ⓓ Ⓔ
75. Ⓐ Ⓑ Ⓒ Ⓓ Ⓔ
76. Ⓐ Ⓑ Ⓒ Ⓓ Ⓔ
77. Ⓐ Ⓑ Ⓒ Ⓓ Ⓔ
78. Ⓐ Ⓑ Ⓒ Ⓓ Ⓔ
79. Ⓐ Ⓑ Ⓒ Ⓓ Ⓔ
80. Ⓐ Ⓑ Ⓒ Ⓓ Ⓔ

# GRE COMPUTER SCIENCE
## TEST 3

**TIME:** 170 Minutes
80 Questions

---

**DIRECTIONS:** Each of the questions or incomplete statements below is followed by five suggested answers or completions. Select the one that is best in each case. Refer to Pages vii – ix for *Notations and Conventions*.

---

1. Which of the following sorting algorithms yield approximately the same worst-case and average-case running time behavior in $0(n \log n)$?

   (A) Bubble sort and Selection sort

   (B) Heap sort and Merge sort

   (C) Quicksort and Radix sort

   (D) Tree sort and Median-of-3 Quicksort

   (E) Exchange sort and Insertion sort

2. The language accepted by the following FA is:

   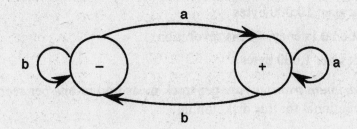

   where "–" is the start state and "+" is the ending state.

   (A) $(a + b) * (a + b)$      (D) $a * b$

   (B) $(a + b) * a$          (E) $a * b *$

   (C) $(a + b) * b$

3.   In order to make the automaton in Questions 2 accept the string of length zero, the language of all words not ending with letter $b$ (and also the null string), the following minor changes will suffice:

(A)   Make right-hand state the start state and left-hand state the final state

(B)   Make right-hand state both the start and final state

(C)   Make left-hand state both the start and final state

(D)   Delete the left-hand state's self loop labeled with $b$

(E)   We need more nodes and significant revisions so that the automaton accepts the null string

4.   RS-232-C:

(A)   Is an interface standard between Data Terminal Equipment and Data Circuit-terminating Equipment

(B)   Is an interface between two Data Circuit-terminating Equipment as exemplified by a local and remote modem

(C)   Specifies only the mechanical characteristics of an interface by providing a 25-pin connector

(D)   Requires only 7 pins out of 25 in order to transmit digital data over public telephone lines

(E)   Both (A) and (D)

5.   Consider a disk with the following characteristics:

Track size: 10,000 bytes

Rotational latency: 10 ms/revolution

Block size: 1,000 bytes

The *maximum transfer rate* per track measured in bits per second as is conventional for this disk unit is:

(A)   400 Mbps          (D)   4,250 Mbps

(B)   8  Mbps           (E)   10 Mbps

(C)   6,400 Mbps

6.  With implementation involving rounding (rather than truncation) and float conversions, the final values of c, i, x, and y in the following C program will be:

```
main( )
{
int i = 97;
char c;
float x = 97.45;
double y;
i = c;
c = i;
y = i;
x = y;
y = x;
}
```

(A)  Both *i* and *c* will have the same value, equal to 0x61 (hexadecimal), which corresponds to lower case ASCII letter *a*. Both *x* and *y* are equal to 97.0.

(B)  Both *i* and *c* will have the same final values, and so will *x* and *y*, regardless of the initial values.

(C)  There will be a compiler error in regard to the *c* = *i* assignment, although all other assignments are legal.

(D)  The final values of *i* and *c* will always be the same regardless of the initial values, but this is not true for *x* and *y*.

(E)  The final values of *i* and *c* will be the same regardless of the order of assignments, but the final values of *x* and *y* depend on the order of assignments.

7.  Which one of the following lattices are Boolean?

(A)                              (D)

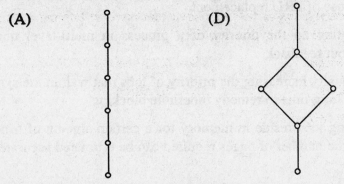

(B)   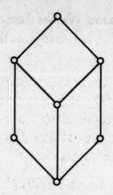   (E)   None of the above

(C)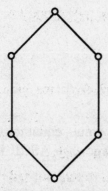

8.   The probability that a single bit will be in error on a typical public telephone line using 4800 bps modem is $10^{-3}$. If no error detection mechanism is used, the residual error rate for a communication line using 9-bit frames is approximately equal to:

(A)  .999                    (D)  .997

(B)  .003                    (E)  .991

(C)  .009

9.   The term "aging" refers to:

(A)  Keeping track of the time a page has been in memory for the purpose of LRU replacement

(B)  Boosting up the priority of a process in multi-level queues without feedback

(C)  Gradually increasing the priority of jobs that wait in the system for a long time to remedy indefinite blocking

(D)  Letting jobs reside in memory for a certain amount of time so that the number of pages required can be estimated accurately

    (E)  Keeping track of the total time a job has been in the system since it was first submitted

10.  A synchronous communication line uses byte-oriented protocol where the size of each frame is equal to 100 characters (including control bytes). If the bit error probability is equal to $10^{-4}$, and each character is 8 bits long without parity bit, the probability that the frame will arrive with one or more bit errors is equal to:

(A)  $1 - (.0001)^8$

(B)  $(.9999)^{100}$

(C)  $(.00001)^{100}$

(D)  $1 - (1 - .0001)^{800}$

(E)  $(.0001)(.999)^{800}$

11.  Which conclusion "logically follows" from the premises given below?

    →  Prices are high

    →  If prices are high, one should sell bonds

    →  If interest rates are not low, one should not sell bonds

(A)  Interest rates are high

(B)  Interest rates are low

(C)  Prices are low

(D)  Do not sell bonds

(E)  No conclusion can be drawn since the relationship between prices and interest rates has not been explicitly defined.

12.  Which of the Pascal declarations correctly sets up a linearly linked structure with X as the first element?

(A)  **type**    $p =$ ^$e$;
                $e =$  **record**
                      $a$: *integer*;
                      $b$: $e$
                      **end**;
      **var** $x : p$;

(B)  **type**    $p =$ ^$e$;
                $e =$  **record**
                      $a$: *integer*;

```
                            b: ^p
                            end;
              var x : e;

(C)   type    p =   ^e;
              e =   record
                    a: integer;
                    b: p
                    end;
              var x : ^e;

(D)   type    p =   ^e;
              e =   record
                    a: integer;
                    b: p
                    end;
              var x: p;

(E)   type    p =   ^e;
              e =   record
                    a: integer;
                    b: e
                    end;
              var x : p;
```

13.  Consider a memory system with the following parameters:

$T_c$ = Cache Access Time = 100 ns

$T_m$ = Main Memory Access Time = 1200 ns

If we would like to have effective (average) memory access time to be no more than 20% higher than cache access time, the hit ratio for the cache must at least be:

(A)  80%                     (D)  99%

(B)  90%                     (E)  95%

(C)  98%

14.  Suppose the cache and main memory access times are 100 and 1200 nanoseconds (ns) as given in Question 13. Moreover, a market survey indicates that:

$C_c$ = Average Cost per Bit of Cache Memory = .02 cents per bit

$C_m$ = Average Cost per Bit of Main Memory = .001 cents per bit

The cost of a 1 MB memory system rounded to the nearest 10 dollars, using cache technology with a cache hit ratio of at least 98% will then be:

(A) $8,000

(B) $8,160

(C) $41,940

(D) $48,960

(E) Not sufficient information to answer the question.

15. Consider the memory system in Question 13. If we would like to use the cache for paging (and for other purposes as before), and the hit ratio of finding the page table entry in the cache is 98%, the same as in Question 13, the effective (or average) paged memory access time in nanoseconds is equal to:

(A) 200          (D) 2400

(B) 1200         (E) 222

(C) 220

16. Using the symbol $\oplus$ for Exclusive Or (XOR); if $A \oplus B = C$ then:

(A) $A \oplus C = B$          (D) All of the above

(B) $B \oplus C = A$          (E) None of the above

(C) $A \oplus B \oplus C = 0$

17. The Signal-to-Noise ratio for a voice-grade line is 30.1 dB (decibels), or a power ratio of 1023:1. The maximum achievable data rate on this line whose spectrum ranges from 300 Hz to 3400 Hz is:

(A) 31,000 bps          (D) 6200 bps

(B) 34,000 bps          (E) 30,100 bps

(C) 9600 bps

18. Assuming 32-bit 2's complement representation for integers and 8-bit ASCII representation for characters, how many bytes of memory are occupied by the following Pascal declaration:

```
var
    block: record
        Field1: record
            Part1: record
                Part11: Char,
                Part12: Integer,
            end;
            Part2: Char,
        end;

        Field2:    array [1.. 2] of record
                        Part_I: Integer,
                        Part_II: array [1.. 3] of Char,
                    end;
    end;
```

(A)  25                    (D)  16

(B)  26                    (E)  21

(C)  20

19.  The diagram:

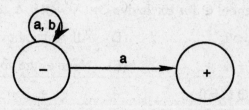

refers to a non-deterministic finite state automaton that accepts:

(A)  All words that contain the substring *ab* and end with *a*

(B)  All words that contain the substring *ba* and end with *a*

(C)  All words that end with *a*, but not the null word lambda ($\lambda$)

(D)  All words that end with a, and also the null word lambda ($\lambda$)

(E)  This is deterministic (ordinary) finite state automaton

20.  The primary quality of a *good* working program in the earlier days of
     software development in the 1950s and 1960s were:

(A) Maintainable

(B) Readable

(C) Fast

(D) On budget and within time

(E) Easy to modify

21. How many comparisons are required to sort an array of length 5 if a straight selection sort is used and the array is already sorted in the opposite order?

(A) 0

(B) 1

(C) 10

(D) 15

(E) 20

22. Let $X = (a, b, c)$ be a set of three elements. The number of algebraic binary operations that can be defined on $X$ are:

(A) $3^3$

(B) $3^2$

(C) $3^8$

(D) $3^9$

(E) $2^3$

23. Regarding software requirements specification, the case that is hardest to "fix" is:

(A) What the software system is to do

(B) How user-friendly the system should be

(C) How fast the software should run

(D) How accurate the outputs should be

(E) How much storage should the software require

24. The number of Boolean functions that can be defined for $n$ Boolean variables over $k$-valued Boolean algebra are:

(A) $2^{(2^n)}$

(B) $(k^{(k^n)})$

(C) $nk$

(D) $n$

(E) $k^2$

25. In the UNIDOS operating system, the time required by a single file read operation has four mutually exclusive components:

   disk seek time - 15 milliseconds

   disk rotational latency time - 10 milliseconds

   disk transfer time - 1 microsecond per byte

   operating system overhead - 2 milliseconds per block

In version 1 of the system, the file read retrieved blocks of 1,024 bytes. In version 2, the file read (along with the underlying layout on disk) was modified to retrieve blocks of 2,048 bytes. The ratio of the time required to read a large noncontiguous file under version 2 to the time required to read the same large file under version 1 is approximately:

(A) 1:2

(B) 1:1.9

(C) 1:1

(D) 1.7:1

(E) 3.6:1

26. Which one of the six element lattices below is complemented?

(A)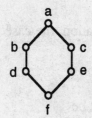

(C)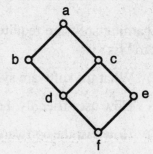

(B)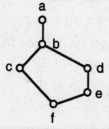

(D)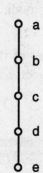

(E)

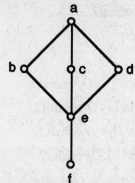

27. The logical expression $((A \wedge B)' \Rightarrow (C' \wedge A)) \Rightarrow (A \equiv 1)$ is:

    (A) A contradiction

    (B) A Well-Formed Formula

    (C) A tautology

    (D) A regular expression

    (E) None of the above

28. Software that measures, monitors, analyzes, and controls real-world events is called:

    (A) System Software

    (B) Business Software

    (C) Real-time Software

    (D) Artificial Intelligence Software

    (E) Scientific Software

29. The context free grammar (CFG) defined by the regular expression $ab*$ is:

    (A) $S \rightarrow Sb \mid a$

    (B) $S \rightarrow XY$
        $X \rightarrow aX$
        $Y \rightarrow bY$

    (C) $S \rightarrow SS \mid baa \mid abb$
        $S \rightarrow \lambda$

    (D) $S \rightarrow SS \mid baa \mid abb \mid \lambda$

    (E) $S \rightarrow aS \mid bS$

30. What is wrong (if anything) with the following pseudocode for evaluating an infix expression using two stacks?

    pop operands stack to get *Operand*1

    **pop** operands stack to get *Operand2*

    **pop** operator stack to get *Token*

    **case** *Token* is

        *'+': New_Value ← Operand1 + Operand2*

        *'-': New_Value ← Operand1 – Operand2*

        *'\*': New_Value ← Operand1 \* Operand2*

        *'/': New_Value ← Operand1 / Operand2*

        *'%': New_Value ← Operand1 % Operand2*

    **end case**

(A) The case '%' which corresponds to **mod** operation requires special handling

(B) The case statement must end with: **psh** *New_Value* unto operands stack

(C) The pseudocode must be concluded with the addition of: **psh** *New_Value* unto operands stack after **end case** statement

(D) The identifier *Token* is inappropriate and must be replaced by Operator

(E) There's nothing wrong with the pseudocode

31. In networks and point-to-point communication links, the data link layer handles transmission errors by requesting retransmission of frames in error. Assume bit errors are independent, each frame is 64-bits long, and the error detection mechanism can catch all the errors. If bit error rate is $2^{-10}$ (on average 1 error in 1024 bits transmitted), what is the mean number of transmissions if acknowledgements are never lost?

(A) 1.050         (D) 2.250

(B) 1.065         (E) 3.050

(C) 1.125

32. Which one of the following is another name for a "record block"?

(A) Record gap         (D) Spanned record

(B) Physical record         (E) Track record

(C) Logical record

33. Generally, maintenance overhead in terms of time spent, and hence the cost, is at least 50% and as high as 65% in the software life-cycle. A good way to reduce maintenance overhead is:

    (A) Stop doing maintenance and concentrate on development

    (B) Change the definition of maintenance

    (C) Use reusable software as often as possible

    (D) Design the package in such a way that it automatically maintains itself while adapting to changing user needs

    (E) Hire staff that require lower pay than the developers to do the maintenance

34. The term "residual error rate" refers to:

    (A) The probability that one or more errors will be detected when an error detection mechanism is used

    (B) The probability that one or more bit errors will occur regardless of whether we use error detection techniques.

    (C) The probability that one or more errors will be undetected when an error detection scheme is in place.

    (D) The number of bit errors per twenty-four hours of continuous operation on an asynchronous 300-bps line

    (E) Signal to noise ratio divided by the ratio of energy per bit to noise per hertz

35. Consider the disk unit specified below where the interblock gaps that do not contain useful data are 250 bytes long. Assume that after a seek the start of data comes under the head after an average of one-half revolution. For this disk, the *average transfer rate* per track is approximately:

    Track size: 10,000 bytes

    Rotational latency: 10 ms/revolution

    Block size: 1,000 bytes

    (A) 7.23 Mbps          (D) 6.00 Mbps

    (B) 4.27 Mbps          (E) 4.00 Mbps

    (C) 6.40 Mbps

36. The primary qualities of a *good* working program in the 1980s and 1990s are:

    (A) Readable and maintainable

    (B) Compact and concise

    (C) Fast and documented in detail

    (D) On budget and within time

    (E) Validated and verifiable

37. Imposing a linear order on all resource types, and letting processes request resources in increasing order of enumeration is an example of:

    (A) Deadlock avoidance where the system will never enter an "unsafe" state

    (B) Deadlock prevention where the maximum needs of each job must also be taken into account

    (C) Deadlock avoidance where hold and wait conditions cannot occur

    (D) Deadlock prevention where circular waits for resources can never take place

    (E) Deadlock detection where out-of-sequence resource requests can easily be identified

38. The following is an example where no information hiding is done:

    (A) **compile** *Prog*1 *Prog*2

    (B) **run** *TestProg*

    (C) **load** $R1, A$

    (D) 001001000010101

    (E) Insertion of an internal modem card into a personal computer

39. A signal of power 1000 milliwatts (mw) is inserted unto a transmission line, and at some distance the measured power is 10 milliwatts. The loss in signal power in decibels is:

    (A) $-30$ dB              (B) $-2$ dB

(C)  – 20 dB                    (D)  – 100 dB

(E)  + 30 dB

40. If memory for the run–time stack is only 150 cells (words), how big can *N* be in *Factorial* (*N*) before encountering stack overflow?

(A) 24                          (D) 50

(B) 15                          (E) 150

(C) 66

41. Bit-vector or bit-map is used in connection with disk space management in order to:

(A) Keep track of allocated space when contiguous allocation method is used

(B) Specify the "bad" sectors on the disk

(C) Optimize the disk space occupied by files when indexed allocation method is used

(D) Keep track of the free space on the disk

(E) Impose priorities upon different types of interrupts.

42. A one-dimensional array *A* has indices 1 .. 75. Each element is a *string* and takes up three memory words. The array is stored starting at location 1120 decimal. The starting address of A[49] is:

(A) 1164                        (D) 1267

(B) 1264                        (E) None of the above

(C) 1169

43. Following is a recursive function for computing the sum of integers from 0 to *N*:

```
function Sum (N: integer) : integer;
begin
        If N = 0 then Sum : = 0
        else _____ .
end;
```

The missing line in the else part is:

(A) **while** $N <> 0$ $Sum := N + Sum(N + 1)$

(B) $Sum := N + Sum(N)$

(C) $Sum := (N - 1) + Sum(N - 1)$

(D) $Sum := N + Sum(N - 1)$

(E) $Sum := (N - 1) + Sum(N)$

44. The volatility of a file refers to:

(A) The number of records added or deleted from a file compared to the original number of records in that file

(B) Percentage of records that has changed in a given time period

(C) Efficiency with which non-sequential files are processed

(D) The extent where the records of the file are contiguous and in proximity to others

(E) Whether the file resides in random access memory or secondary storage

45. Consider the languages:

$r_1 = (a+b)*a$

$r_2 = (a+b)*ab(a+b)*$

$r_3 = (a+b)*(aa+bb)(a+b)*$

According to above:

(A) The machine that accepts $r_1 r_2$ is the same as the machine which accepts $r_2 r_1$

(B) The machine which accepts $r_2 r_3$ is the same as the machine that accepts $r_3 r_2$

(C) The machine that accepts $r_2$ is the same as the machine that accepts $b*aa*b(a+b)*$

(D) The machine which accepts $r_1 r_1$ is the same as the machine which accepts $(r_1)*$

(E) None of the above.

46. The activity of a file:

    (A) Is a measure of the number of records added or deleted from a file compared with the original number of records

    (B) Is a low percentage of number of records that are added to or deleted from a file

    (C) If high, reduces processing efficiency for sequential and nonsequential files

    (D) Is a measure of the percentage of existing records updated during a run

    (E) Refers to how closely the file fits into the allocated space

47. A digital signaling technique is required to operate at 4800 bps (bits per second). Each signal element encodes 8-bit bytes using multilevel phase shift keying. In order to find the minimum bandwidth required, the most appropriate formula to use would be:

    (A) Signal-to-Quantization ratio for the encoding scheme.

    (B) Nyquist's formula for maximum channel capacity.

    (C) Shannon's Law for maximum capacity on a noisy channel.

    (D) Efficiency ratio for digital-to-digital encoding.

    (E) None of the above since the center frequency of the carrier signal is not known.

48. Which phase of the development cycle for a moderately-sized package of 100,000 lines takes more than 50% of the overall time spent?

    (A) Definition (Problem analysis and requirements)

    (B) Design (High-level and low-level)

    (C) Implementation (Coding, compiling, unit testing)

    (D) Testing (Integration and system tests)

    (E) Maintenance (Fine-tuning and re-working)

49. How much space, in terms of memory cells or words, is allocated by the compiler for the following declaration?

**type**

       *PtrType* = *^NodeType*;

       *InfoType* = *Integer*,

       *NodeType* = **record**

           *Info* : *InfoType*;

           *Next* : *PtrType*;

       **end**

**var**

  *List* : *PtrType*;

  *Ptr* : *PtrType*;

(A)  2

(B)  4

(C)  6

(D)  8

(E)  None of the above

50.  Which one of the following is not a "lattice"?

(A)

(C)

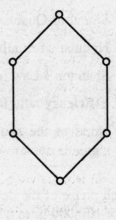

(B)

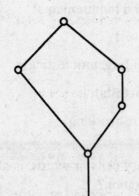

(D)

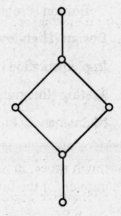

(E)

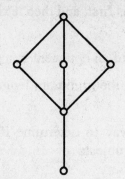

51. Consider the transition diagram of a finite automaton below:

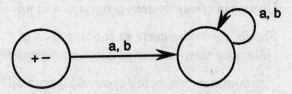

Where the first state with + − is both the starting and the final state. This automaton accepts:

(A) All words over Sigma (*a,b*) such that symbols *a* and *b* alternate

(B) All words over Sigma (*a,b*) including λ (Lambda) which corresponds to no output

(C) Only the λ, meaning this automaton accepts no string of length greater than zero

(D) All words over Sigma (*a,b*) except λ

(E) The diagram does not correspond to finite state automaton

52. As an ordered group of homogeneous elements, a *stack* is more like a(n):

(A) Record            (D) Array

(B) Set               (E) All of the above

(C) File

53. The British Museum procedure is used for:

(A) Exhaustive search involving all branches of a tree in order to reach the goal node

(B) Generating all possible solutions first, and then letting the tester test these one by one

(C) Finding all the possible moves of an opponent in a game tree

(D) Exhaustive search used to find the minimum length path from the start node to the goal node

(E) Labeling line drawings in a way to determine if they correspond to real-world scenes and objects

54. The advantage of a command processor running only built-in commands is:

(A) Users can create system programs and run them as commands

(B) Flexibility to the users in running lists of commands by simply collecting them in named batch command files

(C) The command set being common across different hardware configurations

(D) The processing is much faster than would otherwise be the case when user-defined commands are used

(E) Making the operating system compact in terms of primary memory requirements

55. To send a message $M$, say 1110001 for a letter $G$ in ASCII, we use Cyclic Redundancy Check (CRC) error detection mechanism that generates a 4-bit Frame Check Sequence (FCS). Which of the patterns $P$ below is the best choice?

(A) 1011 (11 decimal)          (D) 1010011 (83 decimal)

(B) 100101 (37 decimal)        (E) 11011 (27 decimal)

(C) 10010 (18 decimal)

56. A search technique where we keep expanding nodes with least accumulated cost so far is called:

(A) Hill-climbing          (D) Breath-first

(B) Best-first             (E) Divide-and-conquer

(C) Branch-and-bound

57. With round-robin CPU scheduling in a time-shared system:

    (A) Using very large time slices (quantas) degenerates into FCFS (First-Come First-Served) algorithm

    (B) Using very small time slices (quantas) degenerates into LIFO (Last-In First-Out) algorithm

    (C) Using extremely small time slices improves performance

    (D) Using medium sized time slices leads to SRTF (Shortest Remaining Time First) scheduling policy

    (E) None of the above.

58. Which is NOT true of truth propagation method:

    (A) Is a type of constraint propagation

    (B) Uses sound rules of inference

    (C) Has a net (graph) used to force truth values for nodes

    (D) May produce contradictions

    (E) Used for proving assertions and facts

59. With a segmentation, if there are 64 segments, and the maximum segment size is 512 words, the length of logical address is how many bits?

    (A) 12          (D) 16

    (B) 14          (E) 13

    (C) 15

60. High block factors typically result in:

    (A) Increased main memory requirements

    (B) Decreased sequential processing times

    (C) Increased random processing times

    (D) Increased disk space utilization

    (E) All of the above.

61. Consider the language $S*$ ($S$ followed by Kleene's star) over the set $S = \{aaa, aab, aba, abb, baa, bab, bba, bbb\}$. Another description of this language may be:

    (A) All words made up of symbols $(a,b)$ of length 3 or more including the word of length 0

    (B) All words over Sigma $(a,b)$ that begin and end with the same symbol

    (C) All words consisting of symbols $\{a,b\}$ of even length

    (D) All words over Sigma $\{a,b\}$ of length divisible by three including the word of length 0

    (E) All words consisting of symbols $\{a,b\}$ of length 24 or more

62. The maximum amount of information that is available with one positioning of the disk access arm for a removable disk pack (without further movement of the arm with multiple heads) is:

    (A) A cylinder of data          (D) A block of data

    (B) A track of data             (E) A surface of data

    (C) A plate of data

63. The intersection of the two regular languages below:
    $L_1 = (a+b)*a$     and   $L_2 = b(a+b)*$

    is given by:

    (A) $b(a+b)*a$

    (B) $(a+b)*ab(a+b)*$

    (C) $a(a+b)*b$

    (D) $(a+b)*ab$

    (E) $ab(a+b)*$

64. A "bug" is a logical fault in a programming system which causes unexpected or undesirable results under certain input conditions. During the life cycle of a software system, a bug can be:

    (A) Detected

(B)   Isolated

(C)   Repaired

(D)   Verified that the repair did fix the problem

(E)   All of the above.

65.   Which of the relations below can also be characterized as a function
      defined on set $I = \{1, 2, 3, 4, 5\}$?

      (A)   $\{ (x,y) \mid x,y \in I, x < y \}$

      (B)   $\{ (x,y) \mid x,y \in I, x > y \}$

      (C)   $\{ (x,y) \mid x,y \in I, x = 1 \}$

      (D)   $\{ (x,y) \mid x,y \in I, x = y/2 \}$

      (E)   $\{ (x,y) \mid x,y \in I, x <> y \}$

66.   If you are not careful in your choice of hash functions, it is possible
      to have collisions in which the search time goes to the order of O(?)
      in a search table of size $N$:

      (A)   1                          (D)   $N!$

      (B)   $\log 2N$                  (E)   None of the above

      (C)   $N$

67.   The number of canonical expressions that we can develop over a 3-
      valued Boolean algebra is:

      (A)   8                          (D)   64

      (B)   16                         (E)   None of the above

      (C)   32

68.   Let $X$ be a set of four elements $\{a, b, c, d\}$. The number of binary
      operations that can be defined on $X$ are:

      (A)   $4^2$                      (D)   $2^{16}$

      (B)   $2^4$                      (E)   $4^{16}$

      (C)   $2^8$

69. What is the Boolean expression for the following circuit:

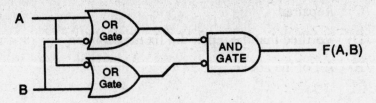

(A) $F(A,B) = (A + B') \cdot (B + A')$

(B) $F(A,B) = 1$ (Tautology)

(C) $F(A,B) = \oplus$ (Inconsistency)

(D) $F(A,B) = A \oplus B$ (*A* exclusive OR'ed with *B*)

(E) $F(A,B) = AB + A'B'$ (Equivalence)

70. A DMA module is transferring characters to main memory using cycle-stealing (getting the system bus from CPU to do DMA transfer). The device is transmitting at 1 Mbps over a Local Area Network. The CPU fetches instructions at the rate of 1 MIPS (one million instructions per second). Assuming each memory location accessible in one bus cycle can hold 16 bits, the CPU instruction fetch speed will degrade down to:

    (A) .9500 MIPS

    (B) .9250 MIPS

    (C) .9375 MIPS

    (D) .9345 MIPS

    (E) The CPU will not be slowed down

71. If $|A| = m$ and $|B| = n$ are sizes (number of members), how many binary relations are there from set *A* to set *B*?

    (A) $mn$        (D) $2^{mn}$

    (B) $(mn)!$        (E) $(m+n-1)! / m!(n-1)!$

    (C) $[Max(m,n)]^2$

72. If a digital data rate of 9600 bps is encoded using the 8-level Phase Shift Keying (PSK) method, the modulation rate is:

    (A) 9600 bauds          (D) 4800 bauds

    (B) 3200 bauds          (E) More information is needed

    (C) 1200 bauds

73. Consider the following recursive definition of 4-*Permutation* (meaning permutations of 4 distinct objects):

    1234 is a 4-*Permutation*

    If *wxyz* is 4-*Permutation*, so are *zyxw* and *xyzw*

    According to this rule, the total number of permutations are:

    (A) 1          (D) 8

    (B) 4          (E) 16

    (C) 24

74. A die is tossed seven times. What is the probability that all six faces appear at least once?

    (A) 63/64          (D) 35/648

    (B) 2/9          (E) 5/324

    (C) 5/54

75. Suppose $(ab)*a$ is a regular expression that defines a language over the alphabet *Sigma* = {$a, b$}. The notation for another regular expression that defines the same language over the same alphabet may be:

    (A) $a(ba)*$

    (B) $a*(ba)*$

    (C) $a*ba$

    (D) Both (A) and (B)

    (E) There's only one regular expression for this language

76. Suppose $X$ and $Y$ are independent continuous random variables whose probability density functions are $f(x) = 2x$, $0 < x < 1$, and $g(y) = y^2 / 9$, $0 < y < 3$, respectively. The range of values that the random variable $Z = XY$ can take on is given by:

(A) $0 < z < 2$                    (D) $0 \leq z \leq 2$

(B) $2/9 \leq z \leq 9$            (E) None of the above.

(C) $1/9 < z < 1/2$

77. Spooling is most beneficial in a multiprogramming environment where:

(A) Most jobs are I/O-bound

(B) Most jobs are CPU-bound

(C) Jobs are evenly divided as I/O-bound and CPU-bound

(D) There is limited primary memory and need for secondary memory

(E) None of the above

78. The memory allocation scheme subject to "external" fragmentation is:

(A) Multiple Contiguous Fixed Partitions

(B) Pure Demand Paging

(C) Swapping

(D) Segmentation

(E) None of the above

79. The reference bit is used for the purpose of:

(A) Implementing LRU page replacement algorithm

(B) Implementing NRU (Not Recently Used) algorithm

(C) To check if the page table entry is in cache memory

(D) Check if the page has been written into recently

(E) Check to see if parameters are passed to a procedure by value or by address

80. Suppose you lived in Chicago, and your number was in the phone book along with the other 3,000,000 people (assume that there is only one phone book for Chicago). What is the maximum number of pages your (intelligent) friend would have to turn in the phone book in order to find your number? Assume 500 people are listed on each face of double-sided pages.

(A) 6000

(D) 12

(B) 3000

(E) 333

(C) 33

# TEST 3

## ANSWER KEY

| | | | | | | | |
|---|---|---|---|---|---|---|---|
| 1. | (B) | 21. | (E) | 41. | (D) | 61. | (D) |
| 2. | (B) | 22. | (D) | 42. | (B) | 62. | (A) |
| 3. | (B) | 23. | (A) | 43. | (D) | 63. | (A) |
| 4. | (A) | 24. | (B) | 44. | (A) | 64. | (E) |
| 5. | (B) | 25. | (B) | 45. | (C) | 65. | (D) |
| 6. | (B) | 26. | (A) | 46. | (B) | 66. | (C) |
| 7. | (E) | 27. | (C) | 47. | (E) | 67. | (D) |
| 8. | (C) | 28. | (C) | 48. | (E) | 68. | (E) |
| 9. | (C) | 29. | (A) | 49. | (A) | 69. | (C) |
| 10. | (D) | 30. | (C) | 50. | (C) | 70. | (C) |
| 11. | (B) | 31. | (B) | 51. | (C) | 71. | (D) |
| 12. | (D) | 32. | (B) | 52. | (D) | 72. | (B) |
| 13. | (C) | 33. | (C) | 53. | (D) | 73. | (D) |
| 14. | (E) | 34. | (C) | 54. | (C) | 74. | (E) |
| 15. | (E) | 35. | (B) | 55. | (E) | 75. | (A) |
| 16. | (D) | 36. | (A) | 56. | (C) | 76. | (E) |
| 17. | (A) | 37. | (D) | 57. | (A) | 77. | (C) |
| 18. | (C) | 38. | (D) | 58. | (B) | 78. | (D) |
| 19. | (C) | 39. | (C) | 59. | (C) | 79. | (B) |
| 20. | (C) | 40. | (C) | 60. | (E) | 80. | (D) |

# DETAILED EXPLANATIONS
# OF ANSWERS
# TEST 3

1.  **(B)**
    If we consider the number of moves in an $n$-element array, construct-ing the heap takes at most $(n/2)\log n$, and afterwards $(n - 1)$ $\log n$ moves are required to sort the array. Thus, both the average and worst cases for the heap sort is in $(3/2)n\log n$ which is considered order of $n\log n$. The merge sort for the same data will take about $n\log n$ moves (corresponding to as many passes involving a pointer manipulation over the list of $n$ elements). There will be anywhere from $\log n$ to $n\log n$ compares with negligible effect on overall running time.

    Following are explanations for the elimination of the other choices: (A) refers to bubble sort whose best-case is $O(n)$ and average case depends on initial ordering. The worst-case is $(1/2)n(n - 1)$ or order of $O(n^2)$. The insertion sort also has $O(n^2)$ moves as the worst-case for random initial order of data. (C) may look promising, but only as far as the average-case is concerned. The radix sort is not directly comparable with other sorting methods; but, its worst-case requires more than $n\log n$ steps if the sort elements contain many digits or letters. As the worst-case, when data is in inverse sort order initially, quicksort requires many more moves than $n\log n$. The tree sort mentioned in (D) is a generic name where we can talk of tree insertion sort, tree selection sort, etc. The median-of-3 quicksort has an average-case of order $O(n\log n)$ but not so quick in the worst-case with order of $O(n^2)$. (E) refers to exchange sort which is another name for bubble sort referred to in (A). Selection sort is a variant of insertion sort and requires $O(n^2)$ moves in the worst-case.

2.  **(B)**
    The definition of each string is as follows:
    (A)  $(a + b) * (a + b)a$ or $b$ repeated zero or more times
    (B)  $(a + b) * a$      $a$ or $b$ repeated zero or more times followed by  an $a$
    (C)  $(a + b) * b$      $a$ or $b$ repeated zero or more times followed by a $b$
    (D)  $a * b$              any number of $a$'s followed by $b$
    (E)  $a * b *$          any number of $a$'s followed by any number of $b$'s (including zero $a$'s or $b$'s)

No matter which state the automaton is in, when it reads an *a*, it goes to the right-hand final state. If it stops there, it must have read the letter *a* as the final input. Before stopping, it may read *a* or *b* as many times as it loops provided *b* is read last. Using Kleene's star, we can designate the string accepted through looping as (*a+b*) *. This means zero or more times of either *a* or *b*. We would then tack the letter *a* to this that must be read in the final leg of the loop.

Therefore, the automaton accepts all strings of the form:

(*a+b*) * *a*.

Note that (*a+b*) * may be null λ, so that the letter *a* by itself is also accepted by this machine. Further, it is clear that this machine will not accept the null string λ.

3.   **(B)**

Making the suggested revision results in the following diagram:

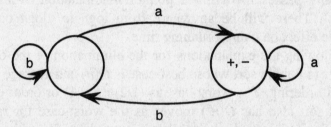

This machine will start in right-hand state, accept 0 or more occurrences of the letters *a* or *b* (through looping). Initially it may accept 0 occurrence of anything or *a*'s through self looping, but the ending letter must always be the letter *a*. In short, this automaton will accept all strings (including null string) that do not end with *b*.

Interchanging the states as suggested in (A) will result in acceptance of the language (*a+b*)**b* instead of (*a+b*)**a* worked out in (2). If we start and stop at the left-hand state, the language accepted will be all words not ending with *a*. Deleting the left-hand self loop will restrict the language accepted since the letter *b* cannot be followed by another *b*. There is no need for more nodes mentioned in alternative (E).

4.   **(A)**

RS-232-C is a physical-layer protocol proposed Electronic Industries Association (EIA) as an interface standard between a DTE (such as a CRT terminal or Computer) and DCE (such as a modem). Since RS-232-C, as with other protocols such as RS-449 etc., is concerned with mechanical, electrical, functional, and procedural characteristics of an interface, the choice (C) is incomplete and incorrect. The protocol between local and remote modems mentioned in (B) is not RS-232-C, but a special modem protocol of the vendor. As for choice (D), it is true that only 7 pins will be sufficient for local DTE-DCE connections without using public telephone lines. However, when public telephone lines are used, two additional pins must be used: one for ring, the other for carrier detect.

5.   **(B)**
    Assuming the data that comes under the disk head is transferred at so high a speed as to be almost instantaneous, we need to simply figure out how much data becomes available for transfer during one rotation (ignoring any other seek time for another track).
    Since in 10 ms (one revolution) 10,000 bytes or 80,000 bits are available; in 1 second we will have:

$$\frac{80,000 \text{ bits /rev}}{0.01 \text{ sec/rev}} = 8,000,000 \text{ bits per second (or 8Mbps).}$$

Notice that this estimate is rather optimistic (hence *maximum rate*) since it assumes that all the data is contiguously available on the track without any interblock gaps, and the disk head comes right on top of start of data after a seek operation.

6.   **(B)**
    In C language, the characters are converted to integers used internally. Thus, the assignments $i = c$ and $c = i$ causes conversions between short and longer integers and leaves the value of $c$ unchanged, assuming short integer is used to represent the characters internally. Now, $y = i$ will result in $y$ having a small integer value that corresponds to an ASCII or EBCDIC character code. Truncation or rounding will take place involving $x$ and $y$ assignments; but the smaller value of $y$ will insure no loss of information and therefore the same final values for both $x$ and $y$.
    Reasons for the rejection of the other choices are as follows. In (A), the initial value of $i$ is 97 but since it is overwritten by the character code value of $c$, its final value is not necessarily equal to 97. Regarding the alternative (C), since C language internally treats the characters as integers, there will be no compiler error involving these assignments. The first part of (D) is true for the particular order of assignments as explained in the correct answer (B). The second part of (D) is not correct. Since $y$ can accommodate numbers equal to greater than $i$, the conversions will not cause truncation, and will lead to same final values for $x$ and $y$. As for (E), changing the order of the assignments between $i$ and $c$ may result in loss of information if the integer is large (16 bits or 32 bits in 2's complement) while the character code is only 8 bits long.

7. **(E)**

Any Boolean lattice over a k-valued Boolean algebra must have $N = 2^k$ elements. Since none of the lattices given above has $2^k$ elements, the answer is (E).

The following are all Boolean lattices corresponding to $k = 1$, $k = 2$, and $k = 3$, respectively:

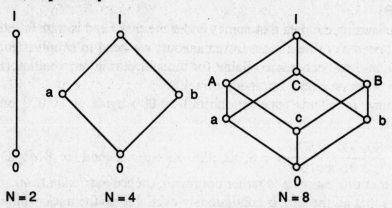

On the other hand, the lattice below, even though it has $2^3 = 8$ elements, is not a Boolean lattice because it does not satisfy the additional requirements for being complemented and distributive.

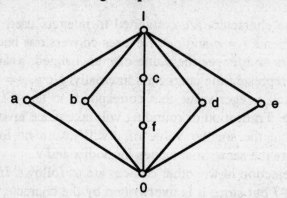

Note that this lattice is complemented but non-distributive.

8. **(C)**

$P_1 = (1 - .001)^9 = .991$ Probability that there are no bit errors
$P_2 = 1 - P_1 = .00896$ or .009 approximately.

9. **(C)**

In a priority scheduling for CPU, where Shortest Processing Time First (SPTF) is a special case, some jobs may never get their turns to run and hence may be blocked indefinitely. This is referred to as "indefinite blocking" or "starvation". This situation can intuitively be envisioned by considering a very long job under SPTF scheduling policy. What happens, if with admittedly low probability, all day long a continuous stream of *shorter* jobs arrive? The long job will never get a chance to run because of SPTF policy that selects the shorter jobs. As a remedy to this situation, the lower priority (or longer jobs under SPTF policy), are *aged*. This means, gradually increasing the priority of a job that has stayed in the system a very long time. If priorities range from 0 (low) to 100 (high), and we increment the priority of a process by one every 5 minutes, even a job with lowest priority of 0 will eventually reach the highest priority of 100. Thus, it would take no more than 8 hours and 20 minutes ($100 \times 5$ minutes) for a process to attain highest priority. It will then be eligible for CPU assignment under any kind of priority scheduling.

10. **(D)**
   The probability that there will be no bit errors is equal to:
   $$P_1 = (1 - P_b)^N \text{ where}$$
   $P_b$ = probability of single bit error
   $N$ = frame size in bits

   Since the probability that one or more bit errors will occur is $1 - P_1$ and the frame size is $8 \times 100 = 800$ bits, the correct answer is:

   Prob (One or more bit errors in the frame) $= 1 - (1 - .0001)^{800}$.

11. **(B)**
   We can use "sound rules of inference" in predicate logic to prove the assertion as follows. Let the variables be:
   
   $H$: Prices are high
   
   $S$: Sell bonds
   
   $L$: Interest rates are low

   The premises can then be listed as
   
   (1) $H$  Prices are high
   
   (2) $H \Rightarrow S$  If prices are high, one should sell bonds
   
   (3) $L' \Rightarrow S'$  If interest is not low, do not sell bonds

   Since $H \Rightarrow S$ ($H$ implies $S$) is the same as $H' \vee S$ (not $H$ or $S$), we may restate premises (1) and (2) as:
   
   (1)  $H$        (2)  $H' \vee S$
   
   which by *modus ponens* resolves to $S$ (one should sell bonds). Now, restate this new fact and (3) as:
   
   (12)  $S$        (3)  $L \vee S'$

which, again by *modus ponens*, resolves into $L$ (interest rates are low).

Based upon this correct conclusion which corresponds to (B), the choice (A) does not apply since it is the very opposite of this one. Choice (C) states the opposite of the original premise (prices are high) and therefore should not be selected. (D) states the opposite conclusion in (12).

12. **(D)**

The other alternatives are not valid because of type mismatches. In (A), the variable $b$ should be of type pointer and not recursively-defined record. In (B), the variable $x$ should be defined as type $p$ (pointer) and not type $e$ (a record). In (C), variable $x$ is defined as type $^\wedge e$ (pointer to E) but there is no such build-in type in Pascal. In (E), the variable $b$ that corresponds to the pointer field of the list element should be of pointer type.

13. **(C)**

The hit ratio of at least 98% can be shown by the following formula:

Effective System Access Time $T_s = H T_c + (1 - H) T_m$

Where $H$ is the hit ratio expressed as .80, ..., .95 etc, and the other parameters as defined in the question. Accordingly:

$$100 H + 1200 (1 - H)$$

should be less than or equal to:

$$T_c + .20 \times T_c = 100 + 20 = 120 \text{ ns}$$

(20% more than cache access time)

Therefore:

$$100 H + 1200 - 1200 H <= 120 \text{ and:}$$

$$H >= 1080/1100 = .98$$

Since H >= .98, the answer of 98% or higher in (C) is the correct one.

14. **(E)**

Even though we know what the hit ratio should be (e.g. 98%) and unit costs of main memory and cache memory, it is not possible to obtain the "optimal" cache memory size. The size of the cache, apart from hit ratio, is sensitive to numerous other factors such as the nature of the application, the work load, and even the design considerations involving chip and board area.

Generally cache sizes vary from 1K to 128K for an 1 MB system depending upon the desired hit ratios. Suppose for the application and work load in question, we do have experimental results involving the hit ratio versus the cache memory size for a 1 MB memory system:

| Cache size per 1 MB memory | Hit ratio for the application |
|:---:|:---:|
| 1 K | .75 |
| 32 K | .80 |
| 64 K | .85 |
| 96 K | .90 |
| 128 K | .95 |
| 196 K | .96 |
| 256 K | .98 |
| 512 K | .99 |

According to the above table, the desired 98% hit ratio requires 256K of cache memory, and therefore the cost of 1 MB system:

$$C = \text{cost of main memory} + \text{cost of cache memory}$$
$$= (2^{20} \times 8 \text{ bits} \times .001 \text{ cents/bit}) + (2^{18} \times 8 \text{ bits})$$
$$\times (.02 \text{ cents/bit})$$
$$= \$(.001 \times 2^{21}) + \$(.02 \times 2^{20})$$
$$= \$20,971.52 + \$20,971.52$$
$$= \$41,943.04$$

Coincidentally, we pay as much for cache as the main memory in this case.

15. **(E)**

We may consider the hit ratio of 98% as the probability of finding the page table entry in the associative memory (cache). Accordingly, with 98% probability the pages memory access time will be:

Cache access time for page number + memory access time

$$= 100 \text{ ns} + 120 \text{ ns}$$
$$= 220 \text{ ns}$$

The other 2% of the time, the search in cache will fail and the page number will be obtained through an *additional* normal memory access. Accordingly:

Cache access time + memory access for page no. + memory access time:

$$= 100 \text{ ns} + 120 \text{ ns} + 120 \text{ ns}$$
$$= 340 \text{ ns}$$

Averaging the two times by weighing these out, we get:

Effective access time $= .98\,(220\text{ ns}) + .02\,(340\text{ ns})$

$$= 215.6\text{ ns} + 6.8\text{ ns}$$

$$= 222.4\text{ ns}$$

Thus, the effective paged memory access time is approximately 222 nanoseconds.

16. **(D)**

XOR or $\oplus$ operation has also been known as Modulo-2 addition of binary values 0 and 1, where for example, $1 \oplus 1 = 0$ (not 2 as in ordinary binary arithmetic). As important result is that a variable XOR'ed with itself must give 0 (false) result.

Take the premise of the question and XOR both sides by $A$:

$$A \oplus A \oplus B = A \oplus C \rightarrow 0 \oplus B = A \oplus C \rightarrow A \oplus C = B.$$

If we XOR both sides with $B$, we will obtain:

$A \oplus 0 = C \oplus B$

$A \quad = B \oplus C$ (commutativity)

By XOR'ing both sides with $C$, and noting that $C \oplus C = 0$, we get the identity in part (C). That is:

Start with: $\qquad A \oplus B = C$

Append: $\qquad A \oplus B \oplus C = C \oplus C$

Result: $\qquad A \oplus B \oplus C = 0$ (since $C \oplus C = 0$ always)

Also note that XOR operation satisfies:

Commutativity: $\quad A \oplus B = B \oplus A$

Associativity: $\quad (A \oplus B) \oplus C = A \oplus (B \oplus C) = A \oplus B \oplus C$

Distributivity: $\quad (A \wedge B) \oplus (A \wedge C) = A \wedge (B \oplus C)$

17. **(A)**

The maximum channel capacity can be calculated using Shannon's law which states that:

$$C = H \log_2 (1 + S/N) \text{ where}$$

$\qquad C:$     maximum channel

$\qquad H:$     minimum bandwidth

$\qquad S/N:$   the power ratio of signal to noise

Note that Signal-to-Noise ratio in decibels for the power ratio of 1023:1 will be equal to:

$$10 \log_{10}(1023) = 10 \times 3.01 = 30.1 \text{ approximately.}$$

Going back to the Shannon's formula, the maximum channel capacity is simply:

$$C = (3400 \text{ Hz} - 300 \text{ Hz}) \log_2(1 + 1023)$$
$$= 3100 \times 10 \quad (\text{Since } 2^{10} = 1024)$$
$$= 31,000 \text{ bps.}$$

18. **(C)**
Field1 is a record that consists of a character, an integer, and another character totaling $1 + 4 + 1 = 6$ bytes. *Field2* consists of two identical records, each with size equal to $4 + 3 = 7$ bytes, totaling 14 bytes. The total allocated memory is then equal to $6 + 2 \times 7 = 20$.

19. **(C)**
Since it must accept at least one letter *a* to go to the final state on the right-hand side, this machine does not accept the null string. (A) is not correct since the machine accepts any number of *a*'s that obviously do not contain the sub string *ab*. Same argument for (B). Concerning (D), this machine does not accept null word $\lambda$ as indicated earlier.

20. **(C)**
This stems from the fact that CPU time was at a premium and there would be significant savings through economy of size and efficient running times. Other undesirable characteristics such as lack of modularity, making changes error-prone, poor readability, etc. had lower priorities.

21. **(E)**
If the array is already sorted in the opposite order, each item will end up being compared with all others. Since there are 5 items, each will require comparison with 4 others, the total number of comparisons will be 20.

22. **(D)**
A binary operator * is a function that maps $X * X \rightarrow X$. We can also regard this as a relation specified by the table on the next page.
Thus, the number of possible binary operations between two sets with three elements is quite large and equal to $3^9 = 19,683$. Note that the table for unary operations will have three entries only, and the answer will then be $3^3 = 27$. The student is encouraged to look at the number of trinery operations over a three element set.

| * | a | b | c |
|---|---|---|---|
| a | <> | <> | <> |
| b | <> | <> | <> |
| c | <> | <> | <> |

a row: ← Each entry can be specified three ways, as $a$, $b$, or $c$.

b row: ← There are $3 \cdot 3 = 9$ entries.

c row: Total number of ways of filling in the table:

$$3^{3 \cdot 3} = 3^9$$

**23. (A)**

The choices (B), (C), (D), and (E) refer to performance requirements that are generally easier to meet than the functional requirements given in (A). The common sense reasoning suggests that it is easier to make a working program friendly, fast, precise, concise, etc., than to make a program work!

**24. (B)**

If there are $n$ Boolean variables, say $W$, $X$, $Y$, ... etc., we need an $n$-dimensional table whose entries define the function's output. Each dimension of the table will list $k$ values, so that the total number of entries will be $k^n$. For example, if there are two variables $X$ and $Y$, the 2-dimensional table will look like this:

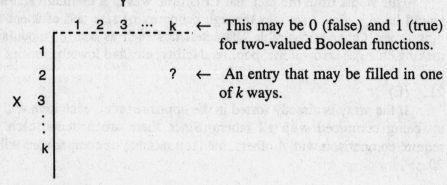

Y

1 2 3 ⋯ k ← This may be 0 (false) and 1 (true) for two-valued Boolean functions.

? ← An entry that may be filled in one of $k$ ways.

X 1, 2, 3, ⋮, k

Thus, the number of possible functions are:

$$k^{(\text{number of entries in the table})} = k^{(k^n)}$$

As a common-sense check, the number of most functions of two variables over two-valued Boolean algebra (e.g., AND, OR, etc.) is:

$$2^{2^2} = 2^4 = 16.$$

25. **(B)**

The exact answer depends upon how the disk space is allocated to files (e.g., contiguous, indexed, linked), and, hence, the word *approximate* is used. Since, presumably the same fixed time overhead will be the case for both 2K and 1K blocks, Version 2 should run faster. This leaves (A) or (B) as two possible answers. The answer cannot be (A) which suggests that the speed will be doubled by simply doubling the blocking factor. This is not the case, since there are components of speed not related to block size, and same for both versions such as disk rotational latency time, etc. Accordingly, even without specific calculations, (B) is the only possibility.

A rough calculation, assuming blocks are randomly positioned on the disk, is given below for files of size 2K and larger multiples:

|              | Version 1 |              | Version 2 |              |
|--------------|-----------|--------------|-----------|--------------|
| Seek time    | 30        | msec         | 15        | msec         |
| Latency      | 20        | msec         | 10        | msec         |
| Transfer     | 2         | msec         | 2         | msec         |
| OS Overhead  | 4         | msec         | 2         | msec         |
| Total:       | 56        | milliseconds | 29        | milliseconds |
| Avg. for 1K: | (28       | msec)        | (14.5     | msec)        |

Since $56/29 = 1.93$ approximately, $1:1.9$ is the correct answer.

26. **(A)**

First, this is a lattice since, for each element, we can uniquely identify a least upper bound and a greatest lower bound. If we take the topmost and bottom nodes ($a$ and $f$) as 1 (true) and 0 (false), we can uniquely identify complements as:

$$a \leftrightarrow f, b \leftrightarrow (c,e), c \leftrightarrow (b,d), d \leftrightarrow (c,e), e \leftrightarrow (b,d)$$

On the other hand: The lattice in (B) is not complemented since $b$ has no complement. In (C), $b$, $c$, $d$, $e$ have no complements. Nodes $b$, $c$, $d$ have no complements in (D). The lattice in (E) is not complemented since nodes $c$ and $e$ do not have complements.

27. **(C)**

First, note that this is not a WFF (Well-Formed Formula) since a WFF would involve quantifiers. It is not a regular expression because of the implies ($\Rightarrow$) operator. It is a logical premise that may be shown to "logically resolve" into (A) or (C). We can show that this is a tautology (always true) as follows. Because of the definition of implication $\Rightarrow$ operator:

$$(A \wedge B)' \Rightarrow (C' \wedge A) \quad \text{same as} \quad (A \wedge B) \vee (C' \wedge A)$$

Now: $(A \wedge B) \vee (C' \wedge A) \Rightarrow (A \equiv 1)$    is the same as:

$\{(A \wedge B) \vee (C' \wedge A)\}' \vee (A \equiv 1)$    (by definition of $\Rightarrow$)

$(A \wedge B)' \wedge (C' \wedge A)' \vee (A \equiv 1)$    (by DeMorgan's law)

$(A' \vee B') \wedge (C \vee A') \vee A$    (since $A$ equivalent to 1 means the same as $A = $ true)

$A' \vee (B' \wedge C) \vee A$    (replace $A' \vee A$ by 1)

Last: $1 \vee (B' \wedge C)$

The last expression involves OR'ing a true value with something else. Regardless of the truth value of that "something else"—in this case $(B'C)$—the result will be true. Therefore, the last expression is a tautology.

28.  **(C)**
Real-time software measures, monitors, analyzes, and controls real-world events as they occur. Specifically, such software provides for: data capture from the external environment; analysis of data in order to transform it into forms required by the application; controls to respond to external events; monitoring of the external environment; and the coordination of system components. A real-time system *must* respond within strict time constrains that usually range from 1 millisecond to 1 minute.

A related definition is *embedded software*, which is characterized by the code residing in Read-Only Memory (ROM) and lack of peripherals such as disks or slower devices. In fact, in some cases, the embedded software implements the device interfaces such as Liquid Crystal Display (LCD) pads, CRT keyboards, etc. The other options do not correspond to the stated main features. System software means the operating system software, which may have real-time components if the operating system is used for real-time applications.

Business and scientific software corresponds to business applications, which for the most part involve large amounts of data and data moves, and scientific applications that engender CPU-intensive mathematical calculations and require a high degree of numerical precision. Artificial-intelligence software has distinct features that include a rules database and inference engine for expert systems, and may, in some cases, involve real-time software, as would be needed for vision and robotics, for example.

29.  **(A)**
First, $ab*$ means the letter $a$ followed by 0 or more $b$'s. An example would be words like $a$, $ab$, $abbb$, $abbbb$, etc. Since the letter $a$ must

always be the first to appear in the word, we required a transition from nonterminal $S$ (a symbol) to terminal $a$ (an actual language element). The "followed" by is taken care of by the $Sb$ on the right-hand side for letter $b$, and the terminal symbol $a$ as discussed.

In (B), we can have occurrences of one or more $a$'s followed by one or more $b$'s that can be expressed as $a*b*$. This is obviously different from $ab*$ which must always start with the letter $a$. In (C) the letters $a$ and $b$ will always occur in triples. This can best be expressed as $(baa + abb)*$, where the second production takes care of the 0 occurrence of $(baa$ or $abb)$.

30. **(C)**

The **case** statement correctly computes the new value using the stack assumed to be initialized with the reverse polish string corresponding to the expression. There remains the saving of the new value of the stack that may either be the result or an operand to be used for the next (higher-level) operation.

31. **(B)**

The retransmission of error frames is known as ARQ (automatic repeat request) in the jargon. We must first find the probability, $P_1$, that a frame will have one or more errors. This is referred to as a Class 2 error:

$$(1) \quad P_1 = (1 - 1/1024)^{64} = (1023/1024)^{64}$$

Next, we need to find the probability, $P_2$, of an error-free frame transmission:

$$(2) \quad P_2 = 1 - P_1 = 1 - (1023/1024)^{64}$$

Let $N$ represent the random variable indicating the number of transmissions. The discrete probability mass function for $N$, assuming frame errors are independent, is given by:

$$Pr\,(N = n) = (1 - P_2)P_2^{\,(n-1)}$$

For $n = 1, 2, \ldots$ (Geometric distribution)

$$Pr\,(N = 2) = (1 - P_2)P_2$$

(probability that frame is transmitted twice)

We may verify 3, 4, 5, etc., transmissions similarly. Now, the mean number of transmissions can be calculated by the formula:

$$\overline{N} = \sum_{n=1}^{\infty} n(1 - P_2)P_2^{\,(n-1)} = \frac{1}{1 - P_2}$$

Since from result (2) above, $1 - P_2 = (1023/1024)^{64}$, we have:

$$\overline{N} = (1024/1023)^{64} = 1.0645$$

32. **(B)**

Record block refers to the physical record. Data on magnetic storage media is accessed in blocks that is equivalent to a sector. A sector depends upon the physical characteristics of the media such as magnetic disks. Similarly, chunks of storage areas separated by InterBlock Gaps (IBGs) are used on magnetic tapes. The term physical record thus refers to the characteristics of the media independent of the kind of application.

A "logical record" has no relationships to media characteristics and is user-defined for the application. For example, the amount of data that holds information sufficient for 1990 census purposes, consisting of name, address, social security number, citizenship, political affiliation, race, and so forth is a logical record.

33. **(C)**

Maintenance is necessary for user satisfaction in meeting his needs closely, and therefore, (A) is incorrect. Regardless of definition, maintenance is a necessary activity, so that (B) is not correct. Use of ready-made reusable software cuts down on maintenance that requires reworking of the software without making basic design changes, and at the same time, prudent selection and modification of reusable software can be tailored to user needs. Thus (C) is a viable alternative for reducing maintenance costs. The solution in (D) is desirable, but no one has yet been able to develop such a software package! Hiring lower-pay staff with less expertise jeopardizes the correct functioning and integrity of the software package since errors may be introduced while the software is being modified to suit the user needs closely.

34. **(C)**

This is also known as Class 2 error where:

$P_2 =$ Probability that the frame arrives with one or more undetected bit errors

The other classes of errors that occur in data transmission are:

$P_1 =$ Probability that the frame arrives with no bit errors (detected or undetected, doesn't matter)

$P_3 =$ Probability that the frame arrives with one or more detected bit errors (and no undetected errors)

Since these three probabilities are mutually exclusive and exhaustive over events regarding data transmission errors:

$$P_1 + P_2 + P_3 = 1$$

If there is no error detection mechanism in place then $P_3 = 0$ and the residual error rate $P_2 = 1 - P_1$.

35. **(C)**
In order to calculate the "average" transfer speed per track, we must take into consideration interblock gaps that do not contain any data. Accordingly, during a half revolution (.005 sec) plus a full revolution (.01 sec),

$$\frac{10,000}{1000 + 250} \times 8 = 64,000$$

bits of data becomes available for instantaneous transfer.
Therefore, the "average" rate of transfer:

$$\frac{64,000 \text{ bits}}{.015 \text{ sec}} \times 4,266,667$$

bits per second (or 4.27 Mbps).

36. **(A)**
Since software is developed in shorter periods with larger teams and more automation and reuse of software, the overriding concern is better communication amongst developers about the design. Since the largest times and costs are expended in maintenance phase, it pays to make software maintainable. The characteristics in (B), (C), and (D) are desirable, but not deemed as crucial. The characteristic in (E) is great, but not attainable for moderately complex systems at reasonable costs.

37. **(D)**
First, we distinguish between deadlock prevention where deadlocks simply *cannot* occur and deadlock avoidance where deadlock *may* occur but can be avoided using prudent resource allocation strategies. Deadlock is prevented by making at least one of the necessary conditions (mutual exclusion, hold-and-wait, circular wait, no-preemption) not possible. Since, imposing linear ordering on resource request makes circular waits impossible, the answer is (D).

38. **(D)**
All the information is given explicitly and in detail down to the last bit. Moreover, there's no attempt to make things clear and understandable by symbols and mnemonics as in (A), (B), or (C). In (E), while the purpose of the internal modem is made clear and its installation is simplified, no details are given about signaling, timing, and protocols, etc. (although such details may be obtained on demand perhaps when the modem does not function as expected).

39. **(C)**

The loss in signal strength is measured in decibels where:

$$\text{Loss} = 10 \log \frac{\text{Power at Destination}}{\text{Power at Source}} = 10 \log \frac{10\text{mw}}{1000\text{mw}}$$

$$= 10 \log (.01) = 10 \times (-3) = -30 \text{ dB}$$

40. **(C)**

"Floor" of 150/3, which turns out to be 50. The reason is that each iteration involves three entries in the stack: New_Value, Old_Value, and Operator.

41. **(D)**

The two principal approaches to keeping track of free space on a disk or swapping device (e.g., faster disk, drum, etc.) are bit-map and free list. Free list refers to a single linked list of free blocks that supplies the available nodes to other lists of allocations corresponding to multiple files. Bit map or bit vector is a concise representation indicating whether a block is free (bit is 0) or allocated to some file (bit 1).

For example, if on a disk, blocks 2,4,5,6,9,10,11,15 are free and all others allocated the bit map will look like:

10100011000111011111111.....etc.

Note that we have only one bit map per storage device showing the *free or available* space and not multiple bit maps, say, for several different files showing the *allocated* space. That is why bit map is not used for an allocation suggested in (C) above. The choice (E) above alludes to the interrupt vector that provides unique memory locations for CPU to trap into depending upon the type and priority of an interrupt, and not the correct answer.

42. **(B)**

The offset in number of locations (memory words) from the starting address is:

$3 \times 49 = 147$ words.

Since the array indices start with 1 (and not 0), this will include the 49th item as well. Therefore, the starting address of the 49th item will be:

$1120 + 144 = 1264$.

Note that if array indices started with 0 (and not 1), the starting address of the 49th item would be $1120 + 147 = 1267$.

43. **(D)**

$Sum := N + Sum(N - 1)$ will do this recursively. The while $N <> 0$ in (A) is redundant and confusing since the else part is executed when $N <> 0$ in any case. The other alternatives simply perform incorrect accumulations for the sum of successive values, each one more than the previous value.

44. **(A)**

Volatility is a measure of changes in key fields that are affected when direct access files are updated. The other alternatives may be eliminated for the following reasons. (B) seems close enough to the definition but may only refer to the changes in information part and not key part of the data. Processing efficiency mentioned in (C) depends on many factors involving how the file is organized and accessed, but does not indicate volatility. (D) suggests how clustered or scattered the files are organized on disk. (E) appears to imply volatility by referring to in-core files that will disappear (evaporate) upon completion (if not saved on disk). Nevertheless, this is not volatility as is generally known in file processing terminology.

45. **(C)**

The definition of each string is as follows:

| | | |
|---|---|---|
| $r_1 = (a+b)*a$ | | the language of all words that end with letter $a$ |
| $r_2 = (a+b)*ab(a+b)*$ | | the language of all words that include substring $ab$ |
| $r_3 = (a+b)*(aa+bb)(a+b)*$ | | the language of all words that contain $a$ double letter |

The language $r_2 = (a+b)*ab(a+b)*$ results in the following strings being accepted:

$ab, a\ ab\ b, b\ ab\ a$, etc.

The language $b*aa*b(a+b)*$ results in $ab$ when Kleene's $*$ is interpreted as 0 times whenever it occurs. Using the substring $b*a$ on the left most positions, we can generate $a$ or $b$ on the left, the right-hand side $(a+b)*$ is the same as in $r_2$. Therefore, any string in $r_2$ can be generated by this language.

As for rejecting the other alternatives:

(A)  $r_2 r_1$ must end with letter $a$; $r_2 r_1$ does not have to

(B)  suppose we get rid of the right-most and left-most letters in both $r_2r_3$ and $r_3r_2$. The remaining string will always end with $b$ in the case of $r_3r_2$, where this is not a requirement for $r_2r_3$

(D) $r_1r_1$ must at least contain two $a$'s and does not contain the null string of length 0. $(r_1)*$ does contain the null string.

### 46. (B)

Activity refers to the percentage of existing records changed during a maintenance run. As such, it can serve as a criteria as to how the file should be organized. If the activity is high, sequential organization makes sense (provided there are no compelling reasons for faster access randomly). Accordingly, the alternative in (C) is not correct. If the activity is low, sequential organization is very inefficient since lots of processing is required to update only few records.

### 47. (E)

Nyquist's law for the maximum channel capacity, or the minimum bandwidth required alternatively, is the most appropriate for this case. This formula states that:

$$C = 2\,H \log_2 L \text{ where}$$

$C$: Maximum channel capacity (bps)

$H$: Minimum bandwidth (Hz)

$L$: Number of signaling elements

$\log_2 L$ = Number of bits encoded per signaling element

In the case above, $L = 256$ where 256 phases encode 8-bit bytes each, and the maximum channel capacity is given as 4800 bps. Accordingly:

$$4800 = 2\text{ H} \times 8 \Rightarrow \text{H} = 4800 / 16 = 300 \text{ Hz}$$

Thus Minimum Bandwidth Required is equal to 300 Hertz.

### 48. (E)

For a moderately-sized software development cycle, it is generally agreed that maintenance requires at least 50% and as high as 65% of time in man-hours of effort, and therefore has the largest cost component. If maintenance accounts for 65%, a rough breakdown for other phases is:

Definition: $(10\% + 20\%) \times 35\% = 10.50\%$ of total.

Design: $(15\%) \times 35\%$ $= 5.25\%$ of total.

Operation: $(15\%) \times 35\%$ $= 5.25\%$ (not shown above)

Implementation and

Testing: (40%) × 35% = 14.00% of total.

Subtotal for Nonmaintenance phases: 35.00%.

49. **(A)**
The **type** declaration simply sets up the types and does not require any memory allocation. **var** declaration allocates memory to data items, each being of type *PtrType* (an address) that takes one memory word (cell) by definition. Therefore, the total allocation will be 2 memory cells, independent of hardware or system software (except the size of a memory cell, of course).

50. **(C)**
According to its definition a "lattice" is a partially-ordered set where every pair of elements has a *lub* (least upper bound) and a *glb* (greater lower bound). In all cases above, except (C), we can uniquely identify the *lub* and *glb* for each node. On the other hand, let us take a closer look at the partial ordering in (C):

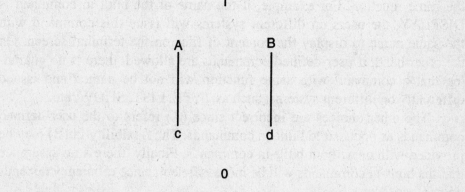

(A), (B) have *lub* of I but no unique *glb* (is it *c* or *d*?). *c,d* have *glb* of *O* but no unique *lub* (is it *A* or *B*?). Therefore, this partial ordering of six elements (namely: *I, A, B, c, d, O*) does not qualify as a lattice.

51. **(C)**
This FA (Finite Automaton) accepts only λ, where the symbol λ stands for lambda. Lambda refers to a string of length zero, or null string with no letters.

All words other than λ cause this machine to go to the right state and stay there.

52. **(D)**

This is because the *stack* contents are homogeneous data items with the same type and also the same requirements for memory. If a *stack* contained items with different types, it would be exceedingly difficult to use the same function, say **psh, pop**, etc., to access and manipulate it. The *array* type also contains elements of the same data type, such as integer, character, etc. In essence, because of this similarity, implementation of queues can be done using either a *stack* or an *array*.

53. **(D)**

The British Museum procedure is a brute-force approach to enumerate all possible paths from start node to goal node on the problem tree. After all possible paths are enumerated, the minimum is chosen as the minimum length path. There are more efficient procedures, such as Branch-and-Bound, that accomplish this for trees with many nodes and branches.

54. **(C)**

Since only built-in commands are allowed, the users across different hardware configurations cannot use different names for commands with the same function. For example, if the name of the built-in command is DISPLAY, the users on different systems will issue this command with the same name to display the content of files on the terminal screen. On the other hand, if user-defined commands are allowed, there is no guarantee that a command with same function will not be named and issued differently on different systems; such as TYPE, LIST, SHOW, etc.

The other choices are incorrect since (A) refers to the user-defined commands as opposed to built-in commands. The flexibility in (B) may be provided with or without built-in commands. Finally, there's no assurance that the built-in commands will be more efficient, since efficiency depends upon other factors.

55. **(E)**

In using the powerful CRC error detection method, the special pattern such as the 17-bit CRC-16 widely used in North America, must be 1 bit longer than the frame check sequence it generates. Since we desire 4-bit FCS, the pattern must be 5 bits long. This eliminates alternatives other than (C) and (E).

The pattern 11011 in (E) is preferable to the pattern 10010 in (C) because it starts and ends with 1. This is required so that the pattern has at least two terms that cannot divide a single bit error which can be expressed as a one-term $E(X) = X^i$ where $i$ is the bit position.

56. **(C)**

Branch-and-bound is a method used to find the minimum length path from the start node to the goal node in a tree which represents the problem domain. It finds the minimal path by keeping track of costs accumulated or distance traveled so far and choosing the next node that will yield least cost (distance) thus far.

57. **(A)**

The round-robin scheduling can be modeled as a *closed queueing system*, meaning that the customers who get the service go back and queue up for the next service until eventual departure as shown below.

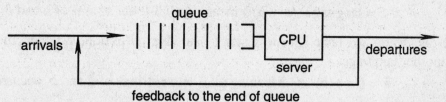

If the time slices are very large, say larger than the largest processing time, then each job will finish on the first round-robin assignment which is done on FCFS basis and will never go back to the tail of the queue. This case can be viewed as an ope*n queueing system* without feedback and corresponds to the FIFO scheduling.

58. **(B)**

The truth propagation method uses truth tables to carry out consequences of operators such as IMPLIES ($\Rightarrow$), AND ($\wedge$), and OR ($\vee$). It does not rely upon resolution theorem and its special cases *modus ponens* and *modus tolens*.

59. **(C)**

With segmentation, a logical address consists of:

| Segment Number | Offset into Segment = Segment Size |
|---|---|

Since there are up to 64 segments, we need 6 bits to indicate segments from 0 to 63 (since $2^6 = 64$). In order to accommodate the offset into the segment for the maximum segment size, we need at least 9 bits (since $2^9 = 512$). Thus, the length of logical address is $6 + 9 = 15$ bits as given in (C).

60. **(E)**

All of the above is a straightforward result since *high blocking factor* means storing and retrieving data in larger "chunks" that holds many records. Although not necessary, it is preferred that the block of records correspond to the physical record block (dictated by media characteristics) exactly.

Since, for homing in a particular record directly we need to read the entire block which is large into the memory, the random processing time will be adversely affected as stated in (C).

61. **(D)**

The language $S = \{aaa, aab, aba, abb, baa, bab, bba, bbb\}$ without Kleene's star (*) tacked to it defines all words of length exactly equal to three. In the nomenclature this can also be expressed as:

$S = $ language $((a + b)^3)$ meaning all 3-letter strings of $a$ and $b$.

Now, when we tack Kleene's star (*) to this definition, we then mean another language:

$L = ((a + b)^3)$*   Meaning all 3-letter strings of $a$ and $b$, occurring

"0 or more times."

The best way to characterize this is in (D). Now, the other choices are not acceptable for the following reasons:

(A): Strings of, say length 4 greater than 3, are not accepted.

(B): Since the original alphabet contains all three-some combinations, this cannot be a requirement.

(C): Strings of, say length 2 or 4, will not be accepted.

(D): This is just a distraction thrown in since the total number of letters in the original alphabet is equal to 24!

62. **(A)**

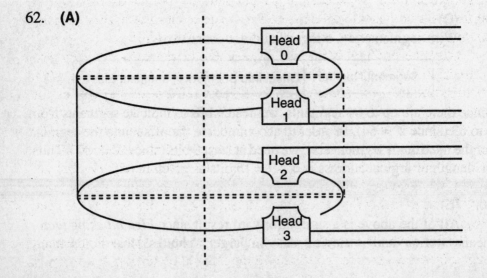

The figure on the previous page assumes double-sided recording surfaces, and the inclusion of four heads illustrates this idea.

63. **(A)**

Note that

$L_1$:   All words ending with $a$

$L_2$:   All words beginning with $b$

If we want both conditions to be true, we need to say:

All words ending with letter $a$

(AND at the same time)

beginning with $b$.

Obviously, a word that satisfies (A)'s statement will belong to $L_1$ (since it ends with a) and will also belong to $L_2$ (since it begins with b).

We can eliminate other alternatives as follows:

(B):   consider *babb*:          Not in $L_1$ since it does not end with $a$

(C):   consider *a aaabb b*:   Not in $L_1$ since it does not end $a$

(D):   consider *aaabbb ab*:   Not in $L_1$ since it does not end with $a$

(E):   consider *ab aaabba*:  Not in $L_2$ since it does not begin with $b$

64. **(E)**

A "bug" is a logical fault in the programming system. Its detection in early stages of integration testing will depend on the nature of integration tests. However, with rigorous testing, the fault in question can usually be uncovered. Afterwards, debugging techniques, desk checks, and code walk-throughs can be used to isolate the fault. This means identification of the component that is responsible for the fault. In other words, the cause of the undesirable behavior is narrowed down to a subsystem, then to module, to a program section, and finally to a group of statements.

Once the problem is isolated, the fix will be done through appropriate revision of the group of statements in question. Care should be taken not to introduce new faults or create adverse effects on the rest of the system (including effects on performance requirements). This is the repair. The verification that the repair did indeed fix the problem must be done by running extensive tests on the "repaired system" and observing the behavior of the modified system. This is the part that unfortunately is often not carried out for expedience, as evidenced by auto mechanics not giving a drive test after fixing the car (they are absolutely sure that the car has been fixed!).

Perhaps the most questionable part in the above scenario is whether a "bug" can always be uncovered during the integration testing. If it is not, it will eventually show itself during the later operational and maintenance phases. What if the "hidden bug" or fault never showed up during the entire software life cycle? Then perhaps it should not be called a "bug" since no harm was done (i.e., no malfunctioning was ever noticed by anybody).

65.  **(D)**
The pair consists of: (1,2) (2, 4). Since by definition a given element appears on the left of only one pair in each case, this is a function. As can be seen, the other alternatives do not satisfy this requirement:

(A)  (1, 2) (1, 3) etc. Member 1 appears as left member twice.

(B):  (2, 1) (3, 1) (4, 1) (5, 1) (3, 2) etc. Member 3 already appears twice.

(C):  (1, 1), (1, 2) (1, 3) etc. Member 1 already reappears on the left hand side.

(E):  (1, 2) (1, 3) ... (5, 1) (5, 2) etc. There are too many repetitions on the left hand side.

66.  **(C)**
Without collisions the hash search is of order O(1), meaning it is extremely efficient search not depending on the size of the table searched. The only thing that slows down a hash search is the collision. A common way to resolve collisions is to store the last items that collide in an overflow area. A pointer to this overflow area is placed in the hash location. If there are N items to be searched; at the worst case, they will all collide to the same hash address. All the items will then be stored sequentially in the overflow area. That means the worst-case search will be sequential search, and if the item searched for is at the end, will take N comparisons.

67.  **(D)**
Each canonical expression will have: $2^3 = 8$ coefficients for each term. Also, we have up to $2^3 = 8$ possible terms. Since we can designate each of the 8 terms involving 3 variables in 8 possible ways, the total number of canonical expressions are:
$$8 \times 8 = 64$$

Thus, there are 64 possible functions with Sum-of-Product (SOP) or Product-of-Sum (POS) canonical forms.
We can use a similar argument over a 2-valued Boolean algebra, where each variable can take on only two values 1 (true) and 0 (false). In this case, the canonical sum-of-products form of a Boolean function with two variables are given as:

$$f(x, y) = a_0 \, x'y' + a_1 \, x'y + a_2 \, xy' + a_3 \, xy$$

Where the coefficients essentially indicate the presence or absence of the corresponding term. Since we can designate each of the 4 terms in 4 ways, the total number of expressions are: $4 \times 4 = 16$

In fact, these functions of two Boolean variables are well known, as shown in the table below:

| Coefficients: | | | | Function | Name of Function | |
|---|---|---|---|---|---|---|
| $a_0$ | $a_1$ | $a_2$ | $a_3$ | $f(x, y)$ | and Symbol for It | |
| 0 | 0 | 0 | 0 | 0 | Inconsistency | F |
| 1 | 0 | 0 | 0 | $x'y'$ | NOR (dagger) | $\downarrow$ |
| 0 | 1 | 0 | 0 | $x'y$ | | |
| 1 | 1 | 0 | 0 | $x'$ | NOT | $\sim x$ |
| 0 | 0 | 1 | 0 | $xy'$ | | |
| 1 | 0 | 1 | 0 | $y'$ | NOT | $\sim y$ |
| 0 | 1 | 1 | 0 | $x'y + xy'$ | XOR | O |
| 1 | 1 | 1 | 0 | $x' + y'$ | NAND (stroke) | $\uparrow$ |
| 0 | 0 | 0 | 1 | $xy$ | AND | $\wedge$ |
| 1 | 0 | 0 | 1 | $xy + x'y'$ | Equivalence | $\equiv$ |
| 0 | 1 | 0 | 1 | $y$ | | |
| 1 | 1 | 0 | 1 | $x' + y$ | Implication | $x \Rightarrow y$ |
| 0 | 0 | 1 | 1 | $x$ | | |
| 1 | 0 | 1 | 1 | $x + y'$ | Implication | $y \Rightarrow x$ |
| 0 | 1 | 1 | 1 | $x + y$ | OR | $\vee$ |
| 1 | 1 | 1 | 1 | 1 | Tautology | T |

68. **(E)**
    A binary operator defines a mapping $S \times S \to S$, where $n = |S|$, the size of set $S$, where:
    $n^{(n^2)}$ operations are possible.

This follows from the fact that a table that lists set-product will have $n \times n = n^2$ entries. Each entry can be filled in one of $n$ ways; corresponding to the members of the set that is mapped to. This indicates multiplying $n$ with itself $n^2$ times to get the total number of possibilities. When $n = 2$, we get the answer in (E).

69. **(C)**

This follows from the fact that, for any Boolean variable, $X$, $XX'$ ($X$ AND NOT $X$) is always equal to 0 (false).

The explicit form of the circuit, before reduction, is:

Inputs:                     Output:

$(A + B')' \cdot (B + A')' = F(A, B)$

Where symbols $+$, $\cdot$, and $'$ indicate OR, AND, and NOT operations respectively. Now, we can begin reductions of the explicit form:

$(A' \cdot B) \cdot (B' \cdot A) = F(A, B)$

DeMorgan's law applied to each term on left separately.

$A'ABB' = F(A, B)$

By commutativity (just changing the order, using product '.' implicitly as done commonly.

$0 \cdot 0 = F(A, B)$

Replace $A'A$ and $BB'$ by 0's, since this is always the case with Boolean algebra.

$0 = F(A, B)$

Since $0 \cdot 0$ (0 AND 0) is equivalent to 0 (false).

Thus, $F(A, B) = 0$ (false) regardless of input values. When the outcome is always false, the Boolean function is referred to as inconsistency or sometimes contradiction.

70. **(C)**

Although DMA (direct memory access) will be considerably faster than interrupt I/O, it will slow down the CPU if a common system bus is used (such as the PDP-11 UNIBUS) by both CPU and DMA module to transfer data to and from main memory. In the case above, we may consider a time period of 1 second to find out about this degradation of performance.

During 1 second, there would have been 1,000,000 fetches by the CPU. On the other hand, the DMA module must transfer 1 million bits corresponding to:

1000000 / 16 = 62500 DMA bus cycles.

Accordingly, the effective CPU instruction fetch speed will be:

$$S = \frac{1,000,000 - 62,500}{1,000,000} \times 1 \text{ MIPS} = .9375 \text{ MIPS}.$$

Note: If we consider 1 Mbps = $2^{20}$ bps = 1,048,576 bps (erroneously!), then there will be 1,048,576 / 16 = 65,436 DMA bus cycles stolen from the CPU. The result be slightly different (.9345 MIPS instead of .9375 MIPS). Nevertheless, using the accepted definition of 1 Mbps as 1 million bits per second the correct answer is .9375.

71. **(D)**
A binary relation involves an instance of the set product $A \times B$ in terms of member pairs being present or absent. The set-product of two sets $A \times B$ contain $mn$ pairs, where $m = |A| = $ size of $A$ and $n = |B| = $ size of $B$. Now, we can find all subsets of the set product, say $C = A \times B$, by including or excluding a pair. This means filling in each slot of the maximal set-product space by 0 or 1, that is, in 2 ways. Therefore:

$2 \times 2 \times 2 \times ... \times 2$ (multiply 2 by itself $mn$ times)

$= 2^{mn}$ (total number of subsets of $mn$ pairs)

Therefore, by definition, the number of binary relations between two sets $A$ and $B$ are $2^{|A||B|}$.

72. **(B)**
When multi-level signaling is used to encode digital data into analog signals, the relationship between data rate in bps and modulation rate (signal level changes per second) in baud is given by:

$C = M \log_2 L$ where

$\quad$ $C$: Data rate or channel capacity

$\quad$ $M$: Modulation rate in bauds

$\quad$ $L$: Number of signal elements

Since $L = 8$ (eight phases encoding 3 bits each), we have:

$\quad M = C / \log_2 L = 9600 \text{ bps} / 3 = 3200 \text{ Bauds}.$

73. **(D)**
Of the 24 possible permutations, only the following 8 can be realized by this definition:

| | | | |
|---|---|---|---|
| 1234 | 4321 | 2341 | 3214 |
| 1432 | 3412 | 2143 | 4123 |

74. **(D)**

The die is tossed seven times. Let $X_i$ denote the number of tosses in which face $i$ comes up, where $i = 1, 2, 3, 4, 5$, and 6. Therefore, we have a series of $n = 7$ independent successive trials, with six possible outcomes for each trial. Each of the outcomes has a constant probability $p_i = 1/6$. The multinomial distribution,

$$P(X_1 = f_1, \ X_2 = f_2, \ ... \ X_k = f_k) = \frac{n!}{f_1! \ f_2! \ ... \ f_k!} \ p_1^{f_1} \ p_2^{f_2} ... \ p_k^{f_k},$$

is called for here.

In seven throws, where each face appears at least once, one of the faces of the die must come up twice. Suppose it is face 1 (i.e., $f_1 = 2$). In the above multinomial distribution, we have

$P(X_1 = 2, X_2 = 1, X_3 = 1, X_4 = 1, X_5 = 1, X_6 = 1)$

$$= \frac{7!}{2! \times 1! \times 1! \times 1! \times 1! \times 1!} \left(\frac{1}{6}\right)^2 \left(\frac{1}{6}\right)^1 \left(\frac{1}{6}\right)^1 \left(\frac{1}{6}\right)^1 \left(\frac{1}{6}\right)^1 \left(\frac{1}{6}\right)^1 = \frac{7!}{2!} \cdot \left(\frac{1}{6}\right)^7$$

This is the probability that all six faces will appear once and that face 1 will appear twice in seven throws. This probability would be the same for any other face appearing twice since $p_i = 1/6$.

Since any of the other faces, 2, 3, 4, 5, or 6, can appear twice, the required probability is the sum of the probabilities of each of the faces appearing twice.

Therefore, the required probability is

$$6 \times \left(\frac{7!}{2!} \cdot \left(\frac{1}{6}\right)^7\right) = \frac{35}{648}.$$

75. **(A)**

Since $(ab)*a$ means nothing ($\lambda$) or one or more $ab$'s followed by $a$; that is:

   *a, aba, ababa, abababa, ....*

Now, $a(ba)*$ means letter $a$ followed by nothing or one or more $ba$'s; that is:

   *a, aba, ababa, abababa, ....*

The two sets of strings accepted are the same and therefore, $a(ba)*$ is another regular expression for the same language.

Now, consider the other alternatives:

(B): *aaaa* accepted but not in the language

(C): *aaaaaba* accepted but not in the language

(D):  not correct since alternative (B) is already rejected

(E):  As was shown, there may be two distinct regular expressions defining the same language.

76.  **(E)**
The minimum value for $Z = XY$ will occur when $X = 0$ and $Y = 0$. This is equal to $0 \times 0 = 0$. The maximum value of $Z = XY$ will occur when $X = 1$ (maximum) and $Y = 3$ (maximum). This is equal to $1 \times 3 = 3$. Thus, the range of random variable $Z$ is 0 to 3. None of the other alternatives state this and they are eliminated.

77.  **(C)**
Spooling overlaps the computation of a job with the input-output of other jobs in the system. If most jobs are CPU-bound, the input-output buffers will be empty most of the time, and the jobs will be subject to queueing delays waiting for CPU. If most jobs are I/O-bound, the buffers will be full most of the time, and the jobs will experience queueing delays waiting for I/O buffers. In short, if all jobs are CPU-bound, CPU is overloaded and I/O devices are underutilized; if all jobs are I/O-bound, I/O devices are overloaded while CPU is idled.
The best we can hope for is an even split between CPU-bound and I/O-bound jobs, so that while approximately half of the jobs compete for I/O resources, the remaining half compete for CPU resources.

78.  **(D)**
Segmentation involves logically meaningful variable-sized parts of the programs being brought into main memory. There is no "internal" fragmentation since each segment will exactly occupy the amount of space equal to its size (e.g., say in number of equivalent memory words). On the other hand, as the segments come and go to/from main memory, other segments are loaded into free spaces (or holes) released by them. If the subsequent segment is not exactly equal in size to the hole (contiguous free memory) released by the previous segment, some space will be wasted and eventually the memory becomes fragmented "externally." In this sense, segmentation is no different from dynamic allocation of jobs into contiguous variable partitions which is known to cause external fragmentation and require garbage collection to create big enough memory chunks out of small fragments.

79.  **(B)**
The reference bit simply indicates whether a page, since its last allocation, has been referenced (read or written into). This is not sufficient

for determining whether the page is "least recently used — LRU" (the answer). If still set 0, the reference bit indicates that the page has not yet been referenced since the time of allocation (hence Not Recently Used). The page is then a candidate for replacement. The NRU algorithm is a rough approximation to the LRU algorithm which is harder to implement since more information needs to be kept track of regarding page history.

As for the other alternatives, (C) is erroneous not since the cache memory is accessed first with successful or unsuccessful outcome. (D) refers to "dirty bit" which, if set, indicates that not only the page has been referenced, but it has also been modified (written into). This information is used for swapping out only the modified pages back to the disk. (E) suggests "call by reference" and has nothing to do with "reference bit."

80. **(D)**
There are 3000000/500 = 6000 page faces, or 6000/2 = 3000 pages. Your friend can use binary search to home in on the page your name is on (never mind which side and where exactly on a page!). Therefore, the number of double-sided pages will at most be:

$$\log_2 3000 = 12 \text{ pages approximately.}$$

# The Graduate Record Examination in

# COMPUTER SCIENCE

## Test 4

# THE GRADUATE RECORD EXAMINATION IN
# COMPUTER SCIENCE
## TEST 4
## ANSWER SHEET

1. Ⓐ Ⓑ Ⓒ Ⓓ Ⓔ
2. Ⓐ Ⓑ Ⓒ Ⓓ Ⓔ
3. Ⓐ Ⓑ Ⓒ Ⓓ Ⓔ
4. Ⓐ Ⓑ Ⓒ Ⓓ Ⓔ
5. Ⓐ Ⓑ Ⓒ Ⓓ Ⓔ
6. Ⓐ Ⓑ Ⓒ Ⓓ Ⓔ
7. Ⓐ Ⓑ Ⓒ Ⓓ Ⓔ
8. Ⓐ Ⓑ Ⓒ Ⓓ Ⓔ
9. Ⓐ Ⓑ Ⓒ Ⓓ Ⓔ
10. Ⓐ Ⓑ Ⓒ Ⓓ Ⓔ
11. Ⓐ Ⓑ Ⓒ Ⓓ Ⓔ
12. Ⓐ Ⓑ Ⓒ Ⓓ Ⓔ
13. Ⓐ Ⓑ Ⓒ Ⓓ Ⓔ
14. Ⓐ Ⓑ Ⓒ Ⓓ Ⓔ
15. Ⓐ Ⓑ Ⓒ Ⓓ Ⓔ
16. Ⓐ Ⓑ Ⓒ Ⓓ Ⓔ
17. Ⓐ Ⓑ Ⓒ Ⓓ Ⓔ
18. Ⓐ Ⓑ Ⓒ Ⓓ Ⓔ
19. Ⓐ Ⓑ Ⓒ Ⓓ Ⓔ
20. Ⓐ Ⓑ Ⓒ Ⓓ Ⓔ
21. Ⓐ Ⓑ Ⓒ Ⓓ Ⓔ
22. Ⓐ Ⓑ Ⓒ Ⓓ Ⓔ
23. Ⓐ Ⓑ Ⓒ Ⓓ Ⓔ
24. Ⓐ Ⓑ Ⓒ Ⓓ Ⓔ
25. Ⓐ Ⓑ Ⓒ Ⓓ Ⓔ
26. Ⓐ Ⓑ Ⓒ Ⓓ Ⓔ
27. Ⓐ Ⓑ Ⓒ Ⓓ Ⓔ

28. Ⓐ Ⓑ Ⓒ Ⓓ Ⓔ
29. Ⓐ Ⓑ Ⓒ Ⓓ Ⓔ
30. Ⓐ Ⓑ Ⓒ Ⓓ Ⓔ
31. Ⓐ Ⓑ Ⓒ Ⓓ Ⓔ
32. Ⓐ Ⓑ Ⓒ Ⓓ Ⓔ
33. Ⓐ Ⓑ Ⓒ Ⓓ Ⓔ
34. Ⓐ Ⓑ Ⓒ Ⓓ Ⓔ
35. Ⓐ Ⓑ Ⓒ Ⓓ Ⓔ
36. Ⓐ Ⓑ Ⓒ Ⓓ Ⓔ
37. Ⓐ Ⓑ Ⓒ Ⓓ Ⓔ
38. Ⓐ Ⓑ Ⓒ Ⓓ Ⓔ
39. Ⓐ Ⓑ Ⓒ Ⓓ Ⓔ
40. Ⓐ Ⓑ Ⓒ Ⓓ Ⓔ
41. Ⓐ Ⓑ Ⓒ Ⓓ Ⓔ
42. Ⓐ Ⓑ Ⓒ Ⓓ Ⓔ
43. Ⓐ Ⓑ Ⓒ Ⓓ Ⓔ
44. Ⓐ Ⓑ Ⓒ Ⓓ Ⓔ
45. Ⓐ Ⓑ Ⓒ Ⓓ Ⓔ
46. Ⓐ Ⓑ Ⓒ Ⓓ Ⓔ
47. Ⓐ Ⓑ Ⓒ Ⓓ Ⓔ
48. Ⓐ Ⓑ Ⓒ Ⓓ Ⓔ
49. Ⓐ Ⓑ Ⓒ Ⓓ Ⓔ
50. Ⓐ Ⓑ Ⓒ Ⓓ Ⓔ
51. Ⓐ Ⓑ Ⓒ Ⓓ Ⓔ
52. Ⓐ Ⓑ Ⓒ Ⓓ Ⓔ
53. Ⓐ Ⓑ Ⓒ Ⓓ Ⓔ

54. Ⓐ Ⓑ Ⓒ Ⓓ Ⓔ
55. Ⓐ Ⓑ Ⓒ Ⓓ Ⓔ
56. Ⓐ Ⓑ Ⓒ Ⓓ Ⓔ
57. Ⓐ Ⓑ Ⓒ Ⓓ Ⓔ
58. Ⓐ Ⓑ Ⓒ Ⓓ Ⓔ
59. Ⓐ Ⓑ Ⓒ Ⓓ Ⓔ
60. Ⓐ Ⓑ Ⓒ Ⓓ Ⓔ
61. Ⓐ Ⓑ Ⓒ Ⓓ Ⓔ
62. Ⓐ Ⓑ Ⓒ Ⓓ Ⓔ
63. Ⓐ Ⓑ Ⓒ Ⓓ Ⓔ
64. Ⓐ Ⓑ Ⓒ Ⓓ Ⓔ
65. Ⓐ Ⓑ Ⓒ Ⓓ Ⓔ
66. Ⓐ Ⓑ Ⓒ Ⓓ Ⓔ
67. Ⓐ Ⓑ Ⓒ Ⓓ Ⓔ
68. Ⓐ Ⓑ Ⓒ Ⓓ Ⓔ
69. Ⓐ Ⓑ Ⓒ Ⓓ Ⓔ
70. Ⓐ Ⓑ Ⓒ Ⓓ Ⓔ
71. Ⓐ Ⓑ Ⓒ Ⓓ Ⓔ
72. Ⓐ Ⓑ Ⓒ Ⓓ Ⓔ
73. Ⓐ Ⓑ Ⓒ Ⓓ Ⓔ
74. Ⓐ Ⓑ Ⓒ Ⓓ Ⓔ
75. Ⓐ Ⓑ Ⓒ Ⓓ Ⓔ
76. Ⓐ Ⓑ Ⓒ Ⓓ Ⓔ
77. Ⓐ Ⓑ Ⓒ Ⓓ Ⓔ
78. Ⓐ Ⓑ Ⓒ Ⓓ Ⓔ
79. Ⓐ Ⓑ Ⓒ Ⓓ Ⓔ
80. Ⓐ Ⓑ Ⓒ Ⓓ Ⓔ

# GRE COMPUTER SCIENCE
## TEST 4

**TIME:** 170 Minutes
80 Questions

**DIRECTIONS:** Each of the questions or incomplete statements below is followed by five suggested answers or completions. Select the one that is best in each case. Refer to Pages vii – ix for *Notations and Conventions.*

1. What will the following program segment accomplish:

Statement #

```
1    var infile, outfile : text;
2    begin
3            reset (infile, 'indata');
4            rewrite (outfile, 'outdata');
5            while not eof (infile) do
6                    begin
7                            outfile^ := infile^;
8                            put (outfile);
9                            get (infile)
10                   end;
11           close (infile);
12           close (outfile)
13   end.
```

(A) to read an input file *infile*

(B) to print out an output file *outfile*

(C) to copy input file *infile* to output file *outfile*

(D) rewrite the input file *infile*

(E) destroy the output file *outfile*

2. Simplify the following Boolean expression:

$2xyz' + xy'z' + x'yz'$

(A) $xy + y'z' + x'y$      (D) $(y + z')x$

(B) $xy + xz' + x'z'$      (E) $(x + y)z'$

(C) $(x + z')y$

3. The grammar $G = \{\{S\}, \{0,1\}, P, S\}$ where

$$P = \{S \rightarrow SS, S \rightarrow 0S1, S \rightarrow 1S0, S \rightarrow \text{empty}\}$$

will generate a:

(A) context-free language

(B) context-sensitive language

(C) regular language

(D) recursively enumerable language

(E) none of the above

4. In problem 3, the language generated is:

(A) $\{0^n1^n \text{ where } n \geq 0\}$

(B) $\{0^n1^n \text{ where } n \geq 0\} \cup \{1^n0^n \text{ where } n \geq 0\}$

(C) $(\{0^m1^k \text{ where } m, k \geq 0\} \cup \{1^m0^k \text{ where } m, k \geq 0\}) *$

(D) $\{0^m1^k \text{ where } m, k \geq 0\} \cup \{1^m0^k \text{ where } m, k \geq 0\}$

(E) $\{W \text{ where } W \text{ has an equal number of 0's and 1's}\}$

5. Consider a non-linear equation $x \sin(x) - 1 = 0$.

(A) $\exists$ unique solution

(B) $\exists$ no solution

(C) $\exists$ infinitely many solutions and the first solution lies in the interval $(^{\pi}/_4, ^{\pi}/_2)$

(D) $\exists$ infinitely many solutions and the first solution lies in the interval $(\pi, 2\pi)$

(E) $\exists$ exactly two solutions

6. The following program segment constitutes:

```
type
      link = ^node;
      node = record
              left, right : link;
                      data : datatype
              end;
procedure example (var tree : link;
                              newdata: datatype);
begin
      if  tree = nil then
              begin
                      new (tree);
                      with tree^ do
                      begin
                              left : = nil;
                              right : = nil;
                              data : = newdata
                      end (* end with *)
              end
      else
              with tree^ do
              if newdata < data then
                      insert (left, newdata)
      else
              if newdata > data then
                      insert (right, newdata)
              else (* duplicate entry *)
end;
```

(A)   An insertion of an element to a binary tree.

(B)   A deletion of an element from a binary tree.

(C)   An insertion of an element to a stack.

(D)   A deletion of an element from a queue.

(E)   To merge two files into a single file.

7.   Let $L$ be a language recognizable by a finite automaton. The language $Front(L) = \{W$ such that $W$ is the prefix of $V$ where $V \in L\}$ is a:

(A)   context-free language

(B)   context-sensitive language

(C) regular language

(D) recursively enumerable language

(E) none of the above

8. Which expression is computed by the following NAND-gate circuit diagram:

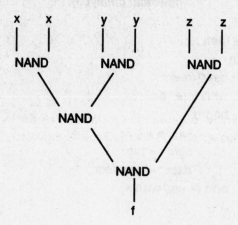

(A) $x'y' + z$

(B) $(x + y) z'$

(C) $xyz'$

(D) $x'y'z'$

(E) $x' + y' + z'$

9. At the Burger-O-Rama, the programmer wrote the code:

```
type fastfood = (bigmac, whopper, chili, fries, whaler);
var x : fastfood ;
begin;
writeln ('Give fast food desired:');
readln (x);
If (x = chili) then writeln ('go to Wendy' 's');
```

At which statement did she go wrong?

(A) type

(B) var

(C) writeln

(D) readln

(E) if

10. Let

$$A = \begin{bmatrix} 4 & 1 & 0 \\ 2 & -1 & 2 \\ x & y & -1 \end{bmatrix}$$

be a 3 × 3 matrix. The values of $x$ and $y$ that could make the following matrix A singular are:

(A)  $x = 1, y = -1$;

(B)  $x = -1, y = 4$;

(C)  $x = 1/2, y = 0$;

(D)  $x = 1, y = 1$;

(E)  $x = 0, y = 2$

11. In order to traverse a binary tree using the **inorder** method, the statements in lines #12, 13, and 14 should be written as:

```
line #
1       type
2               tptr = ^link;
3               link = record
4                       left, right : typtr;
5                       data : datatype
6                   end;
7       procedure traverse (t : tptr);
8       begin
9               If t <> nil
10                  then
11                      begin
12
13
14
15                      end
16      end;
```

(A)  *traverse* $(t^\wedge.right)$;
     *traverse* $(t^\wedge.left)$;
     *root*$(t)$;

(B)  *root*$(t)$;
     *traverse* $(t^\wedge.left)$;
     *traverse* $(t^\wedge.right)$;

(D)  *root*$(t)$;
     *traverse* $(t^\wedge.right)$;
     *traverse* $(t^\wedge.left)$;

(E)  *traverse* $(t^\wedge.right)$;
     *root*$(t)$;
     *traverse* $(t^\wedge.left)$;

(C)  traverse (t^.left);
     root(t);
     traverse (t^.right);

12.  In the following Karnaugh map with don't-care states, which values
     of A and B would minimize the final function's expression length?

|   |   |   |   |
|---|---|---|---|
| 0 | 0 | A | 0 |
| 0 | 1 | 1 | 0 |
| 1 | B | 1 | 0 |
| 0 | 0 | 0 | 0 |

(A)  $A = 0, B = 0$

(B)  $A = 0, B = 1$

(C)  $A = 1, B = 0$

(D)  $A = 1, B = 1$

(E)  All the above give equal length expressions.

13.  How many possible bytes have exactly three bits on (i.e. bit = true)?

(A)  8 * 7                    (D)  8 * 7 * 6

(B)  8 * 3                    (E)  none of the above

(C)  256 * 3/8

14.  What is the value of $F(4)$ using the following procedure:

```
function F(k : integer) : integer ;
begin
      If (k < 3 ) then F :=k else F :=F (k–1) * F(k–2) + F(k–3) ;
end ;
```

(A)  5                       (D)  8

(B)  6                       (E)  26

(C)  7

15.  The language $L = \{0^n 1^n 2^n$ where $n > 0\}$ is a:

(A) context-free language

(B) context-sensitive language

(C) regular language

(D) recursively enumerable language

(E) none of the above

16. What is the value of: *succ* (*ord* ('B') + 1 ) – *ord* (*pred*('B')))

(A) 2          (D) 5

(B) 3          (E) 6

(C) 4

17. With the *lhs* convention, rotating a point clockwise (CW) by angle $\phi$ about the *x*-axis (looking along the positive *x*-axis toward the origin) will move a point on the positive *y*-axis in an arc toward the positive *z*-axis. For any point, the rotational matrix becomes:

(A) $\begin{pmatrix} 1 & 0 & 0 & 0 \\ 0 & \cos\phi & \sin\phi & 0 \\ 0 & -\sin\phi & \cos\phi & 0 \\ 0 & 0 & 0 & 1 \end{pmatrix}$
(D) $\begin{pmatrix} \sin\phi & \cos\phi & 1 & 0 \\ \cos\phi & \sin\phi & 0 & 1 \\ 1 & 0 & 0 & 0 \\ 0 & 0 & 0 & 0 \end{pmatrix}$

(B) $\begin{pmatrix} \cos\phi & 1 & 0 & 0 \\ 0 & \sin\phi & 1 & 0 \\ 1 & 0 & 0 & 0 \\ 0 & \cos\phi & 0 & 1 \end{pmatrix}$
(E) $\begin{pmatrix} 1 & 0 & 1 & 1 \\ 0 & 1 & 0 & 0 \\ 0 & \cos\phi & 1 & 0 \\ 1 & \sin\phi & 0 & 1 \end{pmatrix}$

(C) $\begin{pmatrix} 1 & \sin\phi & 1 & 0 \\ 0 & \cos\phi & 0 & 0 \\ 1 & 0 & 1 & 1 \\ 0 & 0 & 0 & \sin\phi \end{pmatrix}$

18. In the No-Knot Lumber Company, Lumberjack Joe needs to store information like the following data:

| Prod # | Wood | Price Per Pound | Quantity |
|--------|------|-----------------|----------|
| 3117 | Spruce | 2.31 | 499 |
| 4672 | Silver Fir | 19.56 | 69 |
| 9724 | Atlas Cedar | 8.78 | 200 |
| 2953 | Hemlock | 4.44 | 7945 |

Help good ole Joe by choosing the correct coding for this.

(A)   **type** *LUMB* = **record** *PROD:INTEGER*;
*WOOD:CHAR*; *P:REAL*; *Q:INTEGER*; **end;**

(B)   **type** *LUMB* = **record** *PROD:INTEGER*;
*WOOD:STRING*[20]; *P:REAL*; *Q:INTEGER*; **end;**

(C)   **type** *LUMB* = **array** [1..50] **of record** *PROD:INTEGER*;
*WOOD:CHAR*; *P:REAL*; *Q:INTEGER*; **end;**

(D)   **type** *LUMB* = **array** [1..50] **of record** *PROD:INTEGER*;
*WOOD:***array** [1..20] **of** *CHAR*; *P:REAL*; *Q:INTEGER*; **end;**

(E)   none of the above

19.   A ripple carry adder requires _____ time, where $N$ is the number of bits in the sum.

(A)   constant time (i.e. $N$ has no influence)

(B)   logarithmic time ($O(\log (N))$)

(C)   linear time ($O(N)$)

(D)   $O(N\log(N))$

(E)   quadratic time ($O(N^2)$)

20.   The language $L = \{ 0^n 1^n 2^k 3^k$ where $n, k > 0\}$ is a:

(A)   context-free language

(B)   context-sensitive language

(C)   regular language

(D)   recursively enumerable language

(E)   none of the above

21. Let $\Delta$ be the forward difference operator in numerical interpolation, with uniform spacing,

$$h = x_{i+1} - x_i,$$

$$i = 0, 1, 2, \ldots (n-1) \text{ and}$$

$$P_n(x) = b_n x^n + b_{n-1} x^{n-1} + \ldots + b_1 x + b_0$$

be the $n^{th}$ degree polynomial, then

   (A) $\Delta^n P_n(x) = b_n (n+1)! h^n$

   (B) $\Delta^n P_n(x) = b_n n! h^n$

   (C) $\Delta^n P_n(x) = b_n 1/n! h^n$

   (D) $\Delta^n P_n(x) = b_n n! 1/h^n$

   (E) $\Delta^n P_n(x) = b_n (n-1)!$

22. Which of the following is an illegal array definition?

   (A) type *COLOGNE* = (*LIME, PINE, MUSK, MENTHOL*);
       var *a* : array [*COLOGNE*] of *REAL* ;

   (B) var *a* : array [*REAL*] of *REAL* ;

   (C) var *a* : array ['A' .. 'Z'] of *REAL* ;

   (D) var *a* : array [*BOOLEAN*] of *REAL* ;

   (E) var *a* : array [–10 .. –2] of *REAL* ;

23. Which sort will operate in quadratic time relative to the number of elements in the array (on the average)?

   (A) quick sort          (D) heap sort

   (B) radix sort          (E) bubble sort

   (C) merge sort

24. How many 2-input multiplexers are required to construct an 8-input multiplexer?

   (A) 3          (D) 7

   (B) 4          (E) 8

   (C) 6

25. Chevy, Charlie, and Chloe were writing a tick-tack-toe program (i.e. 3 in a "row" wins.) Which line of correct code should they write?

(A) if ($a[1,1]$ = 'x' or $a[2,1]$ = 'x' or $a[3,1]$ = 'x')
   then *writeln* ('win!');

(B) if ($a[2,1]$ = 'x' and $a[1,2]$ = 'x' and $a[1,1]$ = 'x')
   then *writeln* ('win!');

(C) if ($a[3,1]$ = 'x' or $a[2,2]$ = 'x' or $a[1,3]$ = 'x')
   then *writeln* ('win!');

(D) if ($a[3,1]$ = 'x' and $a[2,2]$ = 'x' and $a[1,3]$ = 'x')
   then *writeln* ('win!');

(E) if ($a[1,1]$ = 'x' or $a[2,1]$ = 'x' and $a[3,1]$ = 'x')
   then *writeln* ('win!');

26. $\sum\limits_{2}^{n} (k(k-1)) = ?$

Hint: The answer solves the recurrence

$$F(j) = F(j-1) + j(j-1).$$

(i.e. $1*2 + 2*3 + 3*4 + ... + (n-1)*n$).

(A) $n(n+1)(n+2)/2$

(B) $n^2(n+1)^2/6$

(C) $(n-1)n(n+1)/3$

(D) $(n+1)!/2^n$

(E) $3n^2 + n + 1$

27. Trixie wrote the following program which (when given 4 points) will see if any quadrilateral *ABCD* is a square.

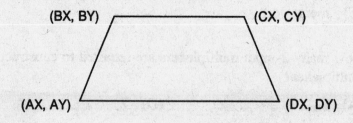

readln ($AX, AY, BX, BY, CX, CY, DX, DY$); ...

Trixie even wrote a subprocedure *Dist(X1, Y1, X2, Y2)* which will compute the distance from *(X1, Y1)* to *(X2, Y2)*. Help Trixie decide which **if** statement will work best.

(A)  **if** *(Dist (AX, AY, BX, BY) = Dist (CX, CY, DX, DY))*
     **then** *writeln* ('This is a square');

(B)  **if** *(Dist (AX, AY, B X, BY) = Dist (CX, CY, DX, DY)*
     **and** *Dist (AX, AY, DX, DY) = Dist (BX, BY, CX, CY))*
     **then** *writeln* ('This is a square');

(C)  **if** *(Dist (AX, AY, BX, BY) = Dist (CX, CY, DX, DY)*
     **and** *Dist (AX, AY, DX, DY) = Dist (BX, BY, CX, CY)*
     **and** *Dist (AX, AY, DX, DY) = Dist (AX, AY, BX, BY))*
     **then** *writeln* ('This is a square');

(D)  **if** *(Dist (AX, AY, BX, BY) = Dist (CX, CY, DX, DY)*
     **and** *Dist (AX, AY, DX, DY) = Dist (BX, BY, CX, CY)*
     **and** *Dist (AX, AY, DX, DY) = Dist (AX, AY, BX, BY)*
     **and** *Dist (AX, AY, CX, CY) = Dist (BX, BY, DX, DY))*
     **then** *writeln* ('This is a square');

(E)  **if** *(Dist (AX, AY, BX, BY) = Dist (CX, CY, DX, DY)*
     **and** *Dist (AX, AY, DX, DY) = Dist (BX, BY, CX, CY)*
     **and** *Dist (AX, AY, DX, DY) = Dist (AX, AY, BX, BY)*
     **and** *Dist (AX, AY, CX, CY) = Dist (BX, BY, DX, DY)*
     **and** *Dist (AX, AY, CX, CY) = Dist (AX, AY, BX, BY))*
     **then** *writeln* ('This is a square');

28. If the control signals $\{a, b, c, d, e, f, g\}$ for some microinstructions and their corresponding MCCs (maximal compatibility classes) are:

    $$\{a\,dfg,\ a\,b\,d,\ b\,c\,g,\ b\,d\,e\,g\}$$

    then to determine the minimal MCC cover, we need to remove:

    (A)  $a\,dfg$

    (B)  $a\,b\,d$

    (C)  $b\,c\,g$

    (D)  $b\,d\,e\,g$

    (E)  none of them can be removed (i.e. all are necessary)

29. Eric the Mediocre conducted a survey of students at V.S.U. (Viking State University). His statistics (for courses) were:

520 took Computer Science (CS)   416 took Plundering (P)

320 took Basket Weaving (BW)   152 took CS and Plundering

96 took CS and Weaving   124 took Plundering and Weaving

60 took All Three

Notation: 520 above took at least CS but may have other courses. Using Venn Diagrams and the Counting Principle (i.e. Inclusion – Exclusion), help Eric compute how many are taking exactly one of the three courses (no more, no less).

(A)  $V < 400$

(D)  $800 < V < 1000$

(B)  $400 < V < 600$

(E)  $1000 < V$

(C)  $600 < V < 800$

30.  A good change–program to compute the fewest number of coins in amount AMT should have which of the following bits of code? Note: dollars should have the number of green bills.

(A)  *AMT*:=371.64;
    *DOLLARS*:=trunc (*AMT*);
    *COINS*:=100 * (*DOLLARS*);
    *QUARTERS*:=*COINS*;
    *DIMES*:=*COINS* mod 10;
    *NICKELS*:=*COINS* mod 5;
    *CENTS*:=*COINS* mod 1;

(B)  *AMT*:=371.64;
    *DOLLARS*:=trunc (*AMT*);
    *COINS*:=100 * (*AMT* – *DOLLARS*);
    *QUARTERS*:=*COINS* div 25;
    *REST*:=(*COINS* – 25 * *QUARTERS*);
    *DIMES*:=*REST* div 10;
    *NICKELS*:=*REST* mod 5;
    *CENTS*:=(*REST* mod 10) mod 5;

(C)  *AMT*:=371.64;
    *DOLLARS*:=trunc (*AMT*);
    *COINS*:=100 * (*AMT* – *DOLLARS*);
    *QUARTERS*:=*COINS* div 25;
    *REST*:=(*COINS* – 25 * *QUARTERS*);
    *DIMES*:=*REST* div 10;

$$NICKELS := REST \text{ div } 5;$$
$$CENTS := REST \text{ mod } 5;$$

(D) $AMT := 371.64;$
$DOLLARS := \text{trunc } (AMT);$
$COINS := 100 * (AMT - DOLLARS);$
$QUARTERS := COINS \text{ mod } 25;$
$DIMES := COINS \text{ mod } 10;$
$NICKELS := COINS \text{ mod } 5;$
$CENTS := COINS - NICKELS;$

(E) $AMT := 371.64;$
$DOLLARS := \text{trunc } (AMT);$
$COINS := 100 * (AMT - DOLLARS);$
$QUARTERS := COINS \text{ div } 25;$
$REST := COINS - 25 * QUARTERS);$
$DIMES := REST \text{ div } 10;$
$NICKELS := (REST \text{ mod } 10) \text{ div } 5;$
$CENTS := REST \text{ mod } 5;$

31. Which decision procedure has at least doubly-exponential time complexity?

    (A) linear programming

    (B) graph-coloring problem

    (C) Traveling Salesman Problem

    (D) Presburger Arithmetic

    (E) Hamiltonian Circuit Problem

32. Who was the FIRST person in the list below to tell the truth?

    (A) Colonel Mustard said "**repeat** – loops test at the top of the loop."

    (B) Mr. Green said "**while** – loops test for the exit condition (i.e. True = exit)."

    (C) Miss Scarlet said "Functions use the command **return** (function name); to send back the answer."

    (D) Mrs. White said "the following code prints the value of (not X)" case X of *TRUE* : *writeln* ('FALSE');

*FALSE* : *writeln* ('TRUE');

end; {*END CASE*}

(E)   Prof. Plum said "writeln; will skip a line"

## QUESTIONS 33 – 34

The next two questions are Water-Jugs search problems in Artificial Intelligence. Assume the following three operations only (i.e. no others):

I.   SPILL        – will spill water down drain (out of system)

II.  FILL         – from faucet; fill one jar full

III. POUR(*a, b*) – pour from jar *a* to jar *b* until either jar *a* is empty or jar *b* is full

Assume these jars are not graduated (i.e. no measurements). Assume all jugs are initially empty. Always determine the MINIMAL number of steps to solve a problem.

33.   Given a three-gallon jug and a four-gallon jug, reach the goal state of precisely two gallons of water in the four-gallon jug. (Each step = 1 operation.)

(A)   4 steps                    (D)   7 steps

(B)   5 steps                    (E)   over seven steps

(C)   6 steps

34.   Given a five-gallon jug and eight-gallon jug, reach the goal state of precisely two gallons in the five-gallon jug.

(A)   4 steps                    (D)   7 steps

(B)   5 steps                    (E)   over seven steps

(C)   6 steps

35.   Riverhead Riveting Company is riveting crossbars to steel girders. Each girder is exactly one foot from the next but the bars are not exactly cut. Help the ailing steel industry by computing the distance of any real number *r* from the closest integer. For example, if *R* is 3.9, compute .1

(A)  *abs (R) – trunc (R)*       (D)  *abs (round (R) – trunc (R))*

(B)  *abs (R – round (R))*       (E)  *abs (trunc (R) – round (R))*

(C)  *abs (R – trunc (R))*

36.  If a disk has a seek time of 20 ms, rotates 20 revolutions per second, has 100 words per block, and each track has a capacity of 300 words, then the total time required to access a one block is: (Choose the closest answer)

(A)  25                    (D)  50

(B)  30                    (E)  60

(C)  40

37.  Which of the following problems is solvable?

(A)  Determining if an arbitrary Turing machine is a universal Turing machine.

(B)  Writing a universal Turing machine.

(C)  Determining if a universal Turing machine can be written in fewer than $k$ instructions for some $k$.

(D)  Determining if a universal Turing machine and some input will halt.

(E)  More than one of the above is solvable.

38.  Is the following a Eulerian graph (i.e., closed Eulerian path)? Is it a (closed) Hamiltonian-cycled graph?

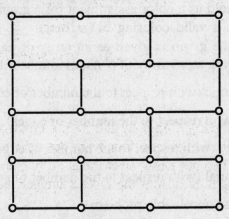

(A)  It is both Hamiltonian and Eulerian

(B)  It is  Hamiltonian, but not Eulerian

(C)  It is Eulerian, but not Hamiltonian

(D)  It is neither Hamiltonian nor Eulerian

(E)  None of the above

39.  How many of the below are FALSE about **constants**?

I.    They may occur on the left of :=

II.   They may occur on the left of =

III.  They may occur on the right of :=

IV.   They may occur on the right of  =

V.    They never change in value (inside the program during execution)

VI.   They may be printed (i.e. used in a **writeln**)

VII.  They make code more easily modifiable if we needed to change something during code maintenance

IX.   They are converted to their actual value (in the program code) at compile time

(A)  1          (D)  4

(B)  2          (E)  more than 4

(C)  3

40.  If a "birdie" told us a color assignment for a graph, we can presently verify if it is a valid coloring in (at best) _____ time. If it helps, assume that the graph is given as an array of pairs (edges) and the coloring is given as an array of $N$ nodes numbered 1 to $N$.

(A)  logarithmic (with respect to the number of edges)

(B)  linear (with respect to the number of edges)

(C)  quadratic (with respect to the number of edges)

(D)  exponential (with respect to the number of edges)

(E)  This is an unsolvable problem

41. If a high-speed 40 ns memory cache has a successful hit ratio of 80 percent, and regular memory has an access time of 100 ns, then the average effective time for CPU to access memory is approximately:

    (A)  50                    (D)  80

    (B)  60                    (E)  90

    (C)  70

42. With local landfills all full, a barge moves debris in different amounts everyday for *n* days. Statistician Tom Trent needs the average amount computed to determine the average daily profit of the barge. Which of the following will compute the average of those *n* numbers?

    (A)  **for** *J*:=1 **to** *N* **do begin**
         *readln* (*K*); *AVE*:=*AVE* + *K*/*J*; **end**;

    (B)  **for** *J*:=1 **to** *N* **do begin**
         *readln* (*K*); *AVE*:=*AVE* + *K*/*N*; **end**;

    (C)  **for** *J*:=1 **to** *N* **do begin**
         *readln* (*K*); *AVE*:=(*AVE* + *K*)/*J*; **end**;

    (D)  **for** *J*:=1 **to** *N* **do begin**
         *readln* (*K*); *AVE*:=(*AVE* + *K*)/*N*; **end**;

    (E)  **for** *J*:=1 **to** *N* **do begin**
         *readln* (*K*); *AVE* :=(*AVE* + *K*) /2; **end**;

43. What is true for the complete bipartite graphs $K(3,3)$ and $K(2,4)$?

    (A)  Both are planar

    (B)  At least one of them requires three colors to be minimally colored

    (C)  Neither is planar

    (D)  Both are isomorphic

    (E)  None of the above are true statements

44. Which code will compute the sine function? One way to compute sine(*x*) is by the series:

    $$sine(x) = x - x^3/3! + x^5/5! - x^7/7! + x^9/9!$$

Which of the following codes will compute sine via the series given? Assume the %%%%%%%% will be resolved by another person.

(A)  *Term:=x*; *k:=1*; *Sum:=0*;
     **repeat** *Term:= − Term\*x\*x / ((k)\*(k − 1))*;
     *Sum:=Sum + Term*;
     *k:=k + 2*; **until** *(%%%%%%%%%%)*;

(B)  *Term:=x*; *k:=1*; *Sum:=0*;
     **repeat** *k:=k + 2*; *Term:= − Term\*x\*x / ((k)\*(k − 1))*;
     *Sum:=Sum + Term*; **until** *(%%%%%%%%%%)*;

(C)  *Term:=x*; *k:=1*; *Sum:=0*;
     **repeat** *Term:= − Term\*x\*x / ((k)\*(k − 1))*;
     *k:=k + 2*; *Sum:=Sum + Term*;
     **until** *(%%%%%%%%%%)*;

(D)  *Term:=x*; *k:=1*; *Sum:=0*;
     **repeat** *Sum:=Sum + Term*; *k:=k + 2*;
     *Term:= − Term\*x\*x / ((k)\*(k − 1))*;
     **until** *(%%%%%%%%%%)*;

(E)  *Term:=x*; *k:=1*; *Sum:=x*;
     **repeat** *k:=k + 2*; *Sum:=Sum + Term*;
     *Term:= − Term\*x\*x / ((k)\*(k − 1))*;
     **until** *(%%%%%%%%%%)*;

45.  Which types of file organizations are supported by magnetic tape?

(A)  contiguous sequential files

(B)  contiguous sequential files and sequential files with extents

(C)  *a* and *b* and indexed sequential files

(D)  random files

(E)  All of the above

46.  At the Fulton Street Fabulous Fried Fish Restaurant, chef Freddie has nine fish (namely, bass, cod, bluefish, sturgeon, Greenland turbot, halibut, swordfish, haddock, barracuda.) Every day, there are exactly three specials. All the fish must be sold during the next three days. No fish may be sold on more than one day. How many different ways can chef Freddie schedule the specials?

Hint: One schedule could be:

DAY 1 cod bass bluefish

DAY 2 sturgeon haddock barracuda

DAY 3 swordfish turbot halibut

Hint: The above is the same as having DAY 1 blue bass cod. (i.e., order inside a specific day is not important)

(A)   $C(9, 6) / (3!)$

(B)   $9!$

(C)   $C(9, 3) * C(6, 3)$

(D)   $C(9, 3)$

(E)   $(9!) / (3!)$

47.   If we needed a subroutine to switch two variables, then we need:

(A)   *procedure Sw (a, b: Real)*; **var** *Temp* : *Real*;
      **begin** *Temp*:=*a*; *a*:=*b*; *b*:=*Temp* **end**

(B)   *procedure Sw (***var** *a, b: Real)*; **var** *Temp* : *Real*;
      **begin** *Temp*:=*a*; *a*:=*b*; *b*:=*Temp* **end**

(C)   *procedure Sw (***var** *a, b: Real) : Real*;
      **var**; *Temp*: integer; **begin** *Temp*:=*a*; *a*:=*b*; *b*:*Temp* **end**

(D)   *function Sw (a, b: Real) : Real*; **var** *Temp* : *Real*;
      **begin** *Temp*:=*a*; *a*:=*b*; *b*:=*Temp* **end**

(E)   *function Sw (***var** *a, b: Real) : Real*;
      **var**; *Temp*: integer; **begin** *Temp*:=*a*; *a*:=*b*; *b*:=*Temp* **end**

48.   $F(x) = (7x^6 + 3x^4 + 17x + 9) / (0.01x^2 * x^{-1})$ is Big-O of WHAT?

(A)   $F$ is $O(n^7)$ but not $O(n^6)$

(B)   $F$ is $O(n^6)$ but not $O(n^5)$

(C)   $F$ is $O(n^5)$ but not $O(n^4)$

(D)   $F$ is $O(n^4)$ but not $O(n^3)$

(E)   $F$ is $O(n^3)$ but not $O(n^2)$

49. According to the debugging methodology "TEST ALL PATHS", what numbers must this code be tested by to verify or debug it completely:

$$readln\ (x,y);\ if\ (x < 10)\ then\ ****\ else\ ++++\ ;$$

$$if\ (y > 5)\ then\ \%\%\%\%\ else\ \$\$\$\$\ ;$$

(A) $(x,y) = (9,7), (11, -2), (2, 9), (8, 6)$

(B) $(x,y) = (-1, 9), (8, -2), (2, 8), (19, 8)$

(C) $(x,y) = (9, 7), (11, 3)\ (19, 11), (3, 4)$

(D) $(x,y) = (9, 19), (5, 3), (6, 11), (11, 3)$

(E) $(x,y) = (9, 7), (11, -2)$

50. What symbol causes a *pop* in the stack-evaluation of fully-parenthesized infix expressions, such as $((2 + 3) * (5 + 7)) <EOF>$ ? Assume the expression is read from left to right. Choose the best or most definite answer.

(A)  2                    (D)  (

(B)  +                    (E)  )

(C)  *

51. Convert

$$x'yz' + x'y'z + x(y + z)$$

into a product of sums.

(A) $x'yz' + x'y'z + xy + xz$

(B) $(x' + y + z')(x' + y' + z)(x + y)(x + z)$

(C) $(x + y' + z)(x + y + z')(x + y + z)$

(D) $(y' + z')(x' + y + z)$

(E) $(y + z)(x + y' + z')$

52. What is the time complexity measure for the following routine which multiplies two square matrices A and B and stores the result in C?

```
for j:=1 to n do
    begin
```

```
for k:=1 to n do
        begin
            sum:=0;
            for l:=1 to n do
                begin
                    sum:=sum + a(j,l) * b(l,k)
                end;
            c(j,k):=sum
end end;
```

(A) linear          (D) quartic

(B) quadratic       (E) quintic

(C) cubic

53. Secret agent 009 is trapped with a bomb in Fort Knox. The probability of it exploding during 1 second is 1/3. What is the probability that 009 will survive for 2 full seconds and be blasted at time = 3 ?

(A) 0               (D) 4/27

(B) 1/27            (E) 1/3

(C) 1/9

54. Queues serve a major role in:

(A) simulation of recursion

(B) simulation of motion of subatomic particles

(C) simulation of arbitrary linked lists

(D) simulation of limited resource allocation

(E) expression evaluation

55. Convert $(a + b) * (c + d)$ to postfix.

(A) $* + ab + cd$          (D) $ab+ cd + *$

(B) $ab + * cd +$          (E) $a + bc + d *$

(C) $abcd ++ *$

56. Which of the choices is an operator grammar equivalent for:

$$S \rightarrow SAS \mid a, A \rightarrow bSb \mid b$$

Assume $S$ is the start symbol.

(A) $S \rightarrow SAS \mid a, A \rightarrow bSb \mid b$

(B) $S \rightarrow SbSbS \mid SbS \mid a$

(C) $S \rightarrow SbAbS \mid a, A \rightarrow b$

(D) $S \rightarrow SbS \mid b$

(E) $S \rightarrow SbS \mid SAS \mid b \mid a$

57. What is the hit-ratio of a cache if a system performs memory access at 30 nanoseconds with the cache and 150 nanoseconds without it? Assume the cache uses 20 nanosecond memory. Choose the closest estimate.

(A) 98%

(B) 92%

(C) 87%

(D) 81%

(E) 75%

58. Which of the following lines of code will delete two successive nodes of a singly linked linear list (WITH MORE THAN 2 NODES)? Assume this code is in the main program, not a subprocedure.

(A) $LINK[X] := LINK\ [LINK[X]]$;

(B) $X := LINK[LINK[X]]$;

(C) $LINK[LINK[X]] := X$;

(D) $LINK[X] := LINK[LINK[LINK[X]]]$;

(E) $X := LINK[LINK[LINK[X]]]$;

59. What is the sum of $6k - 5$ from $k = 1$ to $k = n$?

(i.e. $\displaystyle\sum_{k=1}^{k=n} (6k - 5)$)?

Find the answer on one of the rows below:

(A) It was $6n^2 - n$ or $4n^2 - 5n$ or
$3n^2 - 5n$ or $2n^2 - 6n$

(B)  It was $6n^2 - 3n$ or $5n^2 - 4n$
or $3n^2 - 5n$ or $2n^2 - 5n$

(C)  It was $6n^2 - 5n$ or $5n^2 - 3n$
or $4n^2 - 3n$ or $n^2 + 5n$

(D)  It was $6n^2 - 2n$ or $4n^2 - 2n$ or $2n^2 - 3n$
or $5n^2 - 2n$

(E)  It was $6n^2 - 6n$ or $5n^2 - 2n$ or $2n^2 - 4n$
or $3n^2 - 2n$

60.  How many levels does Frieda need to represent the tree shown below as a binary tree?

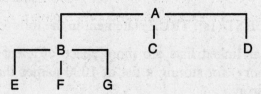

(A)  2            (D)  5

(B)  3            (E)  6

(C)  4

61.  If an original MIB microcomputer operates at 5 MHz with an 8 bit bus and a newer version operates at 20 MHz with a 32 bit bus, compute (approximately) the maximum speed-up possible.

(A)  2            (D)  8

(B)  4            (E)  16

(C)  6

62.  At the Helsinki International Chess Championship, the two contestants must play chess matches until a winner emerges victorious by either winning two successive matches or winning a total of three matches. Find the number of ways that the championship can occur.

(A)  10          (D)  15

(B)  12          (E)  16

(C)  14

63. A complete binary tree of level 5 has how many nodes?

   (A) 15                    (D) 63

   (B) 25                    (E) 71

   (C) 33

64. Which sentence can be generated by: $S \rightarrow aS \mid bA, A \rightarrow d \mid ccA$

   (A) *bccddd*              (D) *aabccd*

   (B) *abbbd*               (E) *aadb*

   (C) *ababccd*

65. Find the FIRST (1st) TRUE statement in the following:

   (A) Linear linked lists are more space efficient (i.e. require less memory) for storing a list of 1000 names than having a plain flat array.

   (B) Linear linked lists are less time efficient (i.e. require more time) for maintaining (i.e. updating) a growing list of over 1000 names (sorted in alphabetic order) than having a plain flat array.

   (C) Arrays are more versatile (i.e. dynamically restructurable) than linked lists.

   (D) A data structure with two links offers more geometrical con-figurations (versatility) than a data structure with one link.

   (E) lists can store dictionaries

66. Using best first search for a shortest path from A to Z, the order in which nodes are considered best for the path is:

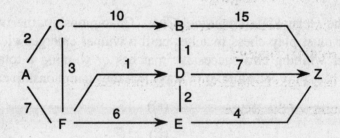

   Note that these are node orders, not full paths.

(A) $A < C < F < D < E$     (D) $A < C < D < F$

(B) $A < C < E < B$     (E) $A < C < B < D$

(C) $A < C < F < E < B$

67. Compute

Fibonacci(8) where Fibonacci(1):=1;

Fibonacci(2):=1;

and Fibonacci(N):=Fibonacci(N – 1)

+ Fibonacci (N – 2);

(A) 8     (D) 34

(B) 13     (E) 55

(C) 21

68. Determining all possible decompositions of sequential machines re-quires _____ time in $N$, where $N$ is the number of states.

(A) logarithmic     (D) quadratic

(B) linear     (E) exponential

(C) $N \log(N)$

69. Fred created a new automaton model which is a pushdown automaton but with two stacks and the added ability of having commands which don't read the input tape but which can pop from one stack and push into the other (and the reverse). This new automaton can recognize: (choose the strongest result)

(A) context-free language

(B) context-sensitive languages

(C) regular language

(D) languages recognizable by Turing machines

(E) none of the above

70. How many of the following relations (over all real numbers) are reflexive?

I.   $A$ is-related-to $B$ means $\quad\quad abs(A - B) \leq 10$

II.  $A$ is-related-to $B$ means $\quad\quad A * B > 8$

III. $A$ is-related-to $B$ means $\quad\quad A \leq B$

IV.  $A$ is-related-to $B$ means $\quad\quad A \leq abs(B)$

(A)  0, none          (D)  3

(B)  1                (E)  all 4

(C)  2

71. In problem 70 (above), how many of the relations are symmetric?

(A)  0, none          (D)  3

(B)  1                (E)  all 4

(C)  2

72. In problem 70 (above), which relation(s) is transitive?

(A)  I, the first

(B)  II, the second

(C)  III, the third

(D)  IV, the fourth

(E)  more than one of the relations are transitive

73. In the disk storage aspect of data bases and applications programs,

(A)  blocked record files and locate mode I/O are faster.

(B)  unblocked record files and locate mode I/O are faster.

(C)  unblocked record files and move mode I/O are faster.

(D)  blocked record files and move mode I/O are faster.

(E)  floppy disks have greater storage capacities than hard disks.

74. Recursively enumerable languages are not closed under:

(A)  intersection

(B)  union

(C)   concatenation

(D)   intersection with a regular set

(E)   complementation

75.   A two input sequential machine for multiplication takes two bits (one from each number) and outputs their product. Assuming arbitrarily long numbers, such a machine:

(A)   requires 2 states          (D)   requires 16 states

(B)   requires 4 states          (E)   is not possible

(C)   requires 8 states

76.   In terms of expressive power (of associations) or generality of representation,

(A)   hierarchical is best, relational worst, and network moderate.

(B)   hierarchical is best, relational moderate, and network worst.

(C)   hierarchical is worst, relational moderate, and network best.

(D)   hierarchical is worst, relational best, and network moderate.

(E)   hierarchical is best, relational worst, and network moderate.

77.   How many boolean functions of three variables $f(x, y, z)$ have the property that $f(x, y, z) = (f(x', y', z'))'$?

(A)   8                          (D)   128

(B)   16                         (E)   256

(C)   64

78.   Which operations require the most memory accesses?

(A)   Register-to-Register Adds

(B)   Branch

(C)   Condition-Code Test

(D)   Shift Register Left

(E)   all are the same

79. Convert FAFAFA in hexadecimal into octal.

    (A) 76767676

    (D) 76575372

    (B) 76737672

    (E) 76576572

    (C) 76727672

80. Inherited attributes are

    (A) passed from son nodes to father nodes.

    (B) passed from father nodes to son nodes.

    (C) both (A) and (B) are possible.

    (D) neither (A) nor (B) are possible.

    (E) genetic traits and have no relevance.

# TEST 4

## ANSWER KEY

| | | | | | | | |
|---|---|---|---|---|---|---|---|
| 1. | (C) | 21. | (B) | 41. | (A) | 61. | (E) |
| 2. | (E) | 22. | (B) | 42. | (B) | 62. | (A) |
| 3. | (A) | 23. | (E) | 43. | (E) | 63. | (D) |
| 4. | (E) | 24. | (D) | 44. | (D) | 64. | (D) |
| 5. | (C) | 25. | (D) | 45. | (A) | 65. | (D) |
| 6. | (A) | 26. | (C) | 46. | (C) | 66. | (A) |
| 7. | (C) | 27. | (D) | 47. | (B) | 67. | (C) |
| 8. | (A) | 28. | (B) | 48. | (C) | 68. | (E) |
| 9. | (D) | 29. | (C) | 49. | (C) | 69. | (D) |
| 10. | (D) | 30. | (E) | 50. | (E) | 70. | (D) |
| 11. | (C) | 31. | (D) | 51. | (E) | 71. | (C) |
| 12. | (B) | 32. | (D) | 52. | (C) | 72. | (C) |
| 13. | (A) | 33. | (C) | 53. | (D) | 73. | (A) |
| 14. | (A) | 34. | (A) | 54. | (D) | 74. | (D) |
| 15. | (B) | 35. | (B) | 55. | (D) | 75. | (E) |
| 16. | (B) | 36. | (E) | 56. | (B) | 76. | (D) |
| 17. | (A) | 37. | (B) | 57. | (B) | 77. | (B) |
| 18. | (D) | 38. | (D) | 58. | (D) | 78. | (E) |
| 19. | (C) | 39. | (A) | 59. | (B) | 79. | (D) |
| 20. | (A) | 40. | (B) | 60. | (C) | 80. | (C) |

# DETAILED EXPLANATIONS
# OF ANSWERS

# TEST 4

1.  **(C)**
    The reset statement opens and sets the input file *infile*. The rewrite statement opens and prepares the the *outfile* for writing. The 7th, 8th and 9th statements copy values from *infile* to *outfile*. Statements 11 and 12 close both *infile* and *outfile*.

2.  **(E)**
    Starting with
    $$2xyz' + xy'z' + x'yz'$$
    separate the $2xyz'$ term to get
    $$(xyz' + xy'z') + (x'yz' + xyz').$$
    Factoring, we get
    $$(xz'(y + y')) + (yz'(x' + x))$$
    reducing to:
    $$(xz'1) + (yz'1) = xz' + yz' = (x + y)z'$$
    hence, answer (E). Choices (A) and (B) have an $xy$ term which can't be since $z'$ occurs in all terms in the original expression. Choices (C) and (D) also have an $xy$ term factored.

3.  **(A)**
    This grammar looks like it generates a recursively enumerable language because of the $S\rightarrow$ empty (e-rule); however, we can delete the e-rule by applying it to every other production. So, we delete the e-rule and add: $S\rightarrow S$, $S\rightarrow 01$, $S\rightarrow 10$. We can ignore the $S\rightarrow S$. The grammar now is clearly context-free.

4.  **(E)**
    By grammar $G$, we derive $S \rightarrow SS \rightarrow 0S10S1 \rightarrow 0101$. Clearly, 0101 is not in choices (A), (B), or (D) because words in any of those have 0's followed by 1's, or 1's followed by 0's. Choice (C) looks good because of

the *-closure and it has 0101. However, $m$ and $k$ are not always equal so choice (C) can generate 000011 which grammar $G$ can't generate. From the productions of $G$, we note that the number of 0's and 1's always stays equal, so choice (E) is best. To see that $G$ can generate all the strings in (E) is a bit more difficult (i.e., requires an induction), but that was not needed for the above problem.

5. **(C)**

$f(x) = x \sin(x) - 1$ is a continuous function in $(\frac{\pi}{4}, \frac{\pi}{2})$

$$f(\tfrac{\pi}{4}) = (\tfrac{\pi}{4})(\tfrac{1}{\sqrt{2}}) - 1 < 0$$

$$f(\tfrac{\pi}{2}) = (\tfrac{\pi}{2})(1) - 1 > 0$$

$\therefore \exists$ a root in $(\pi/4, \pi/2)$

Also, $f(x)$ is continuous in $(0, \pi/4)$, and $f(0) < 0$

$f(\pi/4) < 0$

then $\exists$ no root in $(0, \pi/4)$

$\therefore$ the first root lies in $(\pi/4, \pi/2)$.

Thus, (B) and (D) are clearly wrong. To prove (A) and (E) wrong, do the same thing for $f(nx)$, for $n = 2$ and $n = 3$. Therefore, (C) is the only possible answer.

6. **(A)**

A binary tree consists of two branches identified by pointers *left* and *right*, and a data item part identified by *datatype*.

When using NLR (Node, Left and Right) algorithm, the node value is implemented first, then the left branch and the right branch are created after comparison to the node value.

7. **(C)**

*Front(L)* can be generated by a finite automaton $F$ for language $L$ if we change every state of $F$ to an accept state. In that way, at any point in a string recognition, we can accept the string read so far. Since we have a finite automaton to recognize it, the language must be regular.

8. **(A)**

NAND$(x, x)$ is NOT$(x$ AND $x)$ which reduces to NOT$(x)$. Likewise for $y$ and $z$. So, $f = $ NAND(NAND$(x', y'), z')$. DeMorgan's law reduces NAND$(x', y')$ to OR$(x, y)$, so $f = $ NAND(OR$(x, y), z')$. $f = $ NOT(AND$(x + y, z'))$ distributes into $f = $ NOT$(xz' + yz')$. DeMorgan's law reduces this to $f = ($NOT$(xz'))($NOT$(yz'))$ and again to $f = (x' + z)(y' + z) = x'y' + x'z + y'z + z = x'y' + z$. Choice (B) is the complement of answer (A). Choices (C) and (D) are minterms and hence can't match (A). Choice (E) is a maxterm and can't be equal to (A).

9. **(D)**

(D) assumes that we can read enumerated types like character-strings and is invalid. (A) is a fine declaration of an enumerated type. (B) just declares $x$ to be of that type. (C) is standard character output. (E) is a conditional with the enumerated type variable.

10. **(D)**

Solve $x$ and $y$ by setting determinant of the coefficient $|A| = 0$. Then we have,

$$x - 4y + 3 = 0$$

or $\quad x = 4y - 3.$

Thus, any combination of $(x, y)$ satisfying the above equation gives the correct answer and $x = y = 1$ is one of such combinations.

11. **(C)**

Since the sequence of traversal is to visit the left branch node and then the right branch, therefore the three statements:

```
#
12    traverse (t^.left);
13    root(t);
14    traverse(t^.right);
```

give the correct answer.

12. **(B)**

$B = 1$ is necessary to complete the center 4-cube of four 1's and complete the 2-cube with the 1 to the left of $B$. Since all the 1's are covered at this point, setting $A$ to 1 would require an extra unnecessary term. Therefore, $A$ should be 0. Hence answer (B). Choices (A) and (C) would not complete the inner 4-cube, resulting in two 2-cubes and the 1 to the left of $B$ would remain a 1-cube. Choice (D) would set $A = 1$, creating no savings and adding an unnecessary 2-cube. Consequently, (E) is also false.

13. **(A)**

There are 8 bit positions in a byte. Three of those bits must have a value = true. We can choose the first true bit from 8 possible positions. We can choose the second true bit from the 7 remaining possible positions. Likewise, there are 6 remaining positions (ways) to choose the position of the third true bit. This gives $8 * 7 * 6$, but the order in which we turned them on doesn't matter (i.e., we care only about the final bit patterns). So, we divide by 3!. This gives $(8 * 7 * 6) / (3 * 2 * 1) = 8 * 7$, which is choice (A). We can confirm this by noting that this example fits the concept of "combinations" (i.e., the concept of choosing from an urn without replacement and without order) which gives $C(8, 3) = 8! / (5! * 3!) = (8 * 7 * 6) / (3 * 2 * 1) = 8 * 7$. (B) and (C) make no sense. (D) gives the number of permutations $P(8, 3)$ which is wrong since it counts the following three bit choices as distinct: $\{2, 5, 7\}$ and $\{5, 2, 7\}$ but these are the same bit pattern 01001010, so we really need to divide by 3!.

14. **(A)**
   This problem tests the understanding of recursive calls.

   $F(4) := F(3) * F(2) + F(1)$ where

   $F(3) := F(2) * F(1) + F(0)$

So    $F(4) := 2 * 2 + 1 = 5$

So    $F(3) := 2 * 1 + 0 = 2$

15. **(B)**
   At first, $L$ appears context-free since it resembles $0^n 1^n$, a classical example of one. Intuitively, we can imagine a push-down automaton *PDA* pushing markers for 0's and then popping them to count 1's. At that point, the *PDA* fails since the 2's are unrestricted. Note: pushing two markers for each 0 also fails since the popping phase won't "know" when the 1's should end and the 2's begin, resulting in acceptance of $0^n 1^k 2^{2n-k}$. Time allotted favors this intuitive approach rather than a formal proof via the pumping lemma.

16. **(B)**
   This problem involves ordinal types and functions involving them. The *ord* function computes the numerical value of an ordinal. *succ* and *pred* compute the next and the previous positions in an ordinal type, respectively. Assume $K$ = ordinal position to 'B'. Then, we reduce:

   $succ(ord(\text{'B'}) + 1) - ord(pred(\text{'B'}))$

   $succ(K + 1) - ord(\text{'A'})$

   $(K + 1 + 1) - (K - 1) = 2 + 1 = 3.$

17. **(A)**
   Let $(x, y\, z)$ and $(x', y', z')$ be the original and new coordinates before and after rotation is applied. Then

   $$x' = x \tag{1}$$

$$y' = y * \cos \phi - \sin \phi$$

$$z' = y * \sin \phi + \cos \phi$$

$$(x', y', z', 1) = (x, y, z, 1) * \begin{pmatrix} 1 & 0 & 0 & 0 \\ 0 & \cos \phi & \sin \phi & 0 \\ 0 & -\sin \phi & \cos \phi & 0 \\ 0 & 0 & 0 & 1 \end{pmatrix}$$

The other rotational matrices do not produce the needed rotation to satisfy the system of equation (1).

18. **(D)**

(D) creates type *LUMB* with an array of 50 records, each with the respective type required. (A) and (B) only create one record. (C) creates 50 records but the *WOOD* name only has one character, which will cause trouble with 'Spruce' and 'Silver Fir.'

19. **(C)**

In a ripple carry adder, the output of the Carry-function from one bit is fed to the Add-function of the next sequential bit. So, each of the *N* bits required must wait for the previous bit to be processed. So the time is linear in the number of bits since each individual Add and Carry requires constant time.

20. **(A)**

*L* looks context-sensitive (note problem 15). However, since *n* and *k* differ, we can write a nice context-free set of productions $S \rightarrow AB$, $A \rightarrow 0A1$, $B \rightarrow 2B3$, $A \rightarrow 01$, $B \rightarrow 23$ for generating *L*.

21. **(B)**

$$\Delta P_n(x) = \Delta(b_n x^n + b_n + x^{n-1} + \ldots + b_1 x + b_0)$$
$$= b_n nhx^{n-1} + \text{terms of lower degree in } x$$
$$\Delta^2 P_n(x) = b_n(n-1) h^2 x^{n-2} + \text{terms of lower degree in } x$$
$$\vdots$$
$$\therefore \quad \Delta^n P_n(x) = b_n(n-1)(n-2) \ldots 2 * 1 * h^n x^{n-n} = b_n n! \, h^n$$

22. **(B)**

(B) is illegal since *REAL* is not an ordinal type and hence cannot be used as an array index (since "consecutive" has no meaning with *REAL*). (A) just declares a standard enumerated type and uses it to index an array. Likewise, 'A' .. 'Z' (a subrange type in (C)), *BOOLEAN* (a two value type in (C)), and – 10 .. – 2 (another subrange type in (E)) are all ordinal types and hence are fine indices to arrays.

23. **(E)**
(A), (C), and (D) are $N$log($N$) sort because (A) and (C) use recursive partitioning while (D) uses a static tree-like structure. (B) uses features of the key to operate in linear time with respect to the array size. The bubble sort is quadratic since it has a nested do loop where both loops are bounded by the array size.

24. **(D)**
The following diagram is the minimal solution:

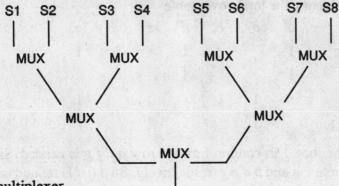

MUX = multiplexer

25. **(D)**
(A), (C), and (E) are wrong since **or** will be true if even one condition is satisfied (i.e. a single 'x' in the right position will trigger a WIN). (B) and (D) will check for the **and** conditions but (B) checks for the wrong ones (they form a corner at [1, 1]). So, (D) is correct since [3, 1], [2, 2], [1, 3] form a diagonal row.

26. **(C)**
Solving the recurrence relation is often an arduous task. Sometimes, it is faster to test the answers by direct substitution. So, at $n = 3$ we have 1 * 2 + 2 * 3 = 8. Choice (A) gives 3 * 4 * 5/2 = 30. Choice (B) gives 9 * 16/6 = 24. Choice (C) gives 2 * 3 * 4/3 = 8. At this point, we can stop but it is best to check the remaining choices (in case a better answer exists). (D) gives 4!/8 = 24/8 = 3. (E) gives 34. Note: if two choices gave the right value for $n = 3$, try $n = 4$, $n = 5$, and so on.

27. **(D)**
(A) only guarantees that Side *AB* – Side *CD*, which is true of any rectangle, so it is insufficient. (B) only guarantees that Side *AB* = Side *CD*

and Side $AD$ = Side $BC$, but notice that $AB$ and $AD$ can be different, so any rectangle can still satisfy this. (C) adds on one more condition to (B), specifically $AD = AB$, so all four sides are equal; however, a rhombus (a "tilted square") fulfills these conditions too, so (C) has a bug. (D) is correct because it checks that Side $AC$ = Side $BD$, which are really the diagonals, and that prevents the tilted case of the rhombus from being accepted as a valid case. (E) is wrong since it has all the conditions of (D) but adds on the inconsistent condition that $AC = AB$ (i.e. side = diagonal) which violates the previous conditions (and reality as well). (E) will never print, no matter what we input.

28. **(B)**
    Constructing the total cover table:

|          | $a$ | $b$ | $c$ | $d$ | $e$ | $f$ | $g$ |
|----------|-----|-----|-----|-----|-----|-----|-----|
| $a\,d\,f\,g$ | 1 |   |   | 1 |   | 1 | 1 |
| $a\,b\,d$ | 1 | 1 |   | 1 |   |   |   |
| $b\,c\,g$ |   | 1 | 1 |   |   |   | 1 |
| $b\,d\,e\,g$ |   | 1 |   | 1 | 1 |   | 1 |

Note that the lone 1 in column f means row $a\,d\,f\,g$ is needed. Similarly, $c$ and $e$ require $b\,c\,g$ and $b\,d\,e\,g$ respectively. So $a\,b\,d$ is redundant.

29. **(C)**
    We have by inclusion-exclusion, those taking Computer Science only

$$\text{CS only} = \text{CS} - (\text{CS with BW}) - (\text{CS with P}) + (\text{CS and BW and P})$$
$$= 520 - 96 - 152 + 60$$
$$= 332$$

Likewise, those who took only Plundering = $416 - 152 - 124 + 60 = 200$ and those who took only Weaving = $320 - 96 - 124 + 60 = 160$. Those taking exactly one course (i.e. three disjoint sets) = $332 + 200 + 160 = 692$. Clearly, choice (C).

30. **(E)**
    First note that everything up to the *COINS*:= statement is correct in all choices above (i.e. *DOLLARS*:=trunc(*AMT*) will copy the non-fractional portion of *AMT* into *DOLLARS*). (A) is wrong since *COINS* should not be computed as 100 ∗ (number of dollars). Choices (B) − (E) avoid that mistake by correctly setting *COINS*:=100∗(*AMT−DOLLARS*), thereby turning a fraction into a "penny count." (B) − (E) correctly use *COINS* **div**

25 to compute quarters. (D) then neglects to compute what remains after removing quarters; (D) erroneously computes *DIMES*:=*COINS* **mod** 10 which double-counts the quarters' value. (B), (C), and (E) avoid that mistake by computing what remains after the quarters in *REST*:=(*COINS*–25\**QUARTERS*) and then compute *DIMES*:=*REST* **div** 10. (C) erroneously computes *NICKELS* as *REST* **div** 5 without first removing the value of the dimes (i.e. another double-counting). (B) computes *NICKELS* as *REST* **mod** 5 which is also wrong since *REST* **mod** 5 gives the remaining *CENTS*. (E) avoids those errors by first removing the dimes and then dividing: *NICKELS*:= (*REST* **mod** 10) **div** 5; (E) correctly finishes by computing cents as *REST* **mod** 5.

31.  **(D)**

Linear programming operates in polynomial time (by ellipsoid and interior methods). Graph coloring, Traveling Salesman, and the Hamiltonian Problems are examples from NP folklore with easily written standard exponential programs (recursively assign and then backtrack if a problem occurs). Presburger Arithmetic is the only alternative left and rightfully so, though hard to prove.

32.  **(D)**

(A) is false; **while** loops test at the top. **repeat** loops test at the bottom. (B) is false since **while** loops test for continuation conditions while **repeat** loops check for termination conditions. (C) is false (in Pascal); functions return values by using assignment statements like:

*FUNCTION_NAME* := *EXPRESSION* ;

(D) is true; the case statement prints false when true and true when false which is what (**not** *X*) computes. (D) is the first true choice. (E) is true but late.

33.  **(C)**

Call the jars *A* with capacity 3 and *B* with capacity 4.

| Operation | Result | |
|---|---|---|
| FILL (*A*) | *A* = 3 | *B* = 0 |
| POUR (*A, B*) | *A* = 0 | *B* = 3 |
| FILL (*A*) | *A* = 3 | *B* = 3 |
| POUR (*A, B*) | *A* = 2 | *B* = 4 |
| SPILL (*B*) | *A* = 2 | *B* = 0 |
| POUR (*A, B*) | *A* = 0 | *B* = 2 |

Minimality is easily shown by noting that other operation sequences easily waste time or are useless (state space tree is easily pruned).

34. **(A)**
    Call the jars $A$ with capacity 5 and $B$ with capacity 8.

| Operation | Result | |
|---|---|---|
| FILL ($A$) | $A = 5$ | $B = 0$ |
| POUR ($A, B$) | $A = 0$ | $B = 5$ |
| FILL ($A$) | $A = 5$ | $B = 5$ |
| POUR ($A, B$) | $A = 2$ | $B = 8$ |

The first step must be FILL ($A$) since FILL ($B$) would set $B = 8$ and then the only meaningful next operation would be POUR($B, A$) giving $B = 3$ but then there are no useful next steps. So the first step must be FILL ($A$) which then leads to POUR($A, B$) since EMPTY or FILL ($B$) would be useless here. In this problem, good objective functions defuse combinatorial explosions.

35. **(B)**
    round($R$) is the closest integer $R$, while $R - round(R)$ gives the displacement between them; taking the absolute values makes it positive (i.e. a distance), so (B) is the answer. (A), (C), (D), and (E) fail since trunc only gives the integer equal or below, which spells disaster for positive numbers with fraction parts above 0.5. For example:

| | Choice | $R$ | Expression | Result |
|---|---|---|---|---|
| | (A) | .9 | $abs(R) - trunc(R)$ | .9 |
| | (C) | .9 | $abs(R - trunc(R))$ | .9 |
| | (D) | .9 | $abs(round(R) - trunc(R))$ | 1.0 |
| | (E) | .9 | $abs(trunc(R) - round(R))$ | 1.0 |
| Correct→ | (B) | .9 | $abs(R - round(R))$ | 0.1 |

36. **(E)**
    Let $Rev = 20$ revolutions per second. $N =$ number of words per track. Let $b =$ number of words per block. Note: $1/20$ sec $= 50$ ms.
    First seek the track, rotate half-way on that track on the average, and then read the data. So:

$$\text{AccessTime} = \text{Seek} + 1/2 * (1/Rev) + (b/N) * (1/Rev)$$
$$= 20 \text{ ms} + .5 * 50 \text{ ms} + 100/300 * 50 \text{ ms}$$
$$= 20 \text{ ms} + 25 \text{ ms} + 16.6 \text{ ms} = 61.6 \text{ (Answer (E))}.$$

37. **(B)**

Choice (A) is insolvable because we would have to determine the behavior of a Turing machine (TM) on ALL inputs ("very" unsolvable). Choice (B) is true; in fact, open any good book on unsolvability and the blueprints of such a universal TM are included (some older texts have the actual machines). (C) is unsolvable using an argument similar to (A). (D) is a rephrasing of the halting problem, also unsolvable.

38. **(D)**

Since there are nodes with odd arity, the graph is not Eulerian. Hamiltonian-ness is harder to test. Rather than test all circuits which hit each node once (too time consuming), try testing a subgraph to see if it can be traversed. Let's try:

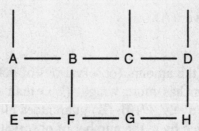

If we come down *A E F G H D* and go up, we miss *C* and *B*. If we also hit *C* and go up, we miss *B*. If we hit *B* also, we will never go back to the upper subgraph. Likewise, if we try *A E F B C D*, we either go up and miss *G* and *H* or we hit *G* and *H* and never return upward. If we try *A B C D*, we lose the bottom nodes. Trying *A B F* will miss *E*. Starting downward at *C* or *D* gives the same results. This exhausts all cases.

39. **(A)**

I is false since constants have no storage space. II and IV are true since a constant has a value and hence may be compared. III is true since a value may be used in an expression. V is true because constants never change (that's one reason why constants are used instead of variables). VI is true because constants have a numerical or character value and therefore can be printed. VII is true since constants may be edited on one line and their values will influence many lines. For example, **const** *Size* = 100; could declare the size of a dozen arrays and then influence all loop bounds for that array; if we didn't use *Size*, every occurrence of 100 must be reviewed in code modification. Lastly, IX is true since **const**ants really cause a textual substitution to occur to code prior to any code-generation.

40. **(B)**

Even though computing a minimal graph coloring requires exponential time, we can take a "magically" given coloring and verify that it is valid in linear time. Just go one pass through the array of pairs (edges) and check both nodes to see if they have the same color. So this requires 2 node-array accesses for each edge, giving linear time. This is known as a certificate problem.

41. **(A)**

$$Average = HitRatio * HighSpeed + MissRatio * LowSpeed$$
$$= .80 * 40 \text{ ns} + (1 - .80) * 100 \text{ ns}$$
$$= 32 \text{ ns} + 20 \text{ ns}$$

So 52 ns is the answer (A).

42. **(B)**

Note that $k$ = the amount (observation) of debris. (A) is wrong since the first observation has more weight ($k/1$) than (for instance) the tenth observation (respectively, $k/10$). (B) guarantees all have equal weight and every value is divided by $n$, the number of observations, thus satisfying the definition of average. (C), (D), and (E) are totally wrong since the *AVE* is redivided every time a new observation comes in, resulting in the first few observations diminishing in significance as new numbers are read in.

43. **(E)**

$K(3, 3)$ is not planar; in fact, it is one of the forbidden subgraphs in Kuratowski's famous planarity theorem and also from the 3-wells problem. Planarity can also be tested by drawing the graph and trying to remove crossings. So (A) is false. (B) is false since any bipartite graph can be split into two sets of disjoint nodes (each of one color); they are both 2-colorable. (C) is false since $K(2, 4)$ can be drawn as:

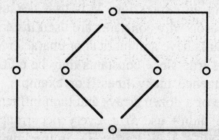

Note: the top and bottom nodes constitute the 2, while the middle row of four nodes is the 4. So $K(2, 4)$ is planar. Finally, (D) is false since $K(3, 3)$ has only nodes of arity three while $K(2, 4)$ has nodes of arity 2 and 4. Thus, (E) is true.

44. **(D)**
    (A) first computes $Term:=-x*x*x/0$, so a division by zero occurs. (B) computes $Term:=-x*x*x/3!$ and then $Sum:=0 - x*x*x/3!$ on the first loop but *Sum* will never have the first term of the series, $x$. (C) also will never have the first term, $x$. (E) will compute $k:=3$, but also computes $Sum=x+x$ which is erroneous. Finally, (D) is correct since at the end of the first loop, we have $k=3$, $Sum=x$, $Term=-x*x*x/6$, then the second loop with $k=5$, $Sum= x - x*x*x/6$, $Term= x*x*x*x*x/120$, and so on.

45. **(A)**
    Tape drives read data sequentially, so choices (C) – (E) are false, since they assume the ability to move to any record at any moment. Sequential files with extents are sequential files fragmented due to the unavailability of large enough contiguous free space. Such fragmentation would make tape file boundaries difficult to manage and so were not made part of taping standards. So (B) is false. Choice (A) is the simplest file organization.

46. **(C)**
    There are $C(9, 3)$ ways on the first day to choose 3 specials from 9 fish. On the second day, since no fish may be used on two days, only 6 fish remain and so there are $C(6, 3)$ ways to choose the 3 specials on day two. Finally, on day three, we choose 3 from 3 giving $C(3, 3) = 1$ way. So for three days, we have $C(9, 3) * C(6, 3)$.

47. **(B)**
    (A) uses call-by-value as the parameter-passing method which prevents any values from being returned to the calling procedure, so the effect of the switch is never recorded. (B) has the magic word **var** which specifies call-by-address parameter-passing, so the switching of $a$ and $b$ will be effective in the calling procedure's variables. (C) is a procedure but attempts to send back a function value (illegal). In fact, (C) and (D) have a fatal flaw in that their integer variable *Temp* which is used to switch two real variables (serious error). (D) uses call-by-value ((A)'s error) and also is a function (unnecessary) without any return type specified (serious error).

48. **(C)**
    We can replace each polynomial by the Big-O of the highest power, so

$$F(x) = (7x^6 + 3x^4 + 17x + 9) / (0.01x^2 * x^{-1})$$

gives

$$O(x^6) / (0.01 \; x^2 / x)$$

$$O(x^6) / (0.01 \; x)$$

$$O(x^6) / O(x)$$

$$O(x^5)$$

49. **(C)**

(E) seems best but is erroneous because $(9, 7)$ and $(11, -2)$ check all the code at least once but not paths that can detect bugs involving the interaction of **** code with $$$$. (A) never tests the $x \geq 10$ and $y > 5$ case (i.e., ++++ %%%%). (B) never tests the $x \geq 10$ and $y \leq 5$ case (i.e. ++++ $$$$). (D) also has the same flaw as (A). (C) is correct since all cases are covered:

| $(9, 7)$, | $(11, 3)$, |
|---|---|
| $x < 10$ and $y > 5$, | $x \geq 10$ and $y \leq 5$, |
| $(19, 11)$, | $(3, 4)$ |
| $x \geq 10$ and $y > 5$, | $x < 10$ and $y \leq 5$ |

50. **(E)**

This question is about interpreter and/or compiler design. (A) seems fine but popping the 2 achieves nothing here. In (B), popping the + would cause trouble in the following:

$$2 + 3 * 4$$

since we really want to multiply prior to taking any action with +. (C) suffers the same problem as (B) if there is a higher priority operator coming and also a *pop* will achieve nothing if the "*" is followed by a "(". (D) would also waste a *pop* because an we would have only started reading the operation that must be completed. (E) is correct because a closed parenthesis signifies that an expression has been read and needs evaluation. This does not negate other popping situations but a ")" is among the strongest indications for popping.

51. **(E)**

$$x'yz' + x'y'z + x(y + z)$$

expands to:

$$x'yz' + x'y'z + xy + xz$$

Using Karnaugh maps:

|  | 00 | 01 | 11 | 10 | $= x, y$ |
|---|---|---|---|---|---|
| $z = 0$ | 0 | 1 | 1 | 0 | |
| $z = 1$ | 1 | 0 | 1 | 1 | |

The 0-cubes are: $(y + z)$ and $(x + y' + z')$. Note that 0-cubes are determined by taking the complement of the literals, so $z = 0$ and $y = 0$ as a 0-cube contributes the term $(y + z)$. So the expression is $(y + z)(x + y' + z')$ choice (E). By expanding out the sum of products, choices (A) through (D) can be shown incorrect. For example, choice (D) expands to:

$$(y'x' + y'y + y'z) + (z'x' + z'y + z'z)$$

and reduces to

$$y'x' + y'z + z'x' + z'y$$

which has $x'y'z'$, not in the original.

52. **(C)**
     The looping is triply nested with each loop bounded by $N$, so the resulting complexity is $O(n*n*n) = O(n^3)$.

53. **(D)**
     Prob(explosion at time 1) = 1/3.

     Prob(no explosion at time 1) = $1 - 1/3 = 2/3$

     Prob(no explosion up to and including time 2)

     = Prob(no explosion at time 1) * Prob(no explosion at time 2)

     = (2/3) * (2/3)

     Prob(explosion at time 3)

     = Prob(no explosion at time 1) * Prob(no explosion at time 2)

     * Prob(explosion at time 3)

     = (2/3) * (2/3) * (1/3) = 4/27

54. **(D)**
     (A) is false since stacks are useful for recursion but not queues. (B) is far-fetched (although queues could be used in ordering the collisions and interactions still to occur in an event oriented simulation, similar to an event oriented billiards simulation). (C) assumes too much of queues; they hardly have the geometric expressive power to match the convoluted structures of arbitrary linked lists. (E) is also a specialty of stacks. So, (D) remains. Queues are used when a limited resource (like a bank-teller, gas

pump, or even a CPU job scheduler) must serve customers (resource requesters).

**55. (D)**

Postfix means "operands first, then operator" (recursively). So,

| $(a + b)$ | becomes | $ab+$ | |
|---|---|---|---|
| $(c + d)$ | becomes | $cd+$ | |
| $(a + b) * (c + d)$ | becomes | $ab+ cd+ *$ | (Choice (D)) |

Since postfix notation is unique, no other choices are possible.

**56. (B)**

An operator grammar has no adjacent nonterminals in the right-hand-side. This is accomplished here by replacing $A$ on the right-hand-side by both $bSb$ and $b$, giving:

$S \rightarrow SbSbS \mid SbS \mid a, A \rightarrow bSb \mid b$

Now $A \rightarrow$ productions are nonproductive, so delete them.

$S \rightarrow SbSbS \mid SbS \mid a$

**57. (B)**

Let $H$ = hit-ratio. Let $C$ = cache speed. Let $R$ = ram speed. Memory access

$$M = H * C + (1 - H) * R.$$
$$30 = H * 20 + (1 - H) * 150.$$
$$30 = 20H + 150 - 150H = -130H + 150.$$
$$H = 120/130 = 24/26 = 12/13 = 92\% \text{ approximately.}$$

**58. (D)**

(D) sets the link field of node $X$ to the link field of a node which is two links ahead. This is the desired operation. (A) only deletes one node ahead. (B) only moves the temporary "pointer" $X$ ahead two nodes but leaves the linked list intact. (C) is bizarre; it will create a small loop in the link structure so that the link of the next node will point back to this node. (E) only moves up temporary "pointer" X three links forward but leaves the list intact.

**59. (B)**

The quickest way to choose a summation formula is to plug numbers in the original and plug into the five choices. Sometimes (as in this problem), this quick test is not practical or possible. In those cases, we use algebra. We know:

$$\sum k = n(n+1)/2.$$

$$\sum_{k=1}^{k=n} (6k - 5) = 6 \sum_{k=1}^{k=n} k - \sum_{k=1}^{k=n} 5 = 6n(n+1)/2 - 5n$$

$$= 6n^2/2 + 6n/2 - 5n$$

$$= 3n^2 - 2n$$

as in Choice (B).

60. **(C)**
The binary tree representation is:

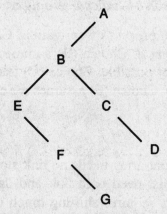

61. **(E)**
Bus expansion increases data flow by a factor of 32 / 8 = 4. Likewise, operating at a higher clock-speed causes a speed-up of at most 20 / 5 = 4. Assuming that operating system and components support it, a speed-up of 4 * 4 = 16 can be achieved totally (answer (E)).

62. **(A)**
Let $A$ = player 1 wins and let $B$ = player 2 wins. The tree of possible outcomes would be as shown in the following figure. The number of

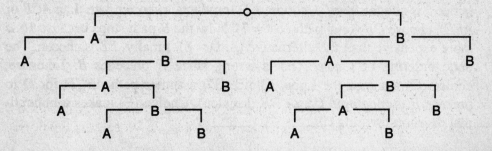

possible outcomes is equal to the number of leaf nodes in the tree. So, we have 10 possible histories.

63.   **(D)**

$63 = 64 - 1 = 2^6 - 1$. The basic progression here is 1 node, then two sons (giving 3 total), then 4 grandsons (giving $7 = 8 - 1 = 2^3 - 1$ total), then 8 great-grandsons ($15 = 16 - 1 = 2^4 - 1$ total) and so on. This is a nice combinatorial property of complete binary trees that matches a feature of $2^n$. Also often useful is the fact (seen here) that a complete binary tree has almost as many leaves as nodes above. This fact is often useful in the combinatorics of binary trees.

64.   **(D)**

$$S \rightarrow aS \rightarrow aaS \rightarrow aabA \rightarrow aabccA \rightarrow aabccd$$

All the others crash in the process of derivation. Choice (A) assumes we can generate more than one $d$. Choice (B) assumes we can generate two successive $b$'s which is not possible. Choice (C) assumes we can generate an $a$ immediately after a $b$. Choice (E) assumes we can generate $d$ immediately after $a$.

65.   **(D)**

(A) is false since a flat array needs no link storage (often as large as the data space), while a list need both link and data.  (B) is false since updating sorted flat arrays requires shifting much of the array, while list modifications are local link surgery of $2 - 3$ nodes. (C) is false since arrays are rigid relative to the physical media that contains them, while the structure of lists is dependent on the value of links which are easily modified. (D) is true since 1 link makes a singly linked list (only), while 2 links give rise to trees, sparse spreadsheets, doubly-linked linear lists, etc. (E) is true though inefficient and late (i.e., it is not first in truth.)

66.   **(A)**

Best first is greedy in that it chooses the immediately most profitable of alternatives. Start at $A$, choose $AC$ (shorter than $AF$), choose $C$ to $F$ (since 5 is shorter than 7), choose $FD$ (products a shorter path than $ACB$ or $AFE$), choose $DB$ (total path cost = 7). Now the $B$ path stops because 15 is more expensive than $DE$ alternative ($A..D = 8$). Finally, $EZ$ is chosen. The node ordering of Choice (B) is wrong since $E$ precedes $B$. Likewise, choice (C) assumes the same. Choice (D) assumes path $ABCD$ for $D$ to precede $F$ (nonoptimal $CB$ or $DB$ decision). Choice (E) makes a nonoptimal decision favoring $CB$.

67. **(C)**
The values of this recursion are more easily computed by noting that each term is the sum of the previous two. If $f(1) = 1$ and $f(2) = 1$ then

$f(3) = 1 + 1 = 2$

$f(4) = 1 + 2 = 3$

$f(5) = 2 + 3 = 5$

$f(6) = 3 + 5 = 8$

$f(7) = 5 + 8 = 13$

$f(8) = 8 + 13 = 21$

68. **(E)**
Determining all possible decompositions requires computing all closed partitions and covers. The set of all covers grows exponentially in $N$.

69. **(D)**
Note that two stacks can simulate a Turing machine tape. Note that a left tape-head movements of the Turing machine corresponds to popping from stack 1 to stack 2 and likewise a right head move will be simulated by a pop off 2 and a push onto 1. Since the stacks are unbound, they can store as much as a Turing machine.

70. **(D)**
I is reflexive since $abs(A - A) = 0$, which is less than 10. II is not reflexive because if $A = 2$, then $A * A = 4$ which is less than 8. III is reflexive since $A \leq A$. IV is also reflexive, since $A \leq abs(A)$. So only three are reflexive.

71. **(C)**
I is symmetric since $abs(A - B) = abs(B - A)$. This is easiest shown by noting $B - A = -(A - B)$, so if we take $abs$ of both sides, we get $abs(B - A) = abs(-(A - B)) = abs(A - B)$, so if one expression is $\leq 10$, then so is the other. Secondly, II is symmetric since $A * B$ equals $B * A$. Thirdly, $A \leq B$ doesn't guarantee $B \leq A$ (for example $2 \leq 4$, not $4 \leq 2$), so III is not symmetric. Finally, IV is not symmetric by the same reasoning as III.

72. **(C)**
I is not transitive since $abs(19 - 11) \leq 10$ and $abs(11 - 6) \leq 10$ but $abs(19 - 6) = 13$ which is not $\leq 10$. Intuitively, relation I is really a locality constraint and two steps are no longer local, so transitivity is violated. II is not transitive since $2 * 5 > 8$ and $5 * 3 > 8$ but $2 * 3$ is not $> 8$. Thirdly, III

is transitive since $A \le B$ and $B \le C$ results in $A \le C$ (a property of real numbers). IV is not transitive since $5 \le abs(-10)$ and $-10 \le abs(0)$ but 5 is not $\le abs(0)$.

73. **(A)**

(A) is true since blocked records move more data per I/O call than unblocked and locate mode I/O avoids all the intermediate buffering of move mode I/O. (B), (C), and (D) deny this and so are false. (E) is insane (floppy disks store from 100 K to 4 Megs while hard drives can have capacities above 1 Gigabyte).

74. **(E)**

Recursively enumerable (r.e.) languages are not closed under complementation because then every r.e. set would be recursive (since we know the theorem that "if $S$ and $S$" are r.e., then both are recursive"). Closure under intersection (A) is proved by simulating the behavior of two Turing machines on one Turing machine on multiple tapes. Closure under union (B) is achieved by creating a new start symbol $S$ and if $A$ and $B$ are start symbols for the two languages, then the union will have the productions of both and $S \to A$ and $S \to B$. Likewise, for concatenation (C), we need only add $S \to AB$. Choice (D) is merely a subcase of choice (A).

75. **(E)**

A sequential machine has finitely many states but the numbers carried past each digit increases without a constant bound in multiplication. So, unlike addition in shift registers, each extra bit of multiplier either requires more adders (in the carry-save multiplier) or intermediate storage (in the shift-and-add standard multiplication algorithm). The shift-and-add multiplier is less expensive but slower. Note that all these algorithms are still finite length multiplication. In addition, the worst carry is 1. So, (E) is the answer.

76. **(D)**

Hierarchical models are rigid tree-like organizations where data is "buried under certain categories" resulting in poor integration. Network models use physical pointers and records in a graph-theoretic way but the limitations of the physical pointers make it less expressive than the relational models. So (D) is the correct choice.

77. **(B)**

A boolean function of 3 variables corresponds to a truth table of $2^3 = 8$ rows. Each row can have a 0 or 1 value, so there are $2^8 = 256$ tables or functions of three variables. However, we are assuming those rows which have complemented values for $x, y, z$ (names, $x'$, $y'$, $z'$) are predestined (or restricted) to the opposite values of $f(x, y\ z)$. So, we may assume four rows are independent and the remaining four rows have no freedom. So, there are $2^4 = 16$ tables with the above property.

78. **(E)**
      During the instruction-fetch phase, all require the same memory access to get the instruction. During the instruction-execution phase, choices (A), (C), and (D) don't access memory since the computations involve CPU entities. (B) seems like it requires a memory access during execute-phase, but that is not true; the instruction fetch phase read the address already into the CPU, either as a real address or as a base-displacement (which computes a real address in the CPU.) That address is then moved to the Instruction Address Register IAR. So the execute phase of a branch requires no memory access. Therefore, (E) is the correct answer.

79. **(D)**

| FAFAFA | = 1111 | 1010 | 1111 | 1010 | 1111 | 1010 | | | (in binary) |
|---|---|---|---|---|---|---|---|---|---|
| | = 111 | 110 | 101 | 111 | 101 | 011 | 111 | 010 | (in binary) |
| | 7 | 6 | 5 | 7 | 5 | 3 | 7 | 2 | (in octal) |

The answer is (D).

80. **(C)**

      Inherited attributes are passed from son nodes to father (such as $E \rightarrow$ real). Inherited attributes are also passed from father to sons (such as in assignment statements, the left son being the target address will have the attribute *ADDRESS* and the right son (right of the equal sign) will have the attribute *VALUE*.)

# Glossary

**ABSOLUTE ADDRESS** — An address that is permanently assigned by the machine designer to a storage location. Synonymous with machine address, specific address.

**ACCESS TIME** — (1) The time interval between the instant at which data are called for from a storage device and the instant delivery begins. (2) The time interval between the instant at which data are requested to be stored and the instant at which storage is started.

**ACCUMULATOR** — A register in which the result of an arithmetic or logic operation is formed.

**ACTUAL PARAMETER** — A variable that is passed to a subroutine by a calling function to dictate the operation of that subroutine. It does not cause any changes outside the subroutine.

**ADDER** — A device whose output is a representation of the sum of the quantities represented by its inputs.

**ADDRESS** — (1) An identification, as represented by a name, label, or number, for a register, location in storage, or any other data source or destination such as the location of a station in a communication network. (2) Loosely, any part of an instruction that specifies the location of an operand for the instruction.

**ADDRESS PART** — A part of an instruction word that specifies the address of an operand instruction, or result.

**ADDRESS REGISTER** — A register in which an address is stored.

**ALGORITHM** — A prescribed set of well-defined rules or processes for the solution of a problem in a finite number of steps, e.g., a full statement of an arithmetic procedure for evaluating sin x to a stated precision.

**ALPHANUMERIC** — Pertaining to a character set that contains letters, digits, and usually other characters such as punctuation marks.

**ANALOG** — Pertaining to representation by means of continuously variable physical quantities.

**AND** — A logic operator having the property that if P is a statement, Q is a statement, R is a statement ..., then the AND of P, Q, R ..., is true if all statements are true, false if any statement is false. P AND Q is often represented by $P \cdot Q$, PQ. Synonymous with logical multiply.

**AND GATE** — A gate that implements the logic "AND" operator.

**ARITHMETIC SHIFT** — (1) A shift that does not affect the sign position. (2) A shift that is equivalent to the multiplication of a number by a positive or negative integral power of the radix.

**ASSEMBLE** — To prepare a machine language program from a symbolic language program by substituting absolute operation codes for symbolic operation codes and absolute or relocatable addresses for symbolic addresses.

**ASSEMBLER** — A computer program that assembles.

**ASSOCIATIVE STORAGE** — A storage device in which storage locations are identified by their contents, not by names or positions.

**ASYNCHRONOUS COMPUTER** — A computer in which each event or the performance of each operation starts as a result of a signal generated by the completion of the previous event or operation, or by the availability of the parts of the computer required for the next event or operation. Contrast with synchronous computer.

**AVL TREE** — A binary search tree in which the heights of two siblings are not permitted to differ by more than one.

**BASE ADDRESS** — A given address from which an absolute address is derived by combination with a relative address.

**BATCH PROCESSING** — (1) Pertaining to the technique of executing a set of computer programs such that each is completed before the next program of the set is started. (2) Pertaining to the sequential input of computer programs or data. (3) Loosely, the execution of computer programs serially.

**BAUD** — A unit of signalling speed equal to the number of discrete conditions or signal events per second. For example, one baud equals one-half dot cycle per second in Morse code, one bit per second in a train of binary signals, and one 3-bit value per second in a train of signals each of which can assume one of eight different states.

**BIG O NOTATION** — A way to represent the running time (T(n)) of a program based on the input size (n).

$$O(f(n)) \Rightarrow T(n) = cf(n) \quad (c = \text{constant})$$

It is often used for comparisons of different sorts and searches.

| | type | worst case | average case |
|---|---|---|---|
| sorts: | quick | $n^2$ | $n \log_2(n)$ |
| | heap | $n \log_2(n)$ | $n \log_2(n)$ |
| | merge | $n \log_2(n)$ | $n \log_2(n)$ |
| | bin/bucket | $n$ | $n$ |
| | bubble | $n^2$ | $n^2$ |
| | insertion | $n^2$ | $n^2$ |
| | selection | $n^2$ | $n^2$ |
| | shell | $n^{1.5}$ | $n^{1.5}$ |
| searches: | binary | $\log_2(n)$ | $\log_2(n)$ |
| | sequential | $n$ | $n/2$ |
| | hash | $n$ | $n$ |

BINARY — (1) Pertaining to a characteristic or property involving a selection, choice, or condition in which there are two possibilities. (2) Pertaining to the number representation system with a radix of two.

BINARY-CODED DECIMAL NOTATION — Positional notation in which the individual decimal digits expressing a number in decimal notation are each represented by a binary numeral. Abbreviated BCD.

BISTABLE — Pertaining to a device capable of assuming either one of two stable states.

BIT — A binary digit.

BOOLEAN — Pertaining to the operations of formal logic.

BOOLEAN OPERATOR — A logic operator each of whose operands and whose result have one of two values.

BOTTOM-UP PARSER — A parser which constructs the parse tree by starting at the leaves and moving towards the root.

BRANCH — (1) a set of instructions that are executed between two successive decision instructions. (2) Loosely, a conditional jump.

BREAKPOINT — A place in a routine specified by an instruction digit, or other condition, where the routine may be interrupted by external intervention or by a monitor routine.

BUFFER — (1) A routine or storage used to compensate for a difference in rate of flow of data, or time of occurrence of events, when transmitting data from one device to another. (2) An isolating circuit used to prevent a driven circuit from influencing the driving circuit.

BUS — One or more conductors used for transmitting signals or power.

BYTE — A sequence of adjacent binary digits operated upon as a unit and usually shorter than a computer word.

CACHE — A high speed buffer memory placed between the processor and the main memory.

CACHE OVERHEAD TIME — The time for the cache to move the data into main memory.

CARRY — (1) One or more digits, produced in connection with an arithmetic operation on one digit place of two or more numerals in positional notation, that are forwarded to another digit place for processing there. (2) The number represented by the digit or digits in (1). (3) Most commonly, a digit as defined in (1), that arises when the sum or product of two or more digits equals or exceeds the radix of the number representation system.

CENTRAL PROCESSING UNIT — A unit of a computer that includes the circuits controlling the interpretation and execution of instructions. Synonymous with main frame. Abbreviated CPU.

CHARACTER — (1) A letter, digit, or other symbol that is used as part of the organization, control, or representation of data. A character is often in the form of a spatial arrangement of adjacent or connected strokes.

CHOMSKY CLASSIFICATION — A classification of grammars.
> type 0 = free grammars
> type 1 = context-sensitive
> type 2 = context-free
> type 3 = regular grammars, finite state automatons

CIRCULAR WAIT QUEUE — A circular wait queue must exist with two or more processes, each of which is waiting for a resource held by the next process in the queue.

CLEAR — To place one or more storage locations into a prescribed state, usually zero or the space character.

CLOCK — (1) A device that generates periodic signals used for synchronization. (2) A register whose content changes at regular intervals in such a way as to measure time.

CLOCK PULSE — A synchronization signal provided by a clock.

CLOSED SUBROUTINE — A subroutine that can be stored at one place and can be linked to one or more calling routines.

CODE — In data processing, to represent data or a computer program in a symbolic form that can be accepted by a data processor.

COMMAND — (1) A control signal. (2) Loosely, an instruction in machine language.

COMPILE — To prepare a machine language program from a computer program written in another programming language by making use of the overall logic structure of the program, or generating more than one machine instruction for each symbolic statement, or both, as well as performing the function of an assembler.

COMPILER — A program that compiles.

COMPUTER PROGRAM — A series of instructions or statements, in a form acceptable to a computer, prepared in order to achieve a certain result.

COMPUTER WORD — A sequence of bits or characters treated as a unit and capable of being stored in one computer location. Synonymous with machine word.

CONDITIONAL JUMP — A jump that occurs if specified criteria are met.

CONNECTOR — (1) On a flowchart, the means of representing the convergence of more than one flowline into one, or the divergence of one flowline into more than one. It may also represent a break in a single flowline for continuation in another area. (2) A means of representing on a flowchart a break in a line of flow.

COPY — To reproduce data in a new location or other destination, leaving the source data unchanged, although the physical form of the result may differ from that of the source. For example, to copy a deck of cards onto a magnetic tape. Contrast with duplicate.

COUNTER — A device such as a register or storage location used to represent the number of occurrences of an event.

CROSSTALK — The unwanted energy transferred from one circuit, called the "disturbing" circuit, to another circuit, called the "disturbed" circuit.

DATA — Any representations such as characters or analog quantities to which meaning is or might be assigned.

DECIMAL — Pertaining to the number representation system with a radix of ten.

DECODER — A matrix of logic elements that selects one or more output channels according to the combination of input signals present.

DESCRIPTOR — In information retrieval, a word used to categorize or index information. Synonymous with keyword.

DESTRUCTIVE READ — A read process that also erases the data from the source.

DIGITAL COMPUTER — (1) A computer in which discrete representation of data is mainly used. (2) A computer that operates on discrete data by performing arithmetic and logic processes on these data.

DIRECT ACCESS — (1) Pertaining to the process of obtaining data from, or placing data into, storage where the time required for such access is independent of the location of the data most recently obtained or placed in storage. (2) Pertaining to a storage device in which the access time is effectively independent of the location of the data. (3) Synonymous with random access (1).

DIRECT ADDRESS — An address that specifies the location of an operand.

DISCRETE — Pertaining to distinct elements or to representation by means of distinct elements such as characters.

DOUBLE PRECISION — Pertaining to the use of two computer words to represent a number.

ENCODE — To apply a set of unambiguous rules specifying the way in which data may be represented such that a subsequent decoding is possible.

ERASE — To obliterate information from a storage medium, e.g., to clear, to overwrite.

ERROR — Any discrepancy between a computed, observed, or measured quantity and the true, specified, or theoretically correct value or condition.

EXCLUSIVE OR — A logic operator having the property that if P is a statement and Q is a statement, then P exclusive OR Q is true if either but not both statements are true, false if both are true or both are false. P exclusive OR Q is often represented by $P \oplus Q$, $P \veebar Q$. Contrast with OR.

EXPONENT — In a floating point representation, the numeral, or a pair of numerals representing a number, that indicates the power to which the base is raised.

FAULT — (1) A physical condition that causes a device, a component, or an element to fail to perform in a required manner.

FIELD — In a record, a specified area used for a particular category of data, e.g., a group of card columns used to represent a wage rate, a set of bit locations in a computer word used to express the address of the operand.

FILE — A collection of related records treated as a unit.

FIXED-POINT PART — In a floating-point representation, the numeral of a pair of numerals representing a number, that is the fixed-point factor by which the power is multiplied.

FIXED-POINT REPRESENTATION — A positional representation in which each number is represented by a single set of digits, the position of the radix point being fixed with respect to one end of the set, according to some convention.

FIXED RADIX NOTATION — A positional representation in which the significances of successive digit positions are successive integral power of a single radix. When the radix is positive, permissible values of each digit range from zero to one less than the radix, and negative integral powers of the radix are used to represent fractions.

FLIP-FLOP — A circuit or device containing active elements, capable of assuming either one of two stable states at a given time. Synonymous with toggle.

FLOATING-POINT BASE — In floating point representation, the fixed positive integer that is the base of the power. Synonymous with floating-point radix.

FLOATING-POINT REPRESENTATION — A number representation system in which each number as represented by a pair of numerals equals one of those numerals times a power of an implicit fixed positive integer base where the power is equal to the implicit base raised to the exponent represented by the other numeral.

FULLY-ASSOCIATIVE CACHE — A placement policy where any memory line can reside in any location.

GATE — A device having one output channel and one or more input channels, such as the output channel state is completely determined by the input channel states, except during switching transients, e.g., AND GATE; OR GATE.

GLOBAL VARIABLES — A variable which can be accessed anywhere throughout a given program.

HALF-ADDER — A combinational logic element having two outputs. S and C, and two inputs, A and B, such that the outputs are related to the inputs according to the following table.

| input | | output | |
|---|---|---|---|
| **A** | **B** | **C** | **S** |
| 0 | 0 | 0 | 0 |
| 0 | 1 | 0 | 1 |
| 1 | 0 | 0 | 1 |
| 1 | 1 | 1 | 0 |

S denotes "Sum Without Carry," C denotes "Carry." Two half-adders may be used for performing binary addition.

HAMMING CODE — A data code which is capable of being corrected automatically.

HEAD — A device that reads, writes, or erases data on a storage medium, e.g., a small electromagnet used to read, write, or erase data on a magnetic drum or tape, or the set of perforating, reading, or marking devices used for punching, reading, or printing on paper tape.

HEXADECIMAL — (1) Pertaining to a characteristic of property involving a selection, choice, or condition in which there are sixteen possibilities. (2) Pertaining to the numeration system with a radix of sixteen.

IDLE TIME — That part of available time during which the hardware is not being used.

INDEX REGISTER — A register whose content may be added to or subtracted from the operand address prior to or during the execution of a computer instruction. Synonymous with B box.

INPUT — Pertaining to a device process, or channel involved in the insertion of data or states, or to the date or states involved.

INSTRUCTION ADDRESS — The address that must be used to fetch an instruction.

INSTRUCTION COUNTER — A counter that indicates the location of the next computer instruction to be interpreted.

INSTRUCTION REGISTER — A register that stores an instruction for execution.

INTERLEAVE — To arrange parts of one sequence of things or events so that they alternate with parts of one or more other sequences of things or events and so that each sequence retains its identity, e.g., to organize storage into banks with independent bases so that sequential data references may be overlapped in a given period of time.

INTERPRETER — A computer program that translates and executes each source language statement before translating and executing the next one.

JOB — A specified group of tasks prescribed as a unit of work for a computer.

JUMP — A departure from the normal sequence of executing instructions in a computer.

LATENCY — The time between the start of an operation and the availability of the result. For moving head disks, it represents the time for the disk to rotate so that the head is located at the beginning of the sector where the information is to be read/written.

LINKER — A program that accepts object modules as input, resolves external references, and produces a single output module ready for loading.

LOADER — A program that moves code from a secondary storage to memory for execution.

LOCAL VARIABLE — A variable whose scope and accessibility are limited to a specific portion of a program (i.e., a subroutine).

LRU — (least recently used) A policy where the page that was referenced the longest time ago is replaced on a page fault.

MACHINE CODE — An operation code that a machine is designed to recognize.

MATRIX — (1) In mathematics, a two-dimensional rectangular array of quantities. Matrices are manipulated in accordance with the rules of matrix algebra. (2) In computers, a logic network in the form of an array of input leads and output leads with logic elements connected at some of their intersections. (3) By extension, an array of any number of dimensions.

MEMORY — (1) Pertaining to a device into which data can be entered, in which they can be held, and from which they can be retrieved at a later time. (2) Loosely, any device that can store data.

MERGE — To combine items from two or more similarly ordered sets into one set that is arranged in the same order.

MODEM — (MOdulator-DEModulator) A device that modulates signals transmitted over communication facilities.

MODULE — A program unit that is discrete and identifiable with respect to compiling, combining with other units, and loading, e.g., the input to, or output from, an assembler, compiler, linkage editor, or executive routine.

MULTIPROCESSING — Pertaining to the simultaneous execution of two or more computer programs or sequences of instructions by a computer or computer network.

MULTIPROCESSOR — A computer employing two or more processing units under integrated control.

MUTUAL EXCLUSION — A mechanism used to guarantee that no more than one process can occur at any one time.

NAND — A logic operator having the property that if P is a statement, Q is a statement, R is a statement ..., then the NAND OF P, Q, R ... is true if at least one statement is false, false if all statements are true. Synonymous with NOT-AND.

NEST — To imbed subroutines or data in other subroutines of data at a different hierarchical level such that the different levels of routines or data can be executed or accessed recursively.

NONDESTRUCTIVE READ — A read process that does not erase the data in the source. Abbreviated NDR.

NONPREEMPETION— Once resources have been assigned to a process they cannot be taken away until the completion of the process and the process releases them.

NO-OP — An instruction that specifically instructs the computer to do nothing, except to proceed to the next instruction in sequence.

NOR — A logic operator having the property that if P is a statement, Q is a statement, R is a statement ..., then the NOR of P, Q, R ... is true if all statements are false, false if at least one statement is true. P NOR Q is often represented by a combination of "OR" and "NOT" symbols, such as ~ (P∨Q). P NOR Q is also called "neither P nor Q." Synonymous with NOT-OR.

NORMALIZE — To multiply a variable or one or more quantities occurring in a calculation by a numerical coefficienct in order to make an associated quantity assume a nominated value, e.g., to make a definite integral of a variable, or the maximum member of a set of quantities, equal to unity.

NOT — A logic operator having the property that if P is a statement, then the NOT of P is true if P is false, false if P is true. The NOT of P is often represented by $\overline{P}$, ~P, ⌐P, P′.

OBJECT CODE — Output from a compiler or assembler which is itself executable machine code or is suitable for processing to produce executable machine code.

OBJECT MODULE — A module that is the output of an assembler or compiler and is input to a linkage editor.

OBJECT PROGRAM — A fully compiled or assembled program that is ready to be loaded into the computer. Synonymous with target program.

OCTAL — (1) Pertaining to a characteristic or property involving a selection, choice or condition in which there are eight possibilities. (2) Pertaining to the number representation system with a radix of eight.

ONES COMPLEMENT — The radix-minus-one complement in binary notation.

OPERATING SYSTEM — Software which controls the execution of computer programs and which may provide scheduling, debugging, input/output control, accounting, compilation, storage assignment, data management, and related services.

OPERATING TIME — That part of available time during which the hardware is operating and assumed to be yielding correct results. It includes development time, production time, and makeup time.

OPERATION — A program step undertaken or executed by a computer, e.g., addition, multiplication, extraction, comparison, shift, transfer. The operation is usually specified by the operator part of an instruction.

OPERATION CODE — A code that represents specific operations. Synonymous with instruction code.

OPERATOR — In the description of a process, that which indicates the action to be performed on operands.

**OR** — A logic operator having the property that if P is a statement, Q is a statement, R is a statement ..., then the OR of P, Q, R ..., is true if at least one statement is true, false if all statements are false. P OR Q is often represented by $P + Q$, $P \vee Q$. Synonymous with inclusive OR, boolean add, logical add. Contrast with exclusive OR.

**OR GATE** — A gate that implements the logic "OR" operator.

**OVERFLOW** — That portion of the result of an operation that exceeds the capacity of the intended unit of storage.

**OVERLAY** — The technique of repeatedly using the same blocks of internal storage during different stages of a program. When one routine is no longer needed in storage, another routine can replace all or part of it.

**PAGE FAULT** — Occurs when the page addressed is not present in memory.

**PAGING** — A form of address transmission where a program is divided into equally sized pages (frames.)

**PARALLEL** — Pertaining to the concurrent or simultaneous occurrence of two or more related activities in multiple devices or channels.

**PARAMETER** — A variable that is given a constant value for a specific purpose or process.

**PARITY BIT** — A check bit appended to an array of binary digits to make the sum of all the binary digits, including the check bit, always odd or always even.

**PARITY CHECK** — A check that tests whether the number of ones (or zeros) in an array of binary digits is odd or even.

**PARTIAL ASSIGNMENT OF RESOURCES** — Processes are assigned resources as they become available. A process does not have to wait for all required resources to become available before an available resource is assigned to the processes.

**PRODUCT OF SUMS** — A boolean algebraic statement designed to recognize (have a '0' value) a specific input combination for which the output produces a '0' result.

**PROGRAMMING MODULE** — A discrete identifiable set of instructions, usually handled as a unit, by an assembler, a compiler, a linkage editor, a loading routine, or other type of routine or subroutine.

QUANTIZE — To subdivide the range of values of a variable into a finite number of nonoverlapping, but not necessarily equal, subranges or intervals, each of which is represented by an assigned value within the subrange.

RADIX — In positional representation, that integer, if it exists, by which the significance of the digit place must be multiplied to give the significance of the next higher digit place.

RADIX COMPLEMENT — A complement obtained by subtracting each digit from one less than its radix, then adding one to the least significant digit, executing all carries required.

RADIX NOTATION — A positional representation in which the significance of any two adjacent digit positions has an integral ratio called the radix of the less significant of the two positions; permissible values of the digit in any position range from zero to one less than the radix of that position.

RADIX POINT — In radix notation, the real or implied character that separates the digits associated with the integral part of a numeral from those associated with the fractional part.

RANDOM ACCESS — An access mode in which specific logical records are obtained from or placed into a mass storage file in a nonsequential manner.

READ — To acquire or interpret data from a storage device, a data medium, or any other source.

RECURSIVE VARIABLE — A variable that is the parameter of a recursive subroutine.

REGISTER — A device capable of storing a specified amount of data such as one word.

RELATIVE ADDRESS — The number that specifies the difference between the absolute address and the base address.

RELOCATE — In computer programming, to move a routine from one portion of storage to another and to adjust the necessary address references so that the routine, in its new location, can be executed.

RESET — To restore a storage device to a prescribed initial state, not necessarily that denoting zero.

ROUNDOFF — To delete the least significant digit or digits of a numeral, and to adjust the part retained in accordance with some rule.

SCOPE — The part of the program during which a particular variable may be accessed.

SEARCH — To examine a set of items for one or more having a desired property.

SEEK TIME — For moving head disks, the time for the head to move to the track to be read/written.

SEQUENTIAL OPERATION — Pertaining to the performance of operations one after the other.

SEQUENTIAL MACHINE — A machine consisting of a finite set of input symbols which can be applied in a sequential fashion, a finite set of internal states, a next state function determined by the present input symbol, and which produces a finite set of output symbols.

SERIAL — Pertaining to the sequential or consecutive occurrence of two or more related activities in a single device or channel.

SET — (1) A collection. (2) To place a storage device into a specified state, usually other than that denoting zero or space character. (3) To place a binary cell into the state denoting one.

SET-ASSOCIATIVE CACHE — A placement policy where the cache is divided into sets and memory lines are placed into different sets based on their relative addresses.

SHIFT — A movement of data to the right or left.

SHIFT REGISTER — A register in which the stored data can be moved to the right of left.

SIGN BIT — A binary digit occupying the sign position.

SIGN DIGIT — A digit occupying the sign position.

SKIP — To ignore one or more instructions in a sequence of instructions.

SOFTWARE — A set of computer programs, procedures, and possibly associated documentation concerned with the operation of a data processing system, e.g., compilers, library routines, manuals, circuit diagrams.

SORT — To segregate items into groups according to some definite rules.

SUBROUTINE — A routine that can be part of another routine.

SUM OF PRODUCTS — A boolean algebraic statement designed to recognize (have a '1' value) a specific input combination for which the output produces a '1' result.

SYMBOLIC ADDRESS — An address expressed in symbols to the computer programmer.

SYNTAX — (1) The structure of expressions in a language. (2) The rules governing the structure of a language.

TERMINAL — A point in a system or communication network at which data can either enter or leave.

TIME SHARING — Pertaining to the interleaved use of the time of a device.

TOP-DOWN PARSER — A parser which constructs the parse tree by starting at the root and proceeding to the leaves.

TRANSMISSION — The sending of data from one location and the receiving of data in another location, usually leaving the source data unchanged.

TRANSMISSION TIME — For moving head disks, the time for data to be moved from the disk into memory.

TRIE — A tree where each path from the root to a leaf corresponds to one word in the represented set. The nodes of the tree correspond to the prefixes of the words in the set.

TRUNCATE — To terminate a computational process in accordance with some rule, e.g., to end the evaluation of a power series at a specified term.

TRUTH TABLE — A table that describes a logic function by listing all possible combinations of input values and indicating, for each combination, the true output values.

TURING MACHINE — An abstract mathematical model consisting of an infinite 'tape' of squares, where each square can contain one symbol

## REALIZATION OF A TURING MACHINE

from a finite number of symbols. The Turing Machine can read and write on the tape by means of a 'head' that can be instructed to move left or right along the tape. Another cell exists which contains the present state of the machine (left, right, read, write)

**2–3 TREE** — A tree where each interior node has two or three children and each path from the root to a leaf has the same length.

**TWOS COMPLEMENT** — The radix complement in binary notation.

**VARIABLE** — A quantity that can assume any of a given set of values.

**VARIABLE PARAMETER** — A variable used in a subroutine which is equivalent to another variable outside the subroutine, where any changes made to it will cause similar changes in its equivalent.

**WORD** — A character string or a bit string considered as an entity.

**WRITE** — To record data in a storage device or a data medium. The recording need not be permanent.

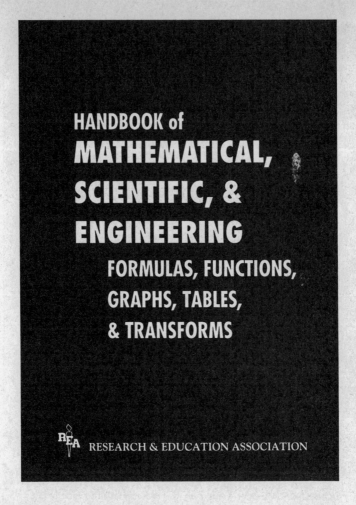

HANDBOOK of
**MATHEMATICAL,
SCIENTIFIC, &
ENGINEERING**
FORMULAS, FUNCTIONS,
GRAPHS, TABLES,
& TRANSFORMS

**R&A** RESEARCH & EDUCATION ASSOCIATION

A particularly useful reference for those in math, science, engineering and other technical fields. Includes the most-often used formulas, tables, transforms, functions, and graphs which are needed as tools in solving problems. The entire field of special functions is also covered. A large amount of scientific data which is often of interest to scientists and engineers has been included.

*Available at your local bookstore or order directly from us by sending in coupon below.*

# REA's Test Preps
# The Best in Test Preparation

- REA "Test Preps" are **far more** comprehensive than any other test preparation series
- Each book contains up to **eight** full-length practice exams based on the most recent exams
- **Every** type of question likely to be given on the exams is included
- Answers are accompanied by **full** and **detailed** explanations

*REA has published over 60 Test Preparation volumes in several series. They include:*

**Advanced Placement Exams (APs)**
Biology
Calculus AB & Calculus BC
Chemistry
Computer Science
English Language & Composition
English Literature & Composition
European History
Government & Politics
Physics
Psychology
Statistics
Spanish Language
United States History

**College-Level Examination Program (CLEP)**
Analyzing and Interpreting Literature
College Algebra
Freshman College Composition
General Examinations
General Examinations Review
History of the United States I
Human Growth and Development
Introductory Sociology
Principles of Marketing
Spanish

**SAT II: Subject Tests**
American History
Biology
Chemistry
English Language Proficiency Test
French
German

**SAT II: Subject Tests (continued)**
Literature
Mathematics Level IC, IIC
Physics
Spanish
Writing

**Graduate Record Exams (GREs)**
Biology
Chemistry
Computer Science
Economics
Engineering
General
History
Literature in English
Mathematics
Physics
Political Science
Psychology
Sociology

**ACT** - American College Testing Assessment

**ASVAB** - Armed Services Vocational Aptitude Battery

**CBEST** - California Basic Educational Skills Test

**CDL** - Commercial Driver's License Exam

**CLAST** - College Level Academic Skills Test

**ELM** - Entry Level Mathematics

**ExCET** - Exam for Certification of Educators in Texas

**FE (EIT)** - Fundamentals of Engineering Exam

**FE Review** - Fundamentals of Engineering Review

**GED** - High School Equivalency Diploma Exam (US & Canadian editions)

**GMAT** - Graduate Management Admission Test

**LSAT** - Law School Admission Test

**MAT** - Miller Analogies Test

**MCAT** - Medical College Admission Test

**MSAT** - Multiple Subjects Assessment for Teachers

**NJ HSPT-** New Jersey High School Proficiency Test

**PPST** - Pre-Professional Skills Tests

**PRAXIS II/NTE** - Core Battery

**PSAT** - Preliminary Scholastic Assessment Test

**SAT I** - Reasoning Test

**SAT I** - Quick Study & Review

**TASP** - Texas Academic Skills Program

**TOEFL** - Test of English as a Foreign Language

**TOEIC** - Test of English for International Communication

---

**RESEARCH & EDUCATION ASSOCIATION**
61 Ethel Road W. • Piscataway, New Jersey 08854
Phone: (732) 819-8880

### Please send me more information about your Test Prep books

Name _____

Address _____

City _____ State _____ Zip _____